Complete Stand Mixer Cookbook

Elevate Your Culinary Creations with 215 Delectable Stand Mixer Recipes

Lindsay G. Cabral

Table of Content

Introduction 7
Stand Mixer vs. Hand Mixer 7
How Stand Mixers Work 8
Tips for How to Use a Stand Mixer 8
Exploring the Best Mixer Attachments 9
Overview of Different Mixer Sizes 9
Bowl Lift and Tilt Head Model Differences 9
Understanding Speed Settings 10
Tips to Minimize Mess 10
Incorporating Ingredients with Ease 10
When should I chill the Bowl? 10
Maintenance Tips for Longevity 11
Proper Cleaning Techniques 11

Bread 12

1. Apple Cinnamon Bread 12
2. Artisan Bread 13
3. Banana Walnut Bread 14
4. Banana Bread 15
5. Banana, Apple, and Blueberry Loaf 16
6. Brioche Bread 17
7. Challah Bread 18
8. Chocolate Chip Banana Bread 19
9. Chocolate Zucchini Bread 20
10. Ciabatta Bread 21
11. French Bread 22
12. Focaccia Bread 24
13. Garlic Bread 25
14. Irish Soda Bread 26
15. Mexican Sweet Bread 27
16. Naan Bread 28
17. Panini Bread 29
18. Pita Bread 30
19. Potato Bread 31
20. Pumpernickel Bread 32
21. Pumpkin Bread 33
22. Sandwich Bread 34
23. Sourdough Bread 35
24. Wheat Bread 36
25. White Bread 37
26. Zucchini Bread 38

Cakes 39

27. Carrot Cake 39
29. Crab Cakes With Herb Salad 40
28. Chocolate Cake 41
30. Honey Bun Cake 42

31. Pound Cake	43
32. Bundt Cake	44
33. Red Velvet Cake	44
34. Vanilla Cake	46
35. Coffee Cake	47
36. Banana Cake	48
37. Lemon Cake	50
38. Strawberry Cake	52
39. Apple Cake	54
40. Coconut Cake	55
41. Yellow Cake	57
42. White Cake	58
43. Everyday Fruit Cake	60
44. Pumpkin Spice Cake	61
45. Black Forest Cake	62
46. Banana cake with coconut sorbet	64
47. Fruit Cake	65
48. Caramel Cake	66
49. Banana Pudding Cake	68
50. Caramel Bundt Cake	70
51. Cheesecake	71
52. Oatmeal Cake	72
53. Chocolate Zucchini Cake	73
54. Cherry Cake	74
55. Pear and Hazelnut Torta Caprese	75
56. Malted Milk Cheesecake	76

Cookies 77

57. Chocolate Chip Cookies	77
58. Sugar Cookies	78
59. Gingerbread Cookies	79
60. Peanut Butter Cookies	80
61. Oatmeal Cookies	81
62. Christmas Cookies	82
63. Shortbread Cookies	83
64. Gluten Free Sugar Cookies	84
65. Crumbl Cookies	86
66. Lemon Cookies	87
67. Pumpkin Cookies	88
68. Vegan Chocolate Chip Cookies	89
69. Almond Cookies	90
70. BUTTERSCOTCH COOKIES	90
71. Banana Cookies	91
72. Brownie Cookies	92
73. Red Velvet Cookies	93
74. Strawberry Cookies	94
75. Apple Cookies	95
76. Blueberry Cookies	96
77. Coconut Cookies	97

78. Ginger Cookies	98
79. Brown Butter Brown Sugar Cookies	99
80. Cinnamon Cookies	100
81. Hazelnut and Apricot Biscotti	101
82. Orange Cookies	102

Rolls 103

83. Cinnamon Roll	103
84. Spring Roll	104
85. Pumpkin Roll	105
86. Dinner Roll	106
87. Crescent Roll	107
88. Sausage Roll	108
89. Jelly Roll	109
90. Egg Roll	111
91. Yeast Roll	112
92. Pepperoni Roll	113
93. French Bread Roll	114
94. Nut Roll	115
95. Caramel Roll	117
96. Potato Roll	118
97. Cheese Roll	119
98. Ciabatta Roll	120
99. Orange Roll	121
100. Garlic Butter Parmesan Roll	122

Buns 125

101. Hamburger Buns	125
102. Hot Cross Buns	126
103. Steamed Bao Buns	128
104. Cinnamon Sticky Buns	129
105. Hot Dog Buns	130
106. Brioche Buns	132
107. Burger Buns	133
108. Pretzel Buns	134
109. Potato Buns	135
110. Red Bean Buns	136

Doughnuts 137

111. Cake Doughnuts	137
112. Glazed Yeast Doughnuts	139
113. Apple Cider Doughnuts	141
114. Sweet Potato Doughnuts	143
115. Mini Doughnuts	145
116. Chocolate Doughnuts	146
117. Cinnamon Sugar Doughnuts	148
118. Jelly Doughnuts	150
119. Gluten Free Doughnuts	151
120. Vegan Doughnuts	152

Meatballs _____ *154*

    123. Turkey Meatball _____ 154
    121. Swedish Meatball _____ 155
    122. Italian Meatball _____ 156
    124. Beef Meatball _____ 157
    125. BBQ Meatball _____ 158
    126. Lamb Meatball _____ 159
    127. Cocktail Meatball _____ 161
    128. Keto Meatball _____ 162
    129. Gluten-Free Meatball _____ 163
    130. Vegan Meatball _____ 164

Pasta and Noodles _____ *165*

    131. Cheese Tortellini _____ 165
    132. Fresh Pasta _____ 166
    133. Shrimp Pasta _____ 167
    134. Salmon Pasta _____ 169
    135. Vodka Pasta _____ 170
    136. Mushroom Pasta _____ 170
    137. Egg Pasta _____ 172
    138. Chinese Noodles _____ 173
    139. Egg Noodles _____ 174
    140. Ramen Noodles _____ 175
    141. Garlic Noodles _____ 176
    142. Rice Noodles _____ 176
    143. GARLIC SHRIMP ZUCCHINI NOODLES _____ 178
    144. Basic EGG NOODLES _____ 179

Dips and Sauces _____ *180*

    145. Guacamole _____ 180
    146. Buffalo Chicken Dip _____ 181
    147. Mashed Potato _____ 181
    148. Taco Dip _____ 182
    149. Margarita Dip _____ 182
    150. Bacon Jalapeno Cheese Dip _____ 183
    151. Cream Cheese Fruit Dip _____ 183
    152. Chocolate Chip Cookie Dough Dip _____ 184
    153. Spinach Artichoke Dip _____ 184
    154. Crab Dip _____ 185
    155. Bean Dip _____ 186
    156. Corn Dip _____ 187
    157. French Dip _____ 188
    158. Sweet Cream Cheese Dip _____ 189
    159. 7 Layer Dip _____ 189
    160. Beer Cheese Dip _____ 190
    161. Chicken Wing Dip _____ 191
    162. Cream Cheese Salsa Dip _____ 191
    163. French Onion Dip _____ 192
    164. Pulled Pork Dip _____ 192

165. Applesauce _____ 193
166. Mayonnaise _____ 193
167. Raw Cranberry Sauce _____ 194
168. Hollandaise Sauce _____ 194
169. Tomato Sauce _____ 195

Frostings _____ *196*

170. Chocolate Buttercream Frosting _____ 196
171. Vanilla Buttercream Frosting _____ 196
172. Buttercream Frosting _____ 197
173. Cream Cheese Frosting _____ 197
174. Peanut Butter Frosting _____ 198
175. White Frosting _____ 198
176. Cookie Frosting _____ 199
177. Whipped Cream Frosting _____ 199
178. Caramel Buttercream Frosting _____ 200
179. Lemon Buttercream Frosting _____ 200
180. Strawberry Frosting _____ 201
181. Vegan Buttercream Frosting _____ 201
182. Cool Whip Frosting _____ 202
183. Frosting Recipe Without Butter _____ 203
184. Coconut Frosting Recipe _____ 203
185. Chocolate Cream Cheese Frosting _____ 204
186. Chocolate Fudge Frosting _____ 204

Doughs _____ *205*

187. Salt Dough _____ 205
188. Pizza Dough _____ 206
189. Cookie Dough _____ 206
190. Pasta Dough _____ 207
191. Puff Pastry Dough _____ 208
192. Bread Dough _____ 209
193. Biscuit Dough _____ 209
194. Pretzel Dough _____ 210
195. Donut Dough _____ 211
196. Sweet Dough _____ 212
197. Tamale Dough _____ 213
198. Dumpling Dough _____ 214
199. Danish Dough _____ 215
200. Pie Dough _____ 216

Ice Cream _____ *217*

201. Peach Ice Cream _____ 217
202. Vanilla Ice Cream _____ 218
203. Coffee Ice Cream _____ 219
204. Coconut Ice Cream _____ 220
205. Blueberry Ice Cream _____ 220
206. Raspberry Ice Cream _____ 222
207. Vanilla Bean Ice Cream _____ 223

208. Cookies & Cream Ice Cream _____ 224
209. Oreo Ice Cream _____ 225
210. Mint Chip Ice Cream _____ 226
211. Butter Pecan Ice Cream _____ 227
212. Pumpkin Ice Cream _____ 228
213. Black Forest Ice Cream _____ 229
214. Peanut Butter Ice Cream _____ 230
215. Strawberry Ice Cream _____ 231

INTRODUCTION

The Stand Mixer Cookbook Is Here! Put your stand mixer to work for you like never before with this helpful kitchen accessory. This cookbook will lead you on a delicious journey through all its possibilities. Make everything from delicious treats to fresh loaves of bread with the help of your stand mixer. The Stand Mixer Cookbook will help you create gourmet masterpieces with ease.

A stand mixer is a strong kitchen tool that makes it easy to mix, beat, and whip ingredients. It has interchangeable attachments for tasks like mixing batter, kneading dough, and whipping cream. The hands-free function lets you do other things while the mixer works. It's popular among home cooks and bakers for its efficiency and versatility.

Among all the kitchen countertop appliances, stand mixers hold a special place in the hearts of baking enthusiasts. If you frequently find yourself baking bread, cookies, or desserts, investing in a stand mixer can significantly reduce your preparation time.

Stand mixers not only deliver professional results but also save time and minimize mess in the kitchen. These electric powerhouses incorporate more air into batters and doughs, resulting in baked goods with superior texture.

Some stand mixers offer exceptional versatility by accommodating various attachments, enabling tasks like vegetable slicing, meat grinding, pasta making, and even ice cream preparation.

STAND MIXER VS. HAND MIXER

The primary differences between a stand mixer and a hand mixer lie in motor size and price. While a hand mixer is suitable for smaller tasks and requires manual handling, a stand mixer offers more freedom of movement in the kitchen. Although a stand mixer occupies more space and has a heavier build, it excels at handling heavy-duty batter, bread doughs, and baking projects, providing quicker results with less mess.

HOW STAND MIXERS WORK

Stand mixers excel not just in convenience but also in their remarkable power. Their strong motors allow them to handle cold butter, achieving a fluffy and light texture that is difficult to replicate by hand or with a hand mixer. The wide paddle attachment swiftly beats cold butter with sugar, creating an airy mixture of fat, air, and sugar crystals. This creaming process is crucial, as butter loses its aeration capacity as it warms up. Stand mixers also offer unique advantages, such as the ability to incorporate ingredients at lower temperatures and whip cold eggs directly from the fridge. In contrast, underpowered hand mixers may result in flat cookies or dense cakes.

TIPS FOR HOW TO USE A STAND MIXER

Here are some helpful tips and tricks for utilizing your stand mixer effectively:

Familiarize yourself with the manual: While it may seem tedious, reading the manual is essential. It provides valuable information about your mixer, such as its capacity and other useful details.

Start with low speed: Begin any task by setting the mixer to low speed and gradually increase it. This prevents ingredients from splattering all over your kitchen.

Avoid scraping while mixing: Although it may be tempting, refrain from scraping the bowl while the mixer is running. Accidental slips of the spatula can damage the beaters.

Adjust the beater: Refer to the manual to learn how to adjust the beater correctly, ensuring optimal mixing without it touching the bottom of the bowl.

Tighten the hinge if needed: If the mixer's head begins to shift or shake, you can tighten the pin. Consult the manual for instructions on how to do this.

Spin the beaters: Once everything is mixed together, slightly lift the beaters while the mixer is on low speed and then high speed. This helps remove excess mixture from the beaters, minimizing waste.

Utilize a towel: To prevent ingredients from flying out of the bowl, especially when using high speed, place a clean kitchen towel over the bowl as a protective barrier.

Chill the bowl: For improved results, chill both the bowl and beaters before using them. This is particularly effective when whipping cream, as it helps achieve fluffy peaks.

Invest in a silicone scraper: A silicone scraper is the ideal tool for scraping down the bowl, ensuring you don't waste any mixture.

Store attachments wisely: Save space by storing attachments in the bowl itself. To prevent scratches, line the stainless steel bowl with a towel.

Consider buying attachments: Explore the variety of attachments available for your stand mixer. Fun options like a pasta maker or meat grinder can enhance your culinary adventures.

By following these tips, you can make the most of your stand mixer and enjoy its full range of capabilities.

EXPLORING THE BEST MIXER ATTACHMENTS

To unlock the full potential of a stand mixer, consider purchasing attachments that expand its functionality. Some popular attachments include:

Paddle (Flat Beater): It works great with thicker mixes like cake batter, frosting, cookies, mashed potatoes, and meatloaf.

Wire Whip: Ideal for incorporating air into mayonnaise, whipped cream, confections, angel food cake, and beaten eggs. Not suitable for dough and heavier mixtures.

Dough Hook: Used for kneading yeast doughs such as white bread, coffee cakes, pizza dough, cinnamon rolls, and pasta.

Scraper: Equipped with flexible rubber or silicone edges, this attachment scrapes down the sides of the mixing bowl while it rotates, eliminating the need to pause and scrape manually. Great for sticky foods like cream cheese and nut butter.

OVERVIEW OF DIFFERENT MIXER SIZES

Selecting the right mixer size depends on your specific needs. For large families, frequent bread making, or regular entertaining, a mixer with at least a 6-quart bowl and a powerful motor is recommended. Smaller kitchens or tighter budgets can make do with a compact 4.5-quart size.

BOWL LIFT AND TILT HEAD MODEL DIFFERENCES

Two main types of stand mixers are available: bowl-lift models and tilt-head models. Here are some key differences between the two:

Height: The tilt-head mixer has a height of 14.0", while the bowl-lift mixer can range from 16 7/16" to 17". The height variation is important to consider, especially if your cabinets are positioned low in relation to the countertop.

Accessibility: If easy access to the beater is a priority for you, the tilt-head model might be more suitable. Its design allows for convenient access to the mixing bowl and attachments.

Bowl removal: While some people appreciate the aesthetic of the bowl-lift mixer, they might find removing the bowl a bit more challenging compared to the tilt-head version. In the bowl-lift mixer, the bowl rests on arms, and you raise it using a lever. On the other hand, the tilt-head mixer has the bowl directly attached to the base, making it simpler to remove.

UNDERSTANDING SPEED SETTINGS

Most stand mixers offer 3 to 12-speed settings, with a "slow start" option for adding ingredients without causing a mess. While 3-speed settings are generally sufficient for most bakers, having more options allows for greater precision in your culinary creations. Here's a breakdown of common speed settings:

Slow Speed: Used for starting the machine and combining dry ingredients.

Speed 2 (Low): Ideal for slow mixing of heavy batter or cutting in butter.

Speed 4 (Medium-Low): Suitable for mixing cookie dough or beating egg whites.

Speed 6 (Medium): Used for creaming butter and beating frostings.

Speed 8 (Medium-High): Enables fast beating or whipping to make meringues and whipped cream.

Speed 10 (High): Allows fast whipping of a small number of egg whites or cream.

TIPS TO MINIMIZE MESS

Some stand mixers come with a splash guard and pouring shield, preventing spills and splatters when adjusting speeds during mixing. You can further reduce splatter by covering the mixer head with a clean kitchen towel.

INCORPORATING INGREDIENTS WITH EASE

For optimal results in baked goods, it's generally recommended to add dry ingredients to wet ones. This method ensures the fat coats the flour, preventing excessive gluten development and yielding light, fluffy baked goods with a tender crumb. While ingredient order may not be crucial for pancake batter, it significantly affects the texture of scones, muffins, and cakes.

WHEN SHOULD I CHILL THE BOWL?

When making whipped cream, chilling the bowl and wire whip for at least 15 minutes before whipping speeds up the process, resulting in faster and better results.

MAINTENANCE TIPS FOR LONGEVITY

To ensure your stand mixer performs optimally for years to come, follow these maintenance tips:

- Adjust the attachment position to ensure it touches the mixing bowl properly.
- Check for loose screws regularly and fix them if you find any.
- Vibration can cause screws to loosen over time, so keep an eye out for this.
- Inspect the mixing bowl for wear and tear, replacing it if it fits loosely or rattles when attached to the base.

PROPER CLEANING TECHNIQUES

Most high-speed kitchen mixers come with stainless steel mixing bowls, but some brands offer alternatives like glass, copper, or porcelain. While these options would work, some would need gentler handling than stainless steel. You may either put the bowl of your mixer in the dishwasher or wash it by hand, and both will be fine. After each use, wipe the stand mixer with a damp cloth to remove any spatter on the undersides. Ensure all components are free from dust and dirt before starting a new project.

BREAD

1. APPLE CINNAMON BREAD

Prep Time: 10 Minutes | Cook Time: 50 Minutes

Total Time: 1 Hour | Serving: 8

Ingredients

- 1 ½ cups of all-purpose flour
- ½ cup of packed light brown sugar
- ½ cup of milk
- 2 eggs
- 1 ½ tsp baking powder
- ½ cup of unsalted butter softened
- 1 ½ tsp ground cinnamon
- 1 large apple, peeled and finely chopped
- ⅔ cup of white sugar
- 2 tsp vanilla extract

Instructions

1. Set oven temperature to 350 degrees.
2. Grease and flour a loaf pan that is 9 by 5 inches.
3. Put the cinnamon and brown sugar in a bowl and set it aside.
4. Mix white sugar and butter in a stand mixer until smooth.
5. Add the eggs and vanilla, and keep beating on medium speed until everything is mixed.
6. Combine the flour, baking powder, and milk.
7. Put half of the batter in the pan that has been prepared.
8. Put half of the apples on top.
9. Use the back of a spoon to press apple slices into the batter.
10. Spread half of the sugar and cinnamon mix on top.
11. Pour the rest of the batter over the apples, then add more apples and the brown sugar/cinnamon mixture on top.
12. With the back of a large spoon, press the topping into the dough. Use a butter knife held vertically to make figure eights in the batter to mix the topping in just a little bit.
13. Bake for around 50 minutes or until a toothpick placed into the center cleans up.
14. Cool in the pan for 10 minutes, then move to a cooling rack.

2. ARTISAN BREAD

Prep Time: 15 Minutes | Cook Time: 45 Minutes | Resting Time: 1 Hour 30 Minutes

Total Time: 2 hours, 30 Minutes | Serving: 12

Ingredients

- 300 ml (1+¼ cups of) warm water
- 5 g (1 tsp) sugar (caster or superfine)
- 8.5 g (1 + ½ tsp) salt (regular table salt/Kosher salt)
- 450 g (3 + ¾ cup) of plain (all-purpose) flour - PLUS ½ cup of (60g) for dusting and shaping the Bread
- 7 g (2 tsp) Instant yeast

Instructions

1. First, Put the yeast, sugar, and warm water in the bowl of the stand mixer or a big bowl. Let the yeast sit for 5 minutes or until it starts to foam.
2. The flour goes in first, then the salt. Apply the dough hook attachment to your stand mixer or use your hands to mix until everything is well combined.
3. Knead the dough for around 10 minutes on medium speed with the dough hook. If you want to do this with your hands, put a little olive or vegetable oil on the work surface and your hands, and knead the dough for 10 minutes. It will be a sticky dough, and that's fine.
4. When the dough has been kneaded, place it in an oiled bowl (wiped with a little olive or vegetable oil). Cover with plastic wrap or wax paper and let rise for 1 hour or until it has doubled in size.
5. Sprinkle 1/4 cup of (30g) of flour on the work surface, then tip the dough out onto the flour. You may need to use your hands to get it out of the bowl because it will still be very sticky. Put a tbsp of flour on top.
6. At this point, we don't want to knock the air out of the dough. We just want to shape the dough by grabbing a piece from the outside and pulling it into the middle.
7. Pull the dough in all the way around until it no longer wants to stay in place. You might need a bit more flour to keep it from sticking together.
8. Then flip the dough over and finish making it round with your hands.
9. Place the dough, seam side down, in a well-floured proving basket or bowl.
10. Warp it with plastic wrap or wax paper and let it rise for 30 minutes.
11. In the meantime, put a Dutch oven with a diameter of about 25cm/10" in the oven and warm it to 230 C/450 F.
12. When the second rise is done, take off the lid and put a long piece of parchment or greaseproof paper on top of the bowl.

13. Turning the bowl over, gently put the dough on the paper.
14. Take the Dutch oven out of the oven very carefully and remove the lid.
15. Carefully lower the Bread into the Dutch oven with the help of the edge of the baking paper. Put the top on and carefully put the dish back in the oven.
16. Bake for 30 minutes, then take off the lid and cook for another 10-15 minutes or until golden brown.
17. Take the cake out of the oven and let it cool completely on a cooling rack before cutting it into pieces and serving it.

3. BANANA WALNUT BREAD

Prep Time: 20 Minutes | Cook Time: 1 Hour

Total Time: 1 Hour 20 Minutes | Serving: 1 Loaf

Ingredients

- 1/2 tsp vanilla extract
- 1/2 cup of room-temperature unsalted butter, plus more to get the pan ready
- 1 tsp baking soda
- 1/2 tsp fine salt
- 1 cup of sugar
- 2 large eggs at room temperature
- About a cup of mashed, peeled, very ripe bananas (3 bananas)
- 1/2 cup of toasted walnut pieces
- 1 1/4 cups of unbleached all-purpose flour

Instructions

1. Put the flour, baking soda, and salt through a sieve into a medium bowl. Blend the eggs and vanilla in a measuring cup of with a spout, then set it aside. Brush some butter on a 9-by-5-by-3-inch loaf pan. Preheat oven to 350°F.
2. Sugar and cream the butter in a standing mixer fitted with the paddle connection until light and fluffy. Pour the egg mixture into the butter slowly while continuing to mix. Then take the bowl off the mixer and add the bananas.
3. Combine the flour mixture with a rubber spatula until barely mixed in. Add the nuts to the batter and pour it into the pan. Bake the Bread for around 55 minutes or until a toothpick stuck in the middle cleans up. Let the Bread cool for 5 minutes in the pan on a wire rack. Take the Bread from the pan and place it on a cooling rack. Use plastic wrap to cover. The banana bread tastes best the day after you make it.

4. BANANA BREAD

Prep Time: 10 Minutes | Cook Time: 65 Minutes |

Total Time: 3 Hours | Serving: 1 Loaf

Ingredients

- 1/2 tsp ground cinnamon
- 2 large eggs at room temperature
- 1 tsp pure vanilla extract
- 1/2 cup of (1 stick or 115g) unsalted butter, softened to room temperature
- 1 tsp baking soda
- 3/4 cup of (150g) packed light or dark brown sugar
- optional: 3/4 cup of (100g) chopped pecans or walnuts
- 2 cups of (250g) all-purpose flour (spooned & leveled)
- 1/3 cup of (80g) plain yogurt or sour cream at room temperature
- 2 cups of (460g) mashed bananas (about 4 large ripe bananas)
- 1/4 tsp salt
- 3/4 cup of (100g) chopped pecans or walnuts (optional)

Instructions

1. Prepare the oven to 350°F (177°C) with the rack in the bottom third position. If you move the oven rack down, the top of your Bread won't brown too quickly and too much. Use non-stick spray to grease a 9x5-inch metal loaf pan. Set aside.
2. Mix the flour, baking soda, salt, and cinnamon in a medium-sized bowl. Set aside.
3. Take a stand mixer, and beat the butter and brown sugar on high speed for about 2 minutes until the mixture is smooth and creamy. Mix the eggs one at a time while the mixer is on medium speed, thoroughly combining the mix after each addition. Then add the yogurt, mashed bananas, and vanilla extract and beat until everything is mixed.
4. When no more flour pockets are visible, turn the mixer to low speed and gradually incorporate the dry elements into the wet ones. Do not over-mix. If you're using nuts, mix them in.
5. Now, Pour and spread the batter in the pan set up for baking. Bake the Bread for 60–65 minutes. Halfway through, loosely cover the top with aluminum foil to avoid getting too brown. When the Bread is done, a toothpick stuck in the middle should come clean with a few small moist crumbs. Depending on your oven, this may be after 60–65 minutes, so start checking every 5 minutes around the 60-minute mark.
6. Remove the Bread from the oven and put it on a wire rack to cool for around 1 hour. Take the Bread out of the pan and let it cool on the wire rack until you are ready to cut it and serve.
7. Cover banana bread and store it at room temperature for around 2 days or in the refrigerator for up to 1 week. The best time to eat banana bread is on the second day after the flavors have had time to blend.

5. BANANA, APPLE, AND BLUEBERRY LOAF

Prep Time: 10 Minutes | Cook Time: 1 Hour 15 Minutes

Total Time: 1 Hour 25 Minutes | Serving: 1 Loaf

Ingredients

- 1 3/4 cup of (175g) almond meal
- 1/2 tsp baking powder
- 2 ripe bananas, flesh mashed with a fork
- 1/2 tsp bicarbonate of soda
- 1 vanilla bean, seeds scraped
- 2 apples, 1 grated, 1 thinly sliced
- 125g blueberries, crushed with a fork
- 3/4 cup of (85g) coconut flour
- 225g unsalted butter, softened
- ½ cup of (100g) rice flour
- 1/4 cup of (90g) honey, plus extra to drizzle
- 3 eggs
- 1 cup of (140g) coconut sugar
- 1/4 cup of (60ml) almond milk

Spice powder:

- 1 pinch saffron threads
- 2 small cinnamon quills
- 2 tsp juniper berries (optional)
- Seeds from 2 tsp cardamom pods
- 1 tsp Murray River sea salt flakes
- 1 tsp white peppercorns
- 2 whole star anise
- 1/2 tsp cloves

Instructions

1. Turn oven on to 180°C. For spice powder, put star anise, peppercorns, cinnamon, cloves, and cardamom in a pan over medium heat and cook for around 1-2 minutes or until the mixture smells good. Mix with the juniper berries, saffron, and salt in a mortar and pestle. Make it into powder.
2. Vanilla, 200g of butter, and sugar are mixed in a stand mixer. Bananas and eggs should be added one at a time. On low, add 1 1/2 tsp spice powder, grated apple, blueberries, flours, almond meal, baking powder, bicarbonate, 1 tsp salt, and almond milk. Beat until everything is well mixed.
3. Pour into a 24 x 12 cm loaf pan that has been oiled. Make it for about 1 hour and 15 minutes or until a clean skewer comes out.
4. Honey and 25g of butter should be put in a pan over medium heat. Add slices of apple. Cook for 3–4 minutes, turning, until the sugars caramelize on top of the Bread.
5. Serve with honey on top.

6. BRIOCHE BREAD

Prep Time: 30 Minutes | Cook Time: 20 Minutes

Total Time: 50 Minutes | Serving: 8

Ingredients

- 1 large egg(s)
- 2 large egg(s)
- 115 grams of unsalted butter
- 250 grams of bleached all-purpose flour
- 11.25 mL active dry yeast 1 packet
- 63 mL whole milk (3.25 % fat) warmed to 110–115ºF
- 1 tsp water
- 5 mL Diamond Crystal fine kosher salt
- 30 mL granulated sugar

Instructions

1. First, put the yeast and warm milk in the bowl of a stand mixer at a paddle connection and stir them together. This will get the yeast wet. Let stand for 8 minutes.
2. Put the flour and salt and mix on low until the mixture is dry and shaggy.
3. Add the eggs and sugar one at a time, beating well after each addition.
4. Change the attachment to the dough hook and beat the dough until it is smooth and the bowl is clean. It will take about 3–4 minutes to do this.
5. Switch back to the paddle, add all the butter to the dough, and then beat it in. When the dough starts to come back together, return to the dough hook and beat on low for roughly 10 minutes, or until the dough is nicely smooth and elastic and the bowl is clean again.
6. Butter a bowl, then place the dough in it. Use Saran wrap to cover. Let it sit out until it has doubled in size (mine took almost 3 hours), then punch it down to deflate it, cover it, and put it in the fridge overnight.
7. The next morning, cut the dough into 8 pieces and roll them quickly into balls on the counter. Don't work the dough for too long or the butter will melt. Put a dough ball in each of the eight holes of a muffin tin that has been buttered. Take the muffin tin on a baking sheet with a rim and cover it with a sheet of waxed paper. Put the sheet in the oven with just the light on (the oven should be off). Let the dough balls rise for about 1.5 hours or until they are twice as big. When the dough has doubled in size, take the pan out of the oven and set it on the counter while you heat the oven to 400oF.
8. Combine the egg with 1 tsp of water and lightly brush each bun. When the oven is ready, Cook for 15–20 minutes until the tops are a deep golden brown. Wait 10 minutes before taking it out of the mold. Serve hot with homemade jam or marmalade and, if you dare, more butter.

7. CHALLAH BREAD

Prep Time: 3 Hours | Cook Time: 30 Minutes

Total Time: 3 Hours 30 Minutes | Serving: 2 Loaves

Ingredients

- 1 tsp sugar
- ¼ cup of olive or vegetable oil
- 2 eggs
- 1 ½ cups of water
- 2 ¼ tsp dry yeast
- 1 egg yolk
- 1 tsp salt
- ½ cup of sugar
- 6 cups of flour

Instructions

1. Add the yeast to a small bowl with 1/4 cup of warm (105–115 F) sugar-dissolved water. Let rise for 5 minutes or until foamy.
2. Mix the eggs, 1/2 cup of sugar, oil, and 1 1/3 cups of water in the bowl of a stand mixer. Mix until everything is even, then add the yeast mixture left to rise. Mix again.
3. Put the flour and salt in a separate bowl. Then, take the flour and salt to the wet mixture and mix to combine. Use a dough hook (or hands to knead) the mixture until it is completely smooth. It shouldn't stick to you. I let the dough hook work for about 7 minutes in my KitchenAid mixer.
4. Put the dough in a bowl that has been lightly greased, then cover it with plastic wrap and a kitchen towel. Let rise in a warm place for 1.5 to 2 hours or until it has doubled in size.
5. When the dough has risen, hit it down and turn it onto a lightly floured surface. Split it in half and let it sit for 10 minutes.
6. Divide each piece into three equal parts (you have a total of six pieces). Make each piece into a long rope about 1" thick. You need to make two loaves, so braid three pieces of dough together, pinch, and tuck the ends under.
7. Take on a baking sheet lined with parchment paper or lightly oiled with oil.
8. Give the loaves an hour to rise.
9. Set the oven temperature to 350 F.
10. Blend the egg yolk with 1 tbsp of water and brush it on the loaves. If you want, you can sprinkle them with poppy seeds.
11. Bake for 30 minutes. Challah should be golden and hollow when you tap it with your finger.

8. CHOCOLATE CHIP BANANA BREAD

Prep Time: 10 Minutes | Cook Time: 1 Hour

Total Time: 1 Hour 10 Minutes | Serving: 10

Ingredients

- 2/3 cup of granulated sugar
- 1/2 cup of unsalted butter (8 Tbsp), softened
- 1 cup of semisweet chocolate chips divided
- 1 tsp baking soda
- 1/2 tsp salt
- 1/2 tsp vanilla extract
- 2 large eggs, room temperature
- 1 1/2 cups of all-purpose flour
- 3 bananas (very ripe)

Instructions

1. Turn the oven on to 350°F. Butter and flour a bread loaf pan that is 9.25"L x 5.25" W x 2.75"D.
2. Mix together 1/2 cup of softened butter and 2/3 cup of sugar, and 1/2 cup of softened butter in a stand mixer with the paddle attachment. Add 2 eggs that have been lightly beaten.
3. With a fork, mash the bananas until they look like chunky applesauce. Add the bananas and 1/2 tsp of vanilla extract to the stand mixer. Mix until blended.
4. Blend all of the dry ingredients in a separate bowl: 1/2 tsp of salt, 1/2 cup of flour, and 1 tsp of baking soda. Put in a stand mixer and mix until everything is mixed in.
5. Mix in 3/4 cup of chocolate chips, then move to a bread pan that has been prepared. Sprinkle the remaining 1/4 cup of chocolate on top, and bake at 350°F for 55–65 minutes, or until a toothpick inserted into the middle comes out clean. Let the banana bread sit for around 10 minutes before cooling it on a rack.

9. CHOCOLATE ZUCCHINI BREAD

Prep Time: 20 Minutes | Cook Time: 1 Hour

Total Time: 1 Hour 20 Minutes | Serving: 8

Ingredients

- 1 pinch ground cloves
- 2 egg
- 1 cup of granulated sugar
- 1 cup of grated zucchini, reserving any juice
- 1/4 cup of unsweetened cocoa powder
- 1/2 tbsp vanilla extract
- 1/2 tsp baking soda
- 1/2 cup of chopped walnuts
- 1/4 tsp baking powder
- 1/2 tbsp ground cinnamon
- 1/2 tsp salt
- 1/2 cup of vegetable oil
- 1 1/2 cups of all-purpose flour
- 1 pinch ground allspice

Instructions

1. First, Warm up the oven to 350 degrees F. Spray baking spray into a 9x5 bread loaf pan, then set it aside.
2. Grate zucchini into a small bowl, making sure to save any juice. Once you have a full cup of zucchini, set it aside.
3. Mix flour, cocoa powder, cinnamon, salt, baking soda, baking powder, cloves, and allspice in a large bowl with a whisk. Set aside.
4. Using a stand mixer, mix the sugar, vegetable oil, egg, and vanilla on medium speed for about 1-2 minutes or until the egg is broken up and creamy.
5. Stop the mixer. Add the zucchini and liquid to the batter, and then mix on low speed for another minute or two until everything is mixed in.
6. Mix the dry ingredients slowly, about 1/2 cup of at a time, while keeping the mixer speed low. Mix for about 2–3 minutes, or until the dry ingredients are mostly mixed in, and there are few clumps.
7. Take the bowl off the blender. Pour in the walnuts and gently fold them in with a spatula.
8. Pour the batter into the loaf pan. The batter should be thin enough to settle in the pan easily. If not, tap the tap on the counter a few times to make it even and get rid of any air bubbles.
9. Bake the Bread for around 60 minutes or until a toothpick added in the middle comes out clean.
10. After 15 minutes, move the Bread to a cooling rack to cool completely. Serve right away.

10. CIABATTA BREAD

Prep Time: 45 Minutes | Cook Time: 30 Minutes | Resting Time: 1 Day

Total Time: 1 Day, 75 Minutes | Serving: 2 Loaves

Ingredients

For the poolish:

- 1 scant cup of (200 ml) of water, room temperature
- 1 ½ cups of (200 g) bread flour
- ¼ tsp instant yeast

For the dough:

- 2 ⅔ cups of (350 g) bread flour
- 1 cup of (240 ml) water, room temperature
- 2 tsp salt
- ½ tsp instant yeast

Instructions

1. Make the poolish: Mix the flour, water, and yeast in a medium-sized bowl. Mix everything with a wooden spoon until everything is smooth. Warp it with plastic wrap and let it sit at room temperature for 15–20 hours to ferment.

Make the dough:

1. Put the poolish and all the dough elements into the bowl of a stand mixer with a paddle connection. Mix on low speed for about 2 minutes or until all the flour is wet. Change the speed to medium-low and mix until the dough starts to move away from the bowl, which should take about 6 minutes.
2. Change to the dough hook and mix at medium-low for about 10 minutes or until the dough is smooth and shiny. Like batter, the dough will be soft, wet, and sticky.
3. Take olive oil or non-stick spray to coat a large bowl lightly. Use a dough scraper made of silicone to move the dough into the bowl. Warp it with plastic wrap and let it sit at room temperature for 1 hour.
4. Using a greased scraper or wet fingers, gently lift and stretch one side of the dough over the other. Turn the bowl 180 degrees and stretch in the same way. Turn 90 degrees, then pull and fold. Turn the paper 180 degrees to fold and stretch the last side. The bottom of the dough should become the top. Warp it with plastic wrap and let it sit at room temperature for 45 minutes. Fold it again twice, then warp it with plastic wrap and let it sit for around 45 minutes after each time.

5. Adjust the oven racks so that one is in the lower third (just below the middle) and the other at the bottom. Place a cast-iron skillet on the bottom rack and a baking sheet turned upside down on the top rack. Make sure the oven is at 450°F. To make sure the oven is hot enough, you should let it heat up for at least an hour.
6. Sprinkle a lot of flour on your work surface and let the dough slide out of the bowl onto it. Try to handle the dough as little as possible and be careful, so you don't knock all the air out of it. Sprinkle flour all over the top of the dough. Carefully shape the dough into a square using 2 bench scrapers dusted with flour. Be careful not to press down on the dough.
7. In the middle of the square, cut the dough in half. Use the bench scrapers to gently shape the sides of each half into loaves.
8. Flip over a large baking sheet and lay a sheet of parchment paper across the top. Use a lot of flour to dust. Slide both bench scrapers under both ends of the dough and move it to the parchment paper that has been prepared. Do the same thing with the other loaf. As you shape each loaf into a rectangle, gently poke the surface with your fingertips.
9. Cover the loaves with a lint-free cloth so they don't dry out. Proof in a place with no drafts until it gets puffy and small bubbles form on the surface, which takes about 30 minutes.
10. Prepare 1 cup of ice. Spray the loaves with water, then gently jerk the parchment with the loaves onto the preheated baking sheet in the oven. Put the ice in the cast-iron pan on the bottom rack right away. Close the oven door quickly.
11. Bake for about 25–35 minutes or until the crust is a deep golden brown. The inside of the Bread should be between 210 and 215°F.
12. Move to a rack to cool completely before slicing and serving.

11. FRENCH BREAD

Prep Time: 15 Minutes | Cook Time: 30 Minutes

Total Time: 2 Hour 15 Minutes | Serving: 2

Ingredients

- 1 ½ pounds of dough (780 g)
- 1 ⅓ cup of (315 g) warm water
- 1 ½ tsp sea salt
- 1 (¼ ounce) packet quick-rise instant yeast or 2 ¼ tsp active dry yeast
- Olive oil or cooking spray
- 3 ½ cups of (480 g) unbleached all-purpose flour

Instructions

1. Mix WARM WATER and YEAST in a stand mixer with a dough hook.
2. Add Flour and Salt. (Save 1/2 cup of the flour to help mix.) Set up a stand mixer to mix the ingredients until a rough dough forms.
3. Mix and knead the dough for around 5 minutes with a stand mixer on low speed until it is stretchy and easy to work with. Sprinkle small amounts of the flour you saved into the bowl as you mix to keep the ingredients from sticking together.
4. Move the dough to a lightly floured surface and shape it into a tight, round shape, tucking the sides under to make a seam on the bottom.
5. For the first proof/rise, place the dough seam side down in a mixing bowl (or Instant Pot) coated with oil. Warp it with a towel or plastic wrap and let it rise until it's twice as big.
6. Deflate (or "punch down") the dough to get rid of air bubbles. You're ready for the next step.
7. Make the dough into a tight round for the second proof/rise.
8. Let's shape these loaves while the oven heats up to 450 degrees Fahrenheit.
9. Move the dough to a surface that has been lightly floured. Press the dough to remove air bubbles and divide it into two or three equal parts.
10. Press each piece into a rectangular shape that isn't too tight.
11. While making the final shape, fold and press the dough into itself until it gets tight.
12. Move to a baking sheet or loaf pan that has been prepared. Brush olive oil on the surface and cover it to keep the air out.
13. For the final proof/rise, leave the forms in a warm place until they are almost twice as big.
14. Using a sharp tool, cut 1/4-inch slits across each loaf of dough.
15. Bake for around 20–25 minutes, turning once or twice to make sure the browning is even.
16. When French Bread is done baking, it will be crisp and golden brown. If you use a thermometer that gives you a quick reading, it should be between 190 and 200 degrees Fahrenheit.
17. Place the loaves on a cooling rack and let them sit there for 5 minutes.
18. Take the loaves out of the pans and let them rest on the cooling rack until completely cool.
19. Keep cooled Bread in a plastic bag or airtight container for around 2 days at room temperature or 5 days in the refrigerator.

12. FOCACCIA BREAD

Prep Time: 75 Minutes | Cook Time: 20 Minutes

Total Time: 1 Hour 35 Minutes | Serving: 8-12

Ingredients

- 3 1/2 cups of all-purpose flour
- 2 tsp of flaky sea salt, plus extra for sprinkling
- 2 sprigs of fresh rosemary
- 1 (0.25 ounce) package of active dry yeast
- 1/4 cup of virgin olive oil, plus more for drizzling
- 1 1/3 cups of hot water (about 110°F)
- 2 tsp sugar or honey

Instructions

1. Check out the yeast. Add warm water (about 110°F), sugar, and a dough hook to the bowl of a stand mixer, and stir to mix. On top of the water, sprinkle the yeast. Give the yeast and water a quick stir to mix them. Then let it sit for around 5–10 minutes until the yeast is foamy.
2. Roll out the dough. Setting the mixer to low speed and add the flour, olive oil, and salt in small amounts. Turn the speed down to medium-low and mix the dough for another 5 minutes.
3. First, let the dough rise. Take the dough out of the bowl and roll it into a ball with your hands. Use olive oil or cooking spray to grease the mixing bowl. Put the dough ball back in the bowl and cover it with a damp towel. Place the dough warmly and let it rise for 45–60 minutes or until it is almost twice as big.
4. The second rise. Turn the dough out onto a floured surface and roll it out into a big circle or rectangle until it is about 1/2 inch thick. Again, put the damp towel over the dough, and let it rise for another 20 minutes.
5. Get the dough ready. Turn oven on to 400°F. Put the dough on a big baking sheet lined with parchment paper (9-by-13-inch baking dish). Make deep holes all over the surface of the dough with your fingers. Sprinkle 1 or 2 tbsp of olive oil evenly over the dough's top, then sprinkle the fresh rosemary needles and sea salt evenly over the top.
6. Bake for around 20 minutes or until the dough is cooked all the way through and has a golden color.
7. Serve. Take out of the oven and, if you want, drizzle with a little more olive oil. Cut it up and serve it hot.

13. GARLIC BREAD

Prep Time: 1 Hour 20 Minutes | Cook Time: 30 Minutes

Total Time: 1 Hour 50 Minutes | Serving: 2

Ingredients

- 1 tbsp white sugar
- 1/2 cup of warm water
- 1 tsp active dry yeast
- 1 tsp salt
- 1 tbsp unsalted butter (softened)
- 3 cups of bread flour
- 1/2 cup of milk

Topping:

- some finely chopped fresh parsley leaves
- 2 cloves garlic (finely minced)
- 1 pinch salt
- 4 tbsp butter (melted)

Instructions

1. Warm water goes into the bowl of a stand mixer with a dough hook. Sugar and yeast are added to the water. Let it sit for 5–10 minutes until the foam forms. Mix in the butter, milk, and salt. Slowly stir in the flour. Seven to ten minutes. The dough should cling to the bowl's bottom but slide off the sides, but the sides should be clear. Divide the dough into 2 equal portions.
2. Mix the butter, salt, parsley leaves, and garlic in a small bowl. Cut small rounds of dough and dip them in the butter mixture. Put the dough balls in one regular loaf pan or two mini loaf pans. Cover and let rise for about an hour or until doubled in size. Save the butter mixture that is left over.
3. Bake for around 30 minutes at 350°F (176°C) or until golden brown. Spread the butter mixture on the garlic bread, which you can pull apart after it comes out of the oven.

14. IRISH SODA BREAD

Prep Time: 15 Minutes | Cook Time: 45 Minutes

Total Time: 1 Hour | Serving: 3

Ingredients

- 1 1/2 cups of buttermilk
- 2 eggs
- 1/3 cup of sugar
- 1 tsp salt
- 3 tbsp caraway seeds
- 1 cup of dried cranberries
- 1 tsp baking soda
- 1/2 tsp baking powder
- 4 cups of bread flour
- 3 tbsp UNSALTED melted butter

Instructions

1. Turn oven on to 350. Using greased parchment paper, prepare a baking sheet. Mix the flour, sugar, baking soda, salt, baking powder, cranberries, and caraway seeds in the bowl of a stand mixer.
2. In a separate bowl, combine eggs, buttermilk at room temperature (not cold!), and melted butter that has cooled down. You can make buttermilk by adding two tbsp of apple cider vinegar to a little less than 1 1/2 cups of milk (taking out about 2 tbsp of milk.) Wait a few minutes before you use this.
3. Mix the wet and dry elements to make dough. To get the dough to come together, knead it for two to three minutes using a dough hook attachment. If the dough is too sticky or shiny, add more flour. You should not have to do this using a stand mixer.
4. Shape the dough into three small, 4-5" circles. Place on a baking sheet that has been prepared. Spread melted butter on each round. Make an "X" on each loaf with a sharp knife.
5. About 45 minutes. Cook until a toothpick stuck in the middle comes out clean. After 30 minutes, turn the loaves.

15. MEXICAN SWEET BREAD

Prep Time: 20 Minutes | Cook Time: 30 Minutes

Total Time: 50 Minutes | Serving: 12

Ingredients

For the Bread:

- Dry yeast (¼ ounce)
- Salt
- Whole Milk
- All Purpose Flour
- Vanilla Extract
- Oil (for greasing)
- Large Eggs (room temperature, beaten)
- Unsalted butter (melted)
- Granulated sugar (divided)

For the Topping:

- Vanilla Extract
- Unsalted butter (softened)
- Unsweetened Cocoa Powder
- All Purpose Flour
- Powdered Sugar

Instructions

1. Heat Milk: Heat the milk in 20-second bursts in a microwave-safe bowl until it feels warm to the touch (about 110-115 degrees F).
2. Combine the sugar and yeast: Add the yeast and half of the sugar and mix well.
3. Cover the mixture: Wrap it in plastic wrap and let it sit for around 5 minutes or until it bubbles.
4. Mix dry ingredients: Mix the salt, flour, and the rest of the sugar in the bowl of the stand mixer.
5. Mix in yeast mixture: Put the bowl in the stand mixer, then secure the dough hook to the machine. Then add the mixture of melted butter, eggs, and yeast.
6. Combine Dough: Mix the dough on medium speed for around 5–7 minutes or until the dough comes together. If the dough is still sticky, take more flour, one tbsp at a time, until it is no longer sticky and is instead smooth and slightly tacky.

16. NAAN BREAD

Prep Time: 15 Minutes | Cook Time: 75 Minutes

Total Time: 1 Hour 30 Minutes | Serving: 8

Ingredients

Naan ingredients:

- 1/4 cup of plain yogurt
- 1 (0.25 ounce) package of active dry yeast (about 2 1/4 tsp)
- 2 tbsp honey
- 3 1/2 cups of all-purpose flour
- 1 large egg
- 1 cup of warm water (about 110°F)
- 1/2 tsp baking powder
- 2 tsp fine sea salt

Garlic butter ingredients(optional):

- 3 cloves garlic, peeled and minced
- (optional) flaky sea salt
- 1/4 cup of salted butter
- finely- chopped fresh cilantro or parsley

Instructions

1. Turn on the yeast: Stir the warm water and honey together quickly in the bowl of a stand mixer. Spread the yeast over the water and stir it quickly. Then, let the mixture sit for 5–10 minutes until the yeast is foamy.
2. Blend the dough: Mix the flour, yogurt, baking powder, salt, and egg. Mix the dough for two to three minutes on medium-low speed with the dough hook until it is smooth.
3. The dough needs to rise: Take the dough out of the bowl and roll it into a ball with your hands. Lightly spray cooking spray in the mixing bowl, then put the dough ball back in the bowl and warp it with a damp towel. Put the bowl in a warm place (I put mine by a sunny window) and let the dough rise for an hour or until it is almost twice as big.
4. Make the garlic butter(Optional): During the last 10 minutes of the dough's rising time, melt the butter in a small sauté pan at medium heat. Take the garlic and cook it for a minute or two until it smells good. Take the pan off the heat and, if you want, stir in some chopped herbs.
5. To roll out the dough: Once the dough is ready, put it on a floured work surface and shape it into a roughly round circle. Cut the dough into 8 pieces that are all the same size, and roll each piece into a ball with your hands. The dough ball should then be rolled out with a rolling pin until it forms an oval and is about 1/4 inch thick.
6. Make the Bread: Make sure a large cast-iron skillet or non-stick sauté pan is nice and hot over medium-high heat. Put a piece of the rolled-out dough in the pan and cook it for around 1 minute, or until the top starts to bubble and the bottom turns a light golden color. Flip the dough and cook on the other side for around 30–60 seconds or until the bottom is

golden. Then, move the dough to a clean plate. You can sprinkle a pinch of flaky sea salt on the naan if you want. Then, keep a clean towel on top of the naan warm. Repeat with the rest of the dough until all the naan pieces are cooked. Adjust the pan's heat to keep it hot (but not too hot so the Bread burns).
7. Serve: Give it to them hot and enjoy!

17. PANINI BREAD

Prep Time: 15 Minutes | Cook Time: 18 Minutes

Total Time: 1 Hour 10 Minutes | Serving: 12

Ingredients

- Biga/Starter:
- 250 gms Flour
- 2 gms Yeast
- 140 ml Water

Panini Bread Dough:

- 12 gms Yeast
- 300 ml Water
- 25 gms Olive Oil
- 10 gms Honey
- 500 gms Flour
- 50 gms Sun-dried Tomato
- 10 gms Salt

Instructions

1. Make the biga or starter culture first. Everything listed under "Biga Ingredients" should be mixed to make a dough. Here, there's no need to knead the dough. Just mix until a dough forms. Wrap it in plastic wrap and let it sit out overnight or for at least 8 hours.
2. Put the flour, salt, olive oil, honey, and in the stand mixer the next day to make the dough. Mix the yeast and water, then add it to the stand mixer. For 8 minutes, knead the dough.
3. After 8 minutes, add the sun-dried tomatoes and stir for 30 seconds more.
4. Lightly grease the bowl, put the dough in it, and let it rise for 40 minutes. You can also let it rise in the instant pot for 20 minutes.
5. After 40 minutes, weigh and shape the dough into balls of 100 gms each, and let it rise again for 10 minutes.
6. Then, flatten a roundel out so it looks like a torpedo. Just flatten them with a rolling pin into an oval shape about the size of your palm.
7. Put it on a baking sheet that has parchment paper already on it. Let it rise for 10 minutes, then bake it at 160°C for 14–18 minutes in an oven that has been preheated.
8. Before slicing, stuffing, and grilling your preferred sandwich, let it cool completely.

18. PITA BREAD

Prep Time: 10 Minutes | Cook Time: 10 Minutes | Proofing Time: 3 Hours

Total Time: 3 Hours 20 Minutes | Serving: 8

Ingredients
- 1 ½ tsp salt
- 2 tsp. active dry yeast 1 packet
- 2 ½ to 3 cups of all-purpose flour + more for kneading
- 1 cup of warm water
- 2 tsp. sugar
- 2 tbsp. Olive oil + more for oiling bowl

Instructions
1. Add the warm water, yeast, sugar, and oil to the bowl of a stand mixer. Give it a gentle whisk to mix in the yeast.
2. Let the yeast mixture sit for around 5 minutes or until it foams up.
3. Method for Stand Mixer: Attach a dough hook to the stand mixer and slowly add flour and salt. Combine on low to medium speed until the dough pulls away from the bowl. You can use a spatula to get any flour left on the bottom of the bowl by kneading the dough.

19. POTATO BREAD

Prep Time: 10 Minutes | Cook Time: 50 Minutes

Total Time: 1 Hours | Serving: 2

Ingredients

- 2 large eggs
- 2 1/2 tsp (15g) salt
- 6 1/2 cups of (780g) All-Purpose Flour
- 1/2 cup of (99g) granulated sugar
- 1 cup of (198g) of mashed potatoes
- 1 tbsp instant yeast
- 12 tbsp (170g) unsalted butter, softened
- 1 1/4-1 1/2 cups of (283g to 340g) lukewarm water or potato water

Instructions

1. Weigh your flour, gently put it in a cup of with a spoon, and then wipe off any extra. Blend all dough ingredients using the flat beater paddle on the stand mixer. Beat the mixture for 4-5 minutes at medium-high speed, stopping the mixer twice to scrape down the sides and bottom of the bowl. The mixture should start to get smoother and maybe even a little shiny.
2. Make the change to the dough hook, and knead the dough for 7 minutes at medium speed, pausing twice to scrape the dough into a ball. The dough may or may not start to clear the sides of the bowl on its own during this time.
3. Make a ball out of the dough and put it in a bowl or large bag that has been lightly greased. Refrigerate for at least one night and up to 24 hours.
4. Cut the dough from the fridge in half, and roll each into a 9" log. Put each one into a 9-by-5-inch greased loaf pan.

20. PUMPERNICKEL BREAD

Prep Time: 25 Minutes | Cook Time: 40 Minutes | Proof Time: 2 Hours

Total Time: 3 Hours 5 Minutes | Serving: 2

Ingredients

- 1 tbsp salt
- 1 ½ cup of (12flounce/340ml) warm water
- 2 cups of (10ounce/282g) of rye flour (or whole wheat)
- 1 tbsp sugar
- 2 ½ cups of (12 ½ounce/355g) all-purpose flour
- ½ cup of (5ounce/142g) molasses (or treacle)
- 2 tbsp vegetable oil
- 2 tbsp cocoa
- 5 tsp instant dry yeast

Instructions

1. Grease two 9 by 5-inch loaf pans. Set aside.
2. Put the dry ingredients (flour, yeast, salt, cocoa powder, and sugar) in a big bowl. Stir things up.
3. Mix the warm water, molasses, and oil in a separate bowl.
4. Take the wet ingredients into the dry ones until the dough sticks together.
5. Knead the dough for about 6–8 minutes or until it is smooth and no longer sticky. Use a mixer on a stand.
6. Put a little oil in the bowl and put the dough in it. Cover the dough and let it rise until it has doubled, which takes about 60-90 minutes.
7. After the dough has risen, knock it back and shape it into two loaves to put in the pans you have already prepared.
8. Cover it again, and put it in a warm place for about 45 minutes or until it's doubled in size, Place the oven temperature to 375°F (190°C).
9. For about 40 minutes, bake. When you tap the base of the dough, it should sound hollow.
10. Let it cool on a rack before you cut it. Bread can be kept for up to 3 days at room temperature. You can also freeze it for up to eight weeks.

21. PUMPKIN BREAD

Prep Time: 20 Minutes | Cook Time: 1 Hour

Total Time: 1 Hour 20 Minutes | Serving: 12

Ingredients

- 4 eggs
- 1/2 tsp nutmeg (or less)
- 2 tsp baking soda
- 2 cups of (424 g) sugar
- 2 tsp cinnamon
- 15 to 16 ounces (454 g) canned pumpkin (not pie filling)
- 1 to 1.5 tsp (5 to 7 grams) fine sea salt or kosher salt or 1.5 tsp salt now
- 1 cup of (215 g) vegetable or canola oil or other neutral oil
- 3/4 cup of (177 g) water
- 3 cups of (384 g) flour
- 1/2 tsp allspice (optional
- 1/2 tsp cloves (optional)

Instructions

1. Turn the oven on to 350oF. Use butter or non-stick spray to grease two standard (8.5 x 4.5 inch) loaf pans.
2. Combine the oil and sugar using a stand mixer until they are well mixed. Add the eggs one by one, stirring after each one. Mix the pumpkin purée and water until they are well mixed.
3. Take the flour, baking soda, salt, cinnamon, nutmeg, cloves(if using), and allspice; Whisk until everything comes together. Pour the batter into the pans.
4. Cook for about 1 hour, but start checking after 45 minutes. The loaves are done when the center bounces back when touched. The loaves should be ready in less than 45 minutes when the small pans are used. Start checking after 30 minutes.
5. Let it cool in the pan for around 15–20 minutes, then move it to a cooling rack to keep cooling before cutting it and serving it.

22. SANDWICH BREAD

Prep Time: 2 Hours | Cook Time: 30 Minutes

Total Time: 2 Hours 30 Minutes | Serving: 2

Ingredients

- 16 ounce hot water
- 2-1/4 tsp. (1 packet) active dry yeast
- 1 Tbsp. extra virgin olive oil
- 3-1/2 Tbsp. honey
- 1 Tbsp. kosher salt
- 5-1/2 cups of all-purpose flour

Instructions

1. Put the yeast and all the other dry elements into the bowl of the stand mixer. Put warm water, oil, and honey in a separate bowl. Stir well to mix the liquids.
2. Set the mixer's dough hook attachment to low speed for 15 seconds to mix the dry ingredients. Stop the mixer, add the liquid, and set it back to low speed for about a minute and a half or until all the ingredients are mixed. Stop the mixer and let it sit for ten minutes.
3. Set the mixer's speed to 2 and let it run for 3 minutes. Take out the dough hook and turn the dough out onto a floured surface. Knead 3 or 4 times to get rid of any air pockets.
4. Put the dough in a bowl that has been greased and cover it with plastic wrap and a kitchen towel. Let dough rise for around 1 hour in a warm place with no drafts. When the hour is up, punch down the dough, turn it out onto a floured surface, and knead it a few more times. Make loaves out of the dough and put them in two loaf pans.
5. Warp the loaves with a kitchen towel and let them rise for about 45 minutes or until they are twice as big.
6. Drizzle olive oil on top of the loaves and bake them at 375 degrees for 30 to 35 minutes or until the crust is a light golden brown. Take out of the loaf pans and let cool for at least 30 minutes on a rack before cutting.

23. SOURDOUGH BREAD

Prep Time: 30 Minutes | Cook Time: 45 Minutes | Rising Time: 18 Hours

Total Time: 19 Hours 15 Minutes | Serving: 1 Loaf

Ingredients

- 1 tbsp sugar
- 6 cups of bread flour 31.8 ounces/ 900 grams
- 2 cups of lukewarm water 16 ounces/ 440 grams
- 3½ tsp salt
- 1½ cups of active sourdough starter 11.25 ounces/ 330 grams

Instructions

1. Put the bread flour, starter, sugar, and water in the stand mixer's bowl. Mix on low speed until all of the ingredients are mixed in. It will look rough and maybe even a little dry. Let the bowl sit at room temperature for around 30 minutes with a clean, damp tea towel on top.
2. Knead until smooth in the stand mixer. Take the salt, then knead the dough on low for 5-9 minutes until soft. The dough should come together into a ball and not stick to the bowl's sides or bottom. If it's too dry, add more water; if it's too wet, add more flour.
3. Rise until doubled. Make a smooth ball out of the dough and put it in a clean, lightly oiled mixing bowl. Warp it with greased plastic wrap and put it in a warm place for around 3-4 hours or until it has doubled and is very puffy.
4. Split, shape, and come back up. Cut the dough in half and shape each half into a smooth ball by pulling the bottom of the dough smoothly. Place in a floured proofing basket or on a parchment-lined baking sheet. Warp it with greased plastic wrap and put it in the refrigerator for at least 18 hours or overnight.
5. Bake. Put an empty Dutch oven in the morning and heat it to 425 degrees. Use a lame or serrated knife to cut. Put the loaf on a piece of parchment and carefully lower it into the hot Dutch oven. Put the lid on and bake for around 25 minutes with the lid on. Then take the lid off and bake for another 20 minutes with the lid off, until the food is a very deep golden brown color.
6. Cool down and cut. Take the loaf out of the oven and let it cool on a rack for 4 hours before cutting it. You can keep it at room temperature for up to four days.

24. WHEAT BREAD

Prep Time: 45 Minutes | Cook Time: 30 Minutes

Total Time: 1 Hour 15 Minutes | Serving: 2 Loaves

Ingredients

- ¼ cup of vital wheat gluten
- ⅓ cup of oil
- 1 tbsp salt
- 1 ½ tbsp instant yeast
- 1 tbsp lemon juice, bottled or fresh
- ⅓ cup of (113 g) honey
- 5-6 cups of (710 to 852 g) of whole wheat flour,
- 2 ¾ cups of warm water

Instructions

1. Mix 3 cups of whole wheat flour, gluten, and yeast in the stand mixer with a dough hook. Mix well after adding the warm water. Warp the bowl and set it aside for 10 to 12 minutes.
2. Mix in the honey, lemon juice, oil, and salt. On low speed, mix.
3. Put flour 1/2 cup of at a time while the mixer runs low speed until the dough is removed from the bowl's sides.
4. Let the mixer work the dough for 5–6 minutes or until it is smooth and soft.
5. Turn the dough out onto a counter that has been lightly greased and cut it in half. Form each half into a tight loaf and put it in an 8 1/2-by-4 1/2-inch loaf pan that has been lightly greased.
6. Warp the loaf pans and let the loaves rise until they are 1 to 2 inches above the edge of the loaf pan.
7. Prepare the oven temperature to 350 degrees F. Make sure one of the oven racks is in the middle. Bake the loaves for 28–32 minutes or until golden brown and cooked all through (a thermometer should read 180–190 degrees in the center of a loaf).
8. The Bread should be put on a wire rack. If using, brush the tops with butter. Let cool down all the way.

25. WHITE BREAD

Prep Time: 15 Minutes | Cook Time: 30 Minutes | Rising Time: 1 Hour 30 Minutes

Total Time: 2 Hours 15 Minutes | Serving: 2 Loaves

Ingredients

- 2 1/4 tsp of dry yeast or instant yeast
- 1 1/2 Tbsp. butter, melted for brushing
- 1 2/3 cups of lukewarm water divided
- 1 Tbsp honey (or more sugar)
- 1 tsp salt
- 4 1/2 cups of all-purpose flour
- 1 tsp sugar
- 1 1/2 Tbsp of unsalted butter, cubed at room temperature

Instructions

1. Mix the instant yeast, sugar, and half of the hot water in the bowl of a stand mixer with a dough hook. Let sit for 5–10 minutes or 15 minutes (if you use active dry yeast).
2. Add the rest of the water, honey, salt, butter cut into small pieces, and 4 cups of flour to the bowl. Knead the dough slowly until it comes together, is soft but not sticky, and holds its shape. If you need to, add a few more tbsp of flour. Keep kneading for another 6–9 minutes or until the dough pulls away from the bowl's sides and is soft and smooth.
3. Put the dough in a bowl that has been lightly greased and make sure it is fully covered. Warp it with plastic wrap and put it in a warm place without drafts for about 45 minutes or until the size doubles.
4. Dust your work surface with a little flour and turn out the dough on it. Split it into two pieces that are the same size. Use your fingers to gently pat each half into an 8-by-12-inch rectangle while pressing it all over to get rid of any air pockets. Roll the rectangle tightly, starting at the short end, and pinch the seams to seal. To add some tension to the surface, tuck the roll's ends just slightly under the roll. Place each loaf, seam side down, with ends tucked in and seam side down, in a greased 8x4-inch loaf pan. Warp with a piece of greased plastic wrap and let rise in a warm place without drafts for about 45 minutes or until it has doubled in size.
5. Put the oven rack in the lower-middle position and heat the oven to 390 degrees F.
6. Bake loaves for around 25–30 minutes or until golden brown (and reaching 208–210 degrees on a thermometer).
7. Turn the bread over onto a rack for cooling. Turn the loaves over and brush the tops and sides with melted butter. Let it cool all the way down before cutting.

26. ZUCCHINI BREAD

Prep Time: 15 Minutes | Cook Time: 1 Hour

Total Time: 1 Hour 15 Minutes | Serving: 2 Loaves

Ingredients

- 2 cups of divided
- 1 tbsp vanilla extract
- 1 tsp baking powder
- 3 large eggs
- 3 tsp of ground cinnamon
- 2 cups of granulated sugar
- 3 cups of all-purpose flour
- 1/4 cup of light brown sugar, divided
- 2 cups of grated zucchini, packed
- 1 tsp
- 1 cup of vegetable oil
- 1 tsp baking soda

Instructions

1. First, Set the oven to 325 degrees F and use nonstick spray to grease two 9-by-5-inch or 8-by-4-inch bread pans.
2. Eggs, vegetable oil, sugar, and vanilla are mixed in a stand mixer.
3. Mix the flour, salt, cinnamon, baking powder, and baking soda in a separate large bowl.
4. Put the dry ingredients and the wet ingredients in two separate steps, mixing between each one. Then beat for around 1 more minute, pushing the sides down so it gets mixed well. It's fine that the mixture looks dry and thick.
5. Add the grated zucchini and 1 cup of walnuts and beat for around 1 minute, scraping down the sides as needed.
6. Split the batter between the 2 loaf pans. Sprinkle 1/2 cup of chopped walnuts and 2 tbsp of light brown sugar on top of each loaf.
7. Bake the leaves for 50 to 60 minutes or until the center of a toothpick or cake tester comes out clean.
8. Take the bread out of the oven and let it cool in the pans for 20 minutes. Then take the bread out of the pans and let it cool completely.

CAKES

27. CARROT CAKE

Prep Time: 17 Minutes | Cook Time: 35 Minutes

Total Time: 52 Minutes | Serving: 16 slices

Ingredients

For the cake:

- 1 1/2 cups of oil
- 3 cups of grated carrots
- 2 cups of sugar
- 1/2 tsp pure vanilla extract
- 1 tsp salt
- 2 tsp cinnamon
- 2 cups of all-purpose flour
- 4 eggs
- 2 tsp baking soda

For the cream cheese frosting:

- 1 package of cream cheese (8-ounce package)
- 1 stick butter, softened
- 1/2 cup of chopped walnuts
- 1 pound confectioners' sugar (powdered sugar)
- 1 tsp pure vanilla extract

Instructions

For the cake:

1. Set oven temperature to 350 degrees.
2. All the dry ingredients (cinnamon, flour, baking soda, salt, and sugar) should be mixed in a large bowl and set aside.
3. Take the eggs, oil, and vanilla into the bowl of the stand mixer.
4. Slowly add the dry ingredients and shredded carrots while the mixer is on low. Mix until just combined.
5. Put the batter into two greased 9-inch cake pans. Make it for about 35 minutes or until a toothpick comes out clean.

For the cream cheese frosting:

1. Take the cream cheese, butter, powdered sugar, and vanilla and beat with a stand mixer until the mixture is smooth. Begin on low and gradually increase the speed until it resembles frosting (about a minute).
2. Add the walnuts at the end and beat for a few seconds to mix them in.
3. Frost the cake only after it has cooled down completely

29. CRAB CAKES WITH HERB SALAD

Prep Time: 40 Minutes | Cook Time: 10 Minutes

Total Time: 50 Minutes | Serving: 6

Ingredients

For the Mayonnaise:

- ½ tsp Dijon mustard
- ½ tsp kosher salt
- 2 tsp unseasoned rice wine vinegar
- 2 egg yolks
- 1 cup of canola oil
- 1 tbsp fresh lemon juice

For the Crab Cakes:

- ¼ cup of mayonnaise
- ½ cup of panko (Japanese bread crumbs), plus more for breading
- 1 pound cooked fresh jumbo lump crab meat
- 1 large shallot, minced
- 2 tbsp unsalted butter, softened
- Kosher salt, to taste
- 1 lemongrass stalk, trimmed and minced
- Zest of 1 lemon
- Canola oil for frying

For the Herb Salad:

- 1 tbsp fresh lime juice
- 2 tsp olive oil
- Kosher salt, to taste
- 1 cup of cilantro sprigs
- 1 cup of Thai basil leaves
- ½ cup of mint

Instructions

1. To make the mayonnaise: Put the egg yolks, salt, mustard, lemon juice, and vinegar in a food processor and blend until smooth. Pulse it a few times to mix it in. Slowly pour in the oil while the food processor is running until the mixture starts to emulsify. Cover and put in the fridge until ready to use.
2. How to make crab cakes: In a stand mixer with a paddle connection, beat the butter, 1/4 cup of the mayonnaise, the lemongrass, the shallots, and the lemon zest until they are all mixed together.
3. Put the crab in a mixing bowl and gently fold in the butter mixture and 1/4 cup of the panko. Add salt to taste.
4. Separate the crab mixture into 6 equal parts and gently shape them into patties with your hands. Put the crab cakes in the fridge for 15 minutes to cool down and get firmer.
5. In the meantime, pulse the last 1/4 cup of panko in a food processor until it is finely ground. Put the panko in a baking dish that isn't too deep. Coat all sides of the crab cakes with the panko.
6. Put enough oil in a large skillet on medium heat to warp the bottom of the pan.

7. Brown the cakes on both sides, flipping them once, for 6 to 8 minutes, or until they are golden brown and cooked all through.
8. While you do that, make the herb salad: Mix the herbs, lime juice, and oil in a bowl, then add salt.
9. Serve the crab cakes with a spoonful of Vietnamese mayonnaise and the herb salad on top.

28. CHOCOLATE CAKE

Prep Time: 25 Minutes | Cook Time: 35 Minutes

Total Time: 1 Hour | Serving: 8

Ingredients

- 2 tsp pure vanilla extract
- ¾ cup of unsweetened cocoa powder
- 1 tsp baking powder
- 2 eggs
- ½ cup of vegetable oil
- 1 ¾ cups of all-purpose flour
- 1 cup of strong black coffee
- 1 tsp kosher salt
- 2 tbsp Dutch-processed cocoa, optional
- 2 tsp baking soda
- 1 cup of buttermilk
- 2 cups of sugar

Instructions

1. Turn oven on to 350°F. Grease and flour either two 9-inch round pans or one 13-by-9-by-2-inch pan. Set aside. Mix the sugar, flour, cocoa, baking soda, baking powder, and salt in a big bowl with a stand mixer with a whisk attachment. Mix on low until all of the dry ingredients are well blended.
2. Add eggs, buttermilk, coffee, oil, and vanilla. About two minutes at medium speed will make a thin batter.
3. Pour the batter evenly into the pans that have been prepared.
4. Bake in a preheated oven for around 30–35 minutes for round pans and 35–40 minutes for rectangular pans or until a wooden toothpick inserted in the middle comes out clean.
5. Let cool for 10 minutes, then take them out of the pans and place them on wire racks. Cool, all the way.
6. Frost as you want.

30. HONEY BUN CAKE

Prep Time: 10 Minutes | Cook Time: 35 Minutes

Total Time: 45 Minutes | Serving: 15

Ingredients

Cake:

- 2 tsp of cinnamon
- 8 ounce cream cheese softened
- ⅔ cup of oil
- 1 cup of packed brown sugar
- 15.25 ounce yellow cake mix box or homemade substitute
- 4 large eggs

Glaze:

- ½ cup of milk
- 2 ½ cups of powdered sugar
- 1 tsp vanilla extract

Instructions

1. First, set the oven to 350°F (175°C) and grease a 13"x9" baking dish.
2. With a stand mixer and a big bowl, beat the cream cheese until nicely smooth, about 30 seconds. Add the cake mix, eggs, and oil. Mix until everything is well blended.
3. In a different bowl, mix the brown sugar and cinnamon. If you're adding pecans, mix them in too.
4. Pour half of the cake batter into the dish set up for baking. Spread the cinnamon and brown sugar mixture evenly over the batter.
5. Put spoonfuls of the remaining cake batter on top of the brown sugar and cinnamon. Spread it out in an even layer to cover the whole cake.
6. Cook for around 30–35 minutes or until a toothpick inserted in the middle cleans up.
7. While the cake is baking, make the glaze. Whisk the powdered sugar, milk, and vanilla extract together in a small bowl until the mixture is smooth.
8. Take the cake out of the oven when it's done, and let it cool for 5 minutes. Make holes all over the cake.
9. Drizzle the glaze all over the hot cake. Let the cake cool down before you cut it and serve it.

31. POUND CAKE

Prep Time: 15 Minutes | Cook Time: 1 Hour 30 Minutes | Cooling Time: 15 Minutes

Total Time: 2 Hours | Serving: 16

Ingredients

- 4 cups of all-purpose flour 480g
- shortening for pan
- 3 cups of white granulated sugar 600g
- 3/4 cup of milk 180mL
- 2 tsp. vanilla extract 10mL
- flour for dusting pan
- 6 large eggs
- 1 pound of butter room temp (softened) (453g)

Instructions

1. Set the oven to 148 C/300 F. Set the rack so that it is in the middle. Put the softened butter from room temperature into a large bowl. Mix the sugar in with the butter 1/3 at a time. Use a stand mixer.
2. On medium speed, mix the eggs one at a time until they are mixed in. After the last egg, scrape the sides of the bowl.
3. Mix in the flour and milk a bit at a time, switching between the two. And mix into the dough until they are all mixed in. Whenever you need to, scrape the sides of the bowl.
4. Then you can put away the mixer. Mix the vanilla extract into the pound cake batter with a spatula.
5. Grease the sides and bottom of a bundt cake pan, tube cake pan, or two rounds or two bread pans. Then put them in the pan or pans. So the cake won't stick to the pan.
6. Put the pound cake batter in the pans and bake for around 1 hour, 30 minutes-1, hour 40 minutes, or until a toothpick or wooden skewer inserted in the middle comes clean up. Let the cake cool for around 15 minutes in the pan before you serve it.
7. Flip the cake and take it out of the pan. Add whatever toppings you like, and serve! Enjoy.

32. BUNDT CAKE

Prep Time: 15 Minutes | Cook Time: 1 Hour

Total Time: 1 Hour 15 Minutes | Serving: 10-12

Ingredients

- 4 eggs
- 1 tsp baking powder
- 400g caster sugar
- 1 tsp milk
- 200ml buttermilk
- 1 tsp baking soda
- 1 tbsp cream cheese
- 70g icing sugar
- 200g butter, softened
- 300g flour
- 1 tsp ground cinnamon

Instructions

1. First, Put the flour, a pinch of salt, baking powder, ground cinnamon, and baking soda in the stand mixer bowl with a Flat Beater. Mix for 15 seconds at speed 1.
2. Put butter and sugar in another bowl. Mix for 1 minute at speed 4. Mix for another minute after adding the eggs.
3. Slowly add the flour-buttermilk mixture. Mix until you get a smooth batter.
4. Put the batter into a bundt pan that has been greased.
5. Bake at 170°C for 50–60 minutes.
6. Blend cream cheese, milk, and icing sugar in a small bowl until smooth. Spread the frosting on top of the bundt cake. Add fresh cranberries and rosemary to finish.

33. RED VELVET CAKE

Prep Time: 10 Minutes | Cook Time: 30 Minutes | Chilling Time: 1 Hour

Total Time: 1 HourPut 40 Minutes | Serving: 8

Ingredients

Red Velvet Cake Ingredients:

- 1 tsp salt
- 14 ounces of all-purpose flour
- 2 large eggs at room temperature
- 14 ounces of granulated Sugar
- 1 Tbsp white vinegar
- 1 tsp baking soda
- 1 tsp vanilla
- 4 ounces vegetable oil
- 6 ounces unsalted butter melted but not hot
- 1 Tbsp red food coloring
- 2 Tbsp cocoa powder
- 8 ounces of buttermilk at room temperature

Cream Cheese Frosting Ingredients:

- 26 ounces powdered sugar sifted
- 8 ounces unsalted butter softened
- 12 ounces of cream cheese softened
- ¼ tsp salt
- ½ tsp vanilla extract or orange extract

Instructions

Red Velvet Cake:

1. Set your oven to 335°F and put cake goop or your preferred pan release on three 6" by 2" pans or two 8" x 2" pans. It also works well in a bundt pan, a cupcake pan, or any other pan.
2. Mix the eggs, vegetable oil, buttermilk, vinegar, butter, vanilla, and red food coloring in a medium-sized bowl. I think using food coloring gel is better than liquid food coloring.
3. Mix the flour, sugar, cocoa powder, salt, and baking soda in a stand mixer bowl with the paddle attachment. Mix this on low for a few seconds to bring everything together.
4. Take the wet ingredients to the dry and mix on medium-high speed for around 1 minute, or until the batter is smooth and all the ingredients are mixed in. Make sure all the ingredients are evenly mixed by scraping the bowl.
5. Spread the cake batter out evenly in the cake pans that have been prepared.
6. Make the cakes for 35-40 minutes, or until a toothpick added in the middle comes out clean up, and the tops bounce back when lightly touched.
7. Cool down the cakes in the pans for around 10 minutes before turning them out onto a cooling rack to finish cooling.
8. If you want to layer and frost the cake on the same day, you can put the cake layers in the freezer for about an hour without wrapping them. If not, wrap each layer in plastic wrap and put it in the freezer for up to a week.

Cream Cheese Frosting:

1. Put the softened butter into the bowl of your stand mixer with a paddle attachment. Mix on low until there are no lumps, and it is smooth.
2. Put the softened cream cheese and mix on low until the mixture is smooth and uniform. Scrape the bowl to make sure everything is mixed in.
3. Take the powdered sugar 1 cup of at a time, mixing on low so you don't throw powdered sugar out of the bowl.
4. Add the extract of vanilla and the salt. Vanilla extract goes well with cream cheese, but I like to use orange or lemon extract for a different taste.
5. If you're going to wait to use the frosting, put it in the refrigerator and cover it.

34. VANILLA CAKE

Prep Time: 30 Minutes | Cook Time: 35 Minutes

Total Time: 1 Hour 5 Minutes | Serving: 12

Ingredients

- 3 cups of all-purpose flour (375g)
- ½ tsp salt
- 1 Tbsp baking powder
- 1 ½ cups of granulated sugar (300g)
- 1/2 cup of (113g) of unsalted butter at room temperature
- ½ cup of canola or vegetable oil or avocado oil (120ml)
- 1 ¼ cup of buttermilk room temperature preferred (300ml)
- 4 large eggs at room temperature preferred
- 1 Tbsp vanilla extract
- 1 batch of Chocolate Frosting

Instructions

1. To prepare, warm the oven to 350°F (177°C), and lightly grease the sides of two deep 8" round cake pans. Set aside.
2. Cream the butter, canola oil, and sugar together in the bowl of a stand mixer until creamy and well combined.
3. Put the eggs one at a time, beating well after each addition to make sure everything is well mixed.
4. Stir in vanilla extract.
5. Take flour, baking powder, and salt with a whisk in a separate medium-sized bowl.
6. Mix until just combined after each addition of flour mixture and buttermilk to the butter combination, beginning and ending with the flour mixture. The batter should be well mixed, but there may be a few small lumps. Don't mix it too much.
7. Bake the cakes at 350F (175C) for 30-35 minutes. When the cake is done, the top should bounce back when you touch it, and a toothpick stuck in the middle should come out mostly clean with a few moist crumbs but no wet batter.
8. Let cakes cool in their pans for around 10 -15 minutes before turning them over onto a cooling rack to cool totally before frosting.
9. Frost the cake with my chocolate frosting, If you want, you can decorate it with sprinkles.

35. COFFEE CAKE

Prep Time: 20 Minutes | Cook Time: 45 Minutes

Total Time: 1 Hour 5 Minutes | Serving: 12

Ingredients

- Cinnamon Filling:
- 2 tsp ground cinnamon
- 3/4 cup of light brown sugar
- 3/4 cup of all-purpose flour

Crumb Topping:

- 1 cup of all-purpose flour
- 1 cup of light brown sugar
- 6 tbsp butter, melted
- 1 1/2 tbsp ground cinnamon

Cake:

- 1 cup of butter, room temperature
- 3/4 cup of sour cream
- 3 eggs
- 1 tsp kosher salt
- 3 tsp baking powder
- 2/3 cup of light brown sugar
- 3 2/3 cups of all-purpose flour
- 1 cup of granulated sugar
- 1 tbsp vanilla extract
- 1 1/4 cup of milk

Icing:

- 2-3 tbsp milk
- 1 cup of powdered sugar

Instructions

1. Turn oven on to 350°F. Use nonstick spray to cover a 9x13 baking dish. Set aside.
2. Make the cinnamon filling by whisking the brown sugar, flour, and cinnamon in the bowl until well mixed. Set aside.
3. To make the crumb topping, mix the cinnamon, brown sugar, butter to melt, and flour in a medium-sized bowl until it looks like coarse crumbs. Mix with your hands to make bigger pieces of crumb. Set aside.
4. For the cake, mix the butter, granulated sugar, and light brown sugar for around 2 minutes on medium-low to high speed in the bowl of a stand mixer with a paddle included until the mixture is light and fluffy.
5. Add the eggs, vanilla, sour cream, salt, and baking powder. Mix for 1 minute, scraping the sides of the bowl as needed, until combined and smooth.
6. Turn the mixer to low and carefully add the flour and milk, beginning and finishing with the flour. Again, scrape the sides of the bowl as needed, and mix until just combined and smooth.
7. Put half of the cake batter in the pan that has been prepared. Spread the cinnamon filling all over the batter. Place the rest of the cake batter carefully on top of the cinnamon layer. Sprinkle the crumb topping on top in an even way.

8. Bake the cake for around 40–45 minutes or until a toothpick stuck in the center comes out neat.
9. Take the cake out of the oven and set the pan on a wire rack so it can cool down.
10. Put the powdered sugar and milk together until smooth, then drizzle them over the cake once it has cooled. Or, instead of making the icing, you could just sprinkle the cookies with powdered sugar.

36. BANANA CAKE

Prep Time: 30 Minutes | Cook Time: 45 Minutes

Total Time: 5 Hours | Serving: 12

Ingredients

Banana Cake:

- 1 and 1/2 cups of (360ml) buttermilk at room temperature
- 1/2 tsp ground cinnamon
- 1 tsp baking soda
- 2 tsp pure vanilla extract
- 1 cup of (200g) granulated sugar
- 1 and 1/2 cups of (345g) mashed bananas (about 4 medium or 3 big bananas)
- 3 cups of (375g) all-purpose flour (spooned & leveled)
- 1 tsp baking powder
- 3 large eggs at room temperature
- 1/2 cup of (100g) of packed light or dark brown sugar
- 3/4 cup of (12 Tbsp; 170g) of unsalted butter, softened to room temperature
- 1/2 tsp salt

Cream Cheese Frosting:

- 1/8 tsp salt
- 1 tsp pure vanilla extract
- 1/2 cup of (8 Tbsp; 113g) of unsalted butter,
- 3 cups of (360g) confectioners' sugar
- 8 ounces (226g) full-fat brick cream chees

Instructions

1. First, Set the oven to 350°F (177°C) and grease a 913-inch pan.

Make the cake:

1. Mix the bananas up. Use a mixer most of the time. Put aside the mashed bananas.
2. Blend the flour with the cinnamon, baking soda, baking powder, and salt. Set aside.
3. Using a stand mixer with a paddle connection, beat the butter on high speed for around 1 minute until smooth and creamy. Take both sugars and beat on high for about 2 minutes

until smooth and creamy. As needed, use a rubber spatula to scrape the sides and bottom of the bowl. Add the vanilla and the eggs. Beat on medium to high speed until everything is mixed, then put the mashed bananas and beat again. When you need to, scrape the sides and bottom of the bowl. With the mixer on low speed, add the dry elements in three additions, alternating with the buttermilk and mixing just until each addition is incorporated. Don't mix too much. The batter will be a little thick, and it's fine if there are a few lumps.

4. Spread the batter into the pan that has been set up. Bake for 45–50 minutes. Keep an eye on yours because baking times vary. A toothpick stuck in the middle should come out neat and clean when the cake is done. If the top of the cake browns too quickly in the oven, use aluminum foil to cover it loosely.
5. After taking the cake out of the oven, put it on a wire rack. Let it cool down after about half an hour.

To make the frosting:

1. In a bowl, beat the cream cheese and butter on high speed with a stand mixer with a paddle or whisk attachment until smooth and creamy. Mix in 3 cups of powdered sugar, vanilla, and salt. After 30 seconds on low speed, switch to high speed and beat for 2 minutes. Add the extra 1/4 cup of confectioners sugar if you want the frosting to be a little bit thicker. Put the frosting on the cake after it has cooled. Refrigerate for 30 minutes before serving. This helps the frosting harden and makes it easier to cut.
2. Leftover cake can be kept in the refrigerator for 5 days if it is tightly wrapped and sealed.

37. LEMON CAKE

Prep Time: 30 Minutes | Cook Time: 35 Minutes

Total Time: 1 Hour 5 Minutes | Serving: 10

Ingredients

For the Lemon Cake:

- 3 large eggs
- 1 cup of buttermilk (240ml)
- 1½ cups of granulated sugar (300g)
- 1 cup of unsalted butter softened (227g)
- 2 tbsp lemon zest (about 2 lemons)
- 2½ cups of all-purpose flour (300g)
- 1½ tsp baking powder
- ¾ tsp salt
- ½ tsp baking soda
- ¼ cup of lemon juice (about 2 lemons) (60ml)
- 1 tbsp vanilla extract

For the Frosting:

- ½ tsp vanilla extract
- 1 tbsp lemon zest (about 1 lemon)
- 7 cups of powdered sugar (840g)
- 8 ounce of cream cheese (226g)
- 1 cup of unsalted butter at room temperature (227g)
- 2 tbsp lemon juice (about 1 lemon)

Instructions

For the Cake:

1. Turn the oven on to 350F. Prepare two round, 8-inch cake pans by greasing and lining them with parchment paper.
2. Whisk the baking soda, flour, baking powder, and salt in a medium bowl.
3. Mix the ingredients in a big stand mixer bowl with a paddle connection. At medium speed, beat the butter until it is smooth. Put the sugar and lemon zest and beat for about 5 minutes until the mixture is light and fluffy. Add the vanilla and eggs one at a time, scraping the bowl between each one. Beat until the ingredients are well mixed and fluffy.
4. Stir the lemon juice and buttermilk together.
5. With the mixer on low speed, put a third of the mix of flour, then 1/2 of the milk mixture. Alternate between adding flour and milk, mixing just until everything is combined. Stop every so often and scrape the bowl. Divide the batter between the ready cake pans.
6. Bake the cakes for 35 to 40 minutes, or until the middle springs back when you touch it and the sides start pulling away from the pan. After 15 minutes, turn the cakes over and let them cool on a wire rack.

For the frosting:

1. In a large bowl of a stand mixer with a paddle connection, beat the butter and cream cheese together on medium speed until nicely smooth and well mixed. Add the lemon zest and beat for about 3 minutes until the mixture is light and fluffy.
2. Turn the mixer on low and add the confectioners' sugar, a few spoonfuls at a time, alternating with the lemon juice. Stop every so often and scrape the bowl. Add the vanilla to the mix. Once everything is mixed, turn the speed to medium-low and beat for about a minute or until the mixture is smooth and fluffy.

For the Assembly:

1. Take the parchment paper off the layers of the cake. Set one layer on a cake stand or a plate for serving. Spread 1 cup of frosting over the top of the cake and smooth it out to the edges. Place the second cake layer on top and use the rest of the frosting to cover the entire outside of the cake. You can decorate with thin slices of lemon or edible flowers if you want

38. STRAWBERRY CAKE

Prep Time: 1 Hour 30 Minutes | Cook Time: 25 Minutes

Total Time: 6 Hours | Serving: 10-12

Ingredients

Cake:

- 2 tsp baking powder
- 2 tsp pure vanilla extract
- 1 tsp salt
- 2 and 1/2 cups of (285g) cake flour (spooned & leveled)
- 1 and 3/4 cups of (350g) granulated sugar
- 3/4 cup of (12 Tbsp; 170g) of unsalted butter, softened to room temperature
- 5 big egg whites at room temperature
- 1/3 cup of (75g) of sour cream or plain yogurt at room temperature
- 1/2 tsp baking soda
- 1/2 cup of reduced strawberry puree
- 1/2 cup of (120ml) of whole milk at room temperature
- 1-2 drops of food coloring in either red or pink(optional)

Strawberry Puree:

- 1 pound (454g) of fresh strawberries, rinsed and hulled

Strawberry Cream Cheese Frosting:

- 3 cups of (360g) confectioners sugar
- 1/2 cup of (8 Tbsp; 113g) unsalted butter, softened to room temperature
- 1–2 Tbsp milk
- 1 cup of (about 25g) freeze-dried strawberries
- 1 tsp pure vanilla extract
- 8 ounces (226g) full-fat brick cream cheese, softened to room temperature
- salt, to taste

Instructions

1. First, make the strawberry puree and let it cool
2. Puree 1 pound of strawberries that have been washed and hulled. You need a little more than 1 cup. Simmer the puree over medium-low heat, stirring occasionally, until you have about 1/2 cup of or a little more (you need 1/2 cup for the cake). Depending on your pan and how juicy your strawberries were, this could take longer than the minimum of 25–35 minutes. Let it cool down before adding it to the cake batter. I always prepare the reduced puree the day before to give it plenty of time to cool. I put a lid on it and put it in the fridge overnight. Let it reach room temperature again before adding it to the cake batter.

3. Set the oven to 177°C (350°F). Clean and grease two 9-inch round cake pans, then line them with rounds of parchment paper and grease the paper. The parchment paper makes it easy for the cakes to come from the pans.

Make the cake:

1. Blend the salt, baking powder, baking soda, and cake flour with a whisk. Set aside.
2. Using a stand mixer with a paddle connection, blend the butter and sugar on high speed for about 2 minutes or until the mixture is smooth and creamy. As needed, use a rubber spatula to scrape the sides and bottom of the bowl. Mix in the egg whites at high speed for about 2 minutes until everything is mixed. Then put the sour cream and vanilla extract and beat them in. When you need to, scrape the sides and bottom of the bowl. Take the dry ingredients while the mixer runs at a low speed until they are all mixed in. Carefully pour in the milk while the mixer is still going on low until everything is mixed. Don't mix too much. Combine in 1/2 cup of reduced strawberry puree at room temperature. Make sure there are no lumps in the bottom of the bowl. It will be a little bit thick. If you want to, stir in food coloring.
3. Spread the batter out in the cake pans. Bake the cakes for about 24–25 minutes or until they are done. Put a toothpick in the middle of the cake to see if it's done. If it is clean, the job is done. Let the cakes cool down in their pans, and set them on a wire rack. Before frosting and putting the cakes together, they must be completely cool.

To make the frosting:

1. Blend or process the freeze-dried strawberries in a blender until they look like powder. There should be about 1/2 a cup of crumbs. Set aside. Combine the cream cheese in a bowl for 1 minute on high speed with a stand mixer fitted with a paddle. Mix in the butter until it is all mixed in. Add the confectioners' sugar, strawberry powder, 1 tbsp of milk, and vanilla, and beat on medium-high speed until smooth. If you want to make it a little thinner, add 1 more Tbsp of milk. Taste it, and if it needs it, add a pinch of salt. About 3 cups frosting will be made.

Put together and freeze:

1. First, use a large knife with a serrated edge to cut a thin layer off the top of each cake to make it flat. Discard. Put one layer of cake on your cake stand or serving dish. Spread frosting all over the top. Place the second layer on top and use the rest of the frosting to cover the top and sides of the cake. Before cutting, put it in the fridge for at least 45 minutes. This keeps the cake from falling apart when you cut it, which could happen if it hasn't been in the refrigerator for a while.
2. Leftover cake can be kept in the refrigerator for 5 days if it is tightly wrapped and sealed.

39. APPLE CAKE

Prep Time: 25 Minutes | Cook Time: 50 Minutes

Total Time: 1 Hour 15 Minutes | Serving: 8

Ingredients
- oil for baking pan
- 1 1/2 cups of sugar
- 4 eggs
- 1 tsp vanilla extract
- 2 cups of all-purpose flour
- 1 tbsp baking powder
- 1 pinch salt
- 2 cups of grated apples, about 4 medium apples
- 1 cup of oil of light olive, coconut, or avocado

Instructions
1. Mix the eggs, sugar, oil, vanilla extract, and salt in the stand mixer's bowl until the mixture is fluffy.
2. Now, Combine the flour and baking powder in the eggs in small amounts.
3. Peel the apples and use the large side of a cheese grater to shred them. Add the apples to the batter for the cake.
4. Spray oil on the baking dish. Fill the pan with the cake batter. Bake for 50 minutes at 325°F or until a toothpick comes out clean.

40. COCONUT CAKE

Prep Time: 35 Minutes | Cook Time: 22 Minutes

Total Time: 4 HoursMinutes | Serving: 12

Ingredients

- 5 large egg whites at room temperature
- 1 cup of (240ml) unsweetened canned coconut milk at room temperature
- 1/2 cup of (120g) sour cream at room temperature
- 1 and 2/3 cups of (330g) granulated sugar
- 2 and 1/2 cups of (285g) cake flour (spooned & leveled)
- 2 tsp baking powder
- 1 tsp coconut extract
- 1/2 tsp baking soda
- 2 tsp pure vanilla extract
- 3/4 cup of (12 Tbsp; 170g) unsalted butter, softened to room temperature
- 1 tsp salt
- 1 cup of (80g) sweetened shredded coconut

Coconut Cream Cheese Buttercream:

- 2 Tbsp (30ml) canned coconut milk
- 8 ounces (226g) full-fat brick cream cheese
- 1/2 tsp pure vanilla extract
- 1/2 tsp coconut extract
- 1 cup of (16 Tbsp; 226g) unsalted butter
- 2 cups of (160g) sweetened shredded
- 5 cups of (600g) confectioners' sugar

Instructions

1. Set the oven to 177°C (350°F). Grease three 9-inch cake pans, then line them with cuts of parchment paper and grease the paper. The parchment paper makes it easy for the cakes to come from the pans.

Make the cake:

1. Now, Mix the salt, baking powder, baking soda, and cake flour with a whisk. Set aside.
2. Use a stand mixer with a paddle or whisk attachment; combine the butter and sugar on medium-high speed for about 2 minutes or until the mixture is smooth and creamy. As needed, use a rubber spatula to scrape the sides and bottom of the bowl. Then put the sour cream, vanilla extract, and coconut extract. The egg whites should be mixed in until they are all mixed in. Mix by beating. The mixture will look curdled because of the different textures and solid butter. When you need to, scrape the sides and bottom of the bowl. Carefully add the dry ingredients and coconut milk while the mixer is on low speed. Mix on

low speed until everything comes together, then add the coconut. To ensure no butter lumps are at the bottom of the bowl, whisk everything by hand. It will be a little bit thick.
3. Spread the batter out in the cake pans. If you want to be sure, you can weigh them. Bake the cakes for 21–23 minutes or until they are done. Put a toothpick in the middle of the cake to see if it's done. If it's clean, the job is done. Let cakes cool down in their pans, which are set on a wire rack. Before frosting and putting the cakes together, they must be completely cool.

To make the frosting:

1. In a large bowl with a whisk or paddle connection on a stand mixer, combine the butter and cream cheese on medium-low high speed for about 2 minutes or until creamy and smooth. While the mixer is on low, add powdered sugar, coconut milk, vanilla extract, coconut extract, and salt. Turn up the speed to high and keep beating for 3 minutes. If the frosting is too thin, add more confectioners' sugar. If the frosting is too thick, add more coconut milk. If the frosting is too sweet, add an extra pinch of salt.

Put together and decorate:

1. Use a big knife with a serrated edge to cut a thin layer off the top of each cake to make a flat surface. Discard. Put one cake layer on your cake stand, cake turntable, or serving plate. Distribute about 1 1/2 cups of frosting all over the top of the cake. Place the second cake layer on top and over it, evenly distribute about 1 1/2 cups of frosting. Put the third cake layer on top. Distribute the rest of the frosting on top and around the sides. Drizzle coconut on the top and sides of the cake.
2. Before cutting the cake, put it in the fridge for at least 20 minutes. This makes it easier to cut the cake, even though it's still pretty fluffy.
3. Leftover cake can be kept in the refrigerator for up to 5 days if well-wrapped.

41. YELLOW CAKE

Prep Time: 15 Minutes | Cook Time: 30 Minutes

Total Time: 45 Minutes | Serving: 16

Ingredients

- 1 cup of half-and-half, (or 1/2 cup of whole milk plus 1/2 cup of heavy cream.)
- 1 cup of half-and-half (or 1/2 cup of whole milk + 1/2 cup of heavy cream)
- 1 1/2 tsp baking powder
- 4 large eggs
- 1 1/2 tbsp pure vanilla extract
- 12 ounces granulated sugar (341g or about 1 3/4 cup)
- 6 ounces unsalted butter, cubed and at room temperature
- 1 1/2 tsp kosher salt
- 7 ounces all-purpose flour (198g or 1 1/2 cups of + 1 tbsp using Spoon & Level Method)

Instructions

1. Put a rack in the middle of the oven and heat it to 350 degrees F. Grease the bottoms of two 8-inch cake pans very lightly, then place parchment rounds on top. If you can, put the pans on a baking sheet.
2. Mix the flour, cornstarch, baking powder, and salt well in a medium bowl. Half-and-half and vanilla should be mixed together in a liquid measuring cup. Break the eggs into a small bowl or measuring cups for liquids.
3. Using a stand mixer and its paddle attachment, blend the butter and sugar on low speed for 3 minutes until the mixture is light and fluffy. If there are bits of sugar or butter on the sides or bottom of the bowl that have yet to be mixed in, use a spatula to mix them for another 30 seconds.
4. Slowly add the eggs one at a time, stopping after the second and last egg to scrape the bottom of the bowl. At the end of this step, the batter may look a little bit broken, but that's fine.
5. On medium speed, quickly add the dry ingredients first, then the wet ingredients, ending with the dry. We shouldn't need more than a minute for this.
6. Put off the mixer and scrape the bowl to the bottom to ensure no dry spots are hiding in there. Turn the speed up to medium and mix for 30 seconds more to help build the batter's structure. Don't leave this step out.
7. Spread the cake batter out evenly in the ready pans. Use a spatula with a flat edge to even out the tops.
8. Make for 28-30 minutes or until a toothpick inserted in the middle comes out neat and clean. Let it cool to room temperature before it is out of the pan. To help the cake's sides come off the pan, use an offset spatula or knife. Then, put a cardboard round or large cutting board against the pan and gently flip the cake over.

42. WHITE CAKE

Prep Time: 45 Minutes | Cook Time: 30 Minutes

Total Time: 1 Hour 15 Minutes | Serving: 10

Ingredients

For the white cake:

- 1 ¾ cups of granulated sugar (350 grams)
- 1 tbsp baking powder
- 1 cup of buttermilk at room temperature (240 ml)
- 5 large egg whites at room temperature
- 1 cup of unsalted butter softened (230 grams)
- 2 tsp pure vanilla extract or clear vanilla extract
- 2 ¾ cups of cake flour (spooned & leveled) (305 grams)
- ¾ tsp salt

For the vanilla buttercream frosting:

- 1 ½ cups of unsalted butter softened (340 grams)
- 3 tbsp of heavy whipping cream (45 ml)
- 1 tbsp pure vanilla extract or clear vanilla extract
- 4 ½ cups of powdered sugar (540 grams)
- ⅛ tsp salt

Instructions

To make the white cake, you will need to:

1. Set the oven's temperature to 350°F. Use nonstick cooking spray to coat two 9-inch cake pans, place parchment paper on the bottom of each pan, and set them aside.
2. Now, Mix the cake flour, baking powder, and salt in a big mixing bowl using a whisk. Set aside.
3. Mix the buttermilk and vanilla extract well in a measuring cup. Set aside.
4. Using the paddle attachment on a stand mixer's bowl, combine the butter on low speed until it is smooth. Then, slowly mix in the granulated sugar. When all of the sugar is added, turn up the speed to medium and keep mixing for another 4 to 5 minutes or until the mixture is light and fluffy.

5. Add the dry elements in three low-speed parts, alternating with the buttermilk mixture. Make sure you don't overmix the batter by mixing each ingredient in until it's just combined.
6. In a different, clean bowl, whip the egg whites until they form stiff peaks. Start by folding half the egg whites, then add the remaining whites and fold until just combined.
7. Put the cake batter into the cake pans that have been prepared and spread it out evenly. Tap the cake pans gently on the counter a couple of times to get out any air bubbles.
8. Bake the cakes for 28 to 32 minutes, or until a toothpick inserted into the center comes out neat and clean. Remove from the oven and let cool in the pans for about 20 minutes. Then, cool the cakes out of the pans on a wire rack.

To make vanilla buttercream frosting:

1. Combine the butter on medium speed using the paddle attachment on a stand mixer's bowl until smooth.
2. Take the powdered sugar one cup of at a time, mix well after each addition, and stop to scrape down the sides of the bowl as needed.
3. Now, Add the heavy whipping cream, vanilla extract, and salt. Mix on medium speed until it is well mixed, ensuring that the bowl's sides are thoroughly scraped.

To put the cake together, do the following:

1. Use a knife or cake leveler to level the tops of each cake. Put one of the cakes on a cake stand, add a layer of frosting, and smooth it out into one even layer. Place the second layer on top, and then use the rest of the frosting to frost the top and sides of the cake.

43. EVERYDAY FRUIT CAKE

Prep Time: 20 Minutes | Cook Time: 1 Hour 45 Minutes

Total Time: 2 Hours 5 Minutes | Serving: 12

Ingredients

- 1 rounded tablespoon of jam (any flavor)
- 60 ml milk (4 tablespoons)
- 3 large eggs
- 125 g soft brown sugar
- 2 teaspoons mixed spice (10ml)
- 125 g butter at room temperature
- 400 g mixed dried fruit
- 250 g self-raising flour

Instructions

Preparation:

1. Preheat the oven to 170°C/ 150°C fan/ 325°F.
2. Either grease the tin with butter or simply insert the liner.
3. Put the fruit in a bowl and weigh it.

For the Everyday Fruit Cake:

1. In a large mixing bowl , mix all of the ingredients except the fruit.
2. Mix well, but don't overwork it.
3. Scrape down the mixture and stir it again.
4. Incorporate the dry fruit by hand.
5. You don't want to sever the fruit.
6. Carefully place the mixture in the tin/liner and make a little indentation in the top with a knife. This implies you'll have a less domed top.
7. Cook for 1 hour 15 minutes, then check with a toothpick. The cake is done when it comes out clean. If not, return to the oven for another 10 minutes and try again. You may require up to 1 hour 45 minutes.
8. Remove the cake from the oven and set it aside for 10 minutes before taking it out onto a wire rack to cool.
9. When cool, store in an airtight container. (You can keep the liner on the cake until it is served.)

44. PUMPKIN SPICE CAKE

Prep Time: 10 Minutes | Cook Time: 35 Minutes | Cooling Time: 1 Hour 30 Minutes

Total Time: 2 Hours 15 Minutes | Serving:

Ingredients

Cake:

- 1 cup of granulated sugar
- 1 tsp vanilla extract
- 2 tsp pumpkin pie spice
- 1/2 tsp baking soda
- 1 cup of pumpkin puree
- 1 cup of all-purpose flour
- 1 tsp baking powder
- 2 large eggs
- 1/2 tsp salt, or to taste
- 1/2 cup of canola or vegetable oil

Frosting:

- 1/2 tsp salt, or to taste
- 1/4 cup of (half of 1 stick) of unsalted butter, softened
- 6 ounces cream cheese, softened (lite okay)
- 1 1/2 cups of confectioners' sugar
- 1/2 tsp vanilla extract

Instructions

Make the cake:

2. Turn the oven on to 350F. Line an 8 by 8-inch pan with aluminum foil and spray it with cooking spray. Set aside.
3. Put the eggs, sugar, pumpkin, oil, pumpkin pie spice, and vanilla in a bowl and whisk to mix.
4. Then, Blend the flour, baking powder, baking soda, and salt together, but don't mix too much.
5. Put the batter into the pan and lightly smooth the top with a spatula. Bake for about 35 to 40 minutes, or until the center is set and a toothpick inserted in the center comes out neat and clean.
6. Take the cake on a cooling rack to cool it before frosting it so it doesn't melt.

Make the frosting:

1. First, Add the cream cheese, butter, confectioners' sugar, vanilla, and salt to the stand mixer's big bowl. Whisk until smooth and fluffy with the paddle attachment of a stand mixer.
2. Spread frosting over cooled cake with a spatula or knife to create a smooth, even, flat layer (If you have a small amount left over, it will keep airtight in the fridge for at least 2 weeks).Slice up and serve

45. BLACK FOREST CAKE

Prep Time: 45 Minutes | Cook Time: 30 Minutes

Total Time: 1 Hour 15 Minutes | Serving: 12

Ingredients

For the Cake:

- 1 tsp salt 5g
- 2 cups of all-purpose flour 240g
- 1 cup of buttermilk 236mL
- 2 eggs
- 1 1/2 cup of sugar 300g
- 1 tbsp coffee 15mL
- 1/2 tsp baking powder 2g
- 1 cup of unsalted butter 227g, room temperature
- 1/2 tsp baking soda 3g
- 2 egg yolks
- 1/2 cup of cocoa powder 58g

For the Syrup:

- 1/2 cup of sugar 100g
- 1/2 cup of water 120mL
- 1/3 cup of Kirsche

For the Whipped Cream Frosting:

- 1 1/2 tbsp Kirsche 22mL
- 1/3 cup of powdered sugar plus more to taste.
- 1 1/2 pints heavy cream cold

For the Assembly:

- 1 bittersweet chocolate
- 2 cups of cherries plus more for decorating

Instructions

For the Cake:

1. Flour and butter 3 cake pans that are six inches in diameter. Turn the oven on to 350F.
2. Sift the baking soda and powder, salt, cocoa powder, and flour.
3. Combine the butter and sugar until it becomes fluffy and light. The eggs and yolks are mixed in one at a time, and then the coffee is added.
4. Now, Mix in the flour mixture and buttermilk in three separate batches. Don't mix too much!
5. Put the same batter in each pan and bake at 350°F for about 25–30 minutes, or until the centers are done. Allow to cool for 10 minutes in the pans before inverting onto a wire rack.

For the Syrup:

1. Put the water and sugar in a small pot and warm it until it boils. After about a minute, take it off the heat and stir in the cherry liqueur. Put the mixture in a bowl and let it cool before you use it.

For the Whipped Cream Frosting:

1. With the whisk attachment attached, fill the bowl of your stand mixer with the cold cream, powdered sugar, and Kirsche. Beat on high speed until fluffy peaks form.

For the Assembly:

1. Combine about 1/4 cup of dark chocolate and 2 tbsp of cream and melt them together. Mix them and put them aside.
2. Wash, cut in half, and remove the pits from about 2 cups of cherries. Place them in a bowl and set them aside.
3. Use a knife or a vegetable peeler to shave the chocolate carefully, then set it aside.
4. Cover the first layer of cake with whipped cream, and then press cherry halves all over the top. The cherry pieces support the cake because whipped cream is too soft to hold up three layers. Repeat with the other layers until the whole cake is put together.
5. Give the cake a quick smoothing, and any loose cherries should be pushed back in. Put more whipped cream on top of the cake, and then smooth the top and sides.
6. Shave some chocolate and carefully press it on the bottom half of the cake. You can also throw the chocolate at the cake since the frosting is soft and easy to mess up.
7. Pour or pipe ganache on top of the cake, then spread it out evenly. Leave about an inch of space around the edge.
8. Put the rest of the whipped cream in a piping bag with a big closed star tip (849) and set it aside. The cherries go on top of the dollops.

46. BANANA CAKE WITH COCONUT SORBET

Prep Time: 50 Minutes | Cook Time: 2 Hours | Total Time: 2 Hours 50 Minutes | Serving: 8

Ingredients

- Finely grated zest of 1 lemon
- 150g unsalted butter, chopped
- 1 1/2 cups of (225g) self-raising flour
- 3 very ripe bananas, mashed
- 1/2 tsp baking powder
- 2 large eggs, lightly beaten
- 3/4 cup of (165g) caster sugar
- Finely grated lime zest to serve

Coconut sorbet:

- 1 cup of (220g) caster sugar
- 800ml coconut milk
- Finely grated lime peel and the juice of 2 limes

Caramel banana:

- 3 small bananas, halved lengthways
- 1 vanilla bean, split, seeds scraped
- Juice of 1 lemon
- 100g muscovado sugar
- 1/2 cup of (110g) caster sugar

Instructions

1. To make the coconut sorbet, put all the elements in a large saucepan with 1/2 cup of (125ml) water and heat it over low heat. For 2 minutes, stir while cooking to dissolve the sugar. Take it out and let it cool at room temperature for 4 hours or overnight.
2. When the sorbet mixture is cold, place it in an ice cream producer and churn it based on the maker's directions until it is thick but still soft enough to spoon into a container. Move to a container and freeze for at least 4 hours or overnight.
3. Get the oven ready at 160°C. Line a 1L (4-cup) loaf pan with baking paper and grease the bottom and sides.
4. Combine the butter and sugar with a whisk connection on a stand mixer until it is light and fluffy. Mix in the lemon zest and banana puree with a whisk. Whisk in the eggs until the mixture is thick and airy. Mix in the baking powder and flour. Put into a loaf pan and bake for 1 hour or until a skewer stuck in the middle comes out clean.
5. Pour 300ml of water into a saucepan and add the caster sugar and muscovado sugar. Bring to a boil at a medium flame. Cook for 10 minutes without stirring or until thin, golden caramel forms. Add the vanilla pod and seeds, as well as the lemon juice. Mix well, and then turn the heat down to medium-low.
6. Add the banana halves and cook, spooning caramel over them, for 6 to 8 minutes, until the bananas are caramelized and coated with sauce. Take the bananas out of the pan and turn the heat up to medium. Then, reduce the sauce until it's as thick as syrup.
7. Bananas are layered on top of the cake, and syrup is drizzled over them. The cake is then cut into pieces and served with sorbet and lime zest on top.

47. FRUIT CAKE

Prep Time: 30 Minutes | Cook Time: 2 Hours 30 Minutes | Total Time: 3 Hours | Serving: 12

Ingredients

- 50g (½ cup) almond meal
- 190g butter, softened
- 1 medium green apple, peeled & grated
- 3 large eggs
- juice and rind 1 medium orange
- 1 cup of (200g) plain flour
- 1kg dried mixed fruit, roughly chopped
- 1 tsp ground cinnamon
- 100g dark cooking chocolate, chopped
- ¾ cup of (175g) caster sugar
- 100g pitted prunes, roughly chopped
- 115g dried dates, roughly chopped
- 50ml brandy or whisky
- 60g glacé ginger, chopped
- 60g walnuts, chopped

Topping:

- 2 tsp brandy
- 250g of your favorite nuts (blanched almonds, brazil nuts, walnuts)
- 2 tbsp apricot jam

Instructions

1. Mix the dried and glazed fruits, rind, juice, brandy, and apple in a large bowl. Cover and set aside for up to 3 days or overnight.
2. Set the oven to 150C (130C with the fan on). Line the bottom and sides of a KitchenAid Springform Pan (23cm) with two layers of brown paper and 2 layers of baking paper. Let the paper hang over the edge of the pan by 4cm.
3. Put the flat beater on the KitchenAid Stand Mixer. On speed 8, mix the butter and sugar for 5 minutes or until the mixture is light and creamy.
4. Put the eggs, beating well after each one.
5. Shut off the mixer. Mix in the fruit, nuts, chocolate, flour, and cinnamon. Spread the mixtures around the bowl with a spoon. Turn to speed 2 and mix until everything is well mixed, but don't mix too much.
6. Spread the mixture evenly in a pan that has been prepared. Drop the pan twice on the counter to spread the cake out evenly.
7. Put nuts on top of the cake and lightly press them into the batter to make a design.
8. Put the cake on two layers of brown paper on a baking sheet, and cook it for around 2 1/2 hours or until a skewer comes out clean. Cover the cake with foil and let it cool in the pan
9. Warm up the jam and brandy in a small pan, then brush the mixture over the nuts.

48. CARAMEL CAKE

Prep Time: 30 Minutes | Cook Time: 22 Minutes

Total Time: 52 Minutes | Serving: 12

Ingredients

Caramel Cake:

- ½ cup of vegetable oil
- ½ tsp baking soda
- 1 ¼ cups of buttermilk room temp
- 1 cup of granulated sugar
- ½ cup of unsalted butter softened
- ½ tsp fine sea salt
- 4 large eggs at room temperature
- ⅔ cup of light brown sugar packed
- 1 tbsp vanilla extract
- 2 ⅔ cups of all-purpose flour
- 2 tsp baking powder

Caramel Frosting:

- 1 tsp vanilla extract
- ⅓ cup of heavy cream
- ⅓ cup of evaporated milk
- 1 cup of light brown sugar packed
- 2 cups of powdered sugar sifted
- 1 cup of unsalted butter cut into tbsp
- ½ tsp fine sea salt
- 1 cup of dark brown sugar packed

Instructions

1. Turn the oven up to 350°F. Use baking spray to lightly grease two 9-inch round cake pans. In the bottom of each pan, put a circle of parchment paper. Use the baking spray to spray the paper. Set aside.
2. Now, Blend the flour, baking powder, baking soda, and salt in a medium-sized bowl.
3. Oil and butter should be put in the bowl of a stand mixer. Beat until everything is well mixed.
4. Blend in the granulated sugar and brown sugar at a medium speed for 3 minutes or until everything is well mixed.
5. Mix in the vanilla extract until everything is mixed. Next, add the eggs until they are all mixed in.
6. Alternate adding the dry elements and the buttermilk, scraping the sides of the bowl as needed. Split the batter evenly between the cake pans that have been prepared. Use an offset spatula to smooth the top.
7. Bake the cakes for 22 to 27 minutes, or until a toothpick inserted into one of the cakes comes out clean. The cakes should cool all the way down in the pan.
8. Take the cakes out of the pans carefully and set them on a flat surface. Use a large knife with a serrated edge to cut off uneven or domed cake parts.
9. Put one of the cakes on the plate or cake stand. Set aside.

Prepare The Caramel Frosting:

1. In a medium-sized saucepan at medium heat, mix the brown sugar, butter, and salt together. Stir everything together as the butter melts.
2. Now, Mix in the heavy cream and evaporated milk.
3. Bring to a slow boil and keep boiling for 4 minutes. Move the mixture immediately to a bowl that can handle heat or the bowl of a stand mixer that can handle heat.
4. Add the powdered sugar a little at a time using the stand mixer until the mixture is smooth. Add the vanilla extract to the mix.
5. Now is the time to move quickly while the frosting is still easy to spread.
6. Put about 3/4 cup of the frosting over the cake on the cake stand and Spread it evenly on top of the cake with an offset spatula.
7. Carefully place the other cake on top of the caramel frosting, top side down. Spread the rest of the frosting on top and around the sides of the cake as quickly as you can before the frosting starts to get stiff.
8. Let the frosting set for about 2 to 3 hours before cutting and serving the cake.

49. BANANA PUDDING CAKE

Prep Time: 15 Minutes | Cook Time: 25 Minutes

Total Time: 40 Minutes | Serving: 10

Ingredients

For the cake:

- 3 large eggs
- 1 (15.25-ounce) box vanilla or white cake mix
- 1 cup of full-fat sour cream
- 1 (3-ounce) box cook and serve banana cream pudding mix
- Cooking spray
- 1/3 cup of vegetable oil
- 1/2 cup of whole milk

For the frosting:

- 1 1/4 cups of powdered sugar
- 2 tsp vanilla extract
- 8 ounces full-fat cream cheese
- 3 cups of cold heavy cream

For assembly:

- 1 (11-ounce) box Nilla Wafers, divided
- 2 medium ripe (but not spotty) bananas

Instructions

Do the baking:

1. Put 8 ounces of cream cheese for the frosting in the bowl of a stand mixer and let it sit out at room temperature while you make the cake. (You could also use a large bowl and an electric hand mixer.) Put a rack in the middle of the oven and turn the temperature to 350°F. Coat around two 9-inch round cake pans with cooking spray, then put parchment paper circles on the bottoms.
2. Combine 1 cup of full-fat sour cream, 1/2 cup of whole milk, 1/3 cup of vegetable oil, and 3 large eggs in a spacious bowl, stirring until smooth consistency. Whisk together 1 box of cake mix and 1 box of banana cream pudding mix until smooth. Distribute the batter evenly between the baking pans.
3. 20 to 25 minutes, or until the cakes are light brown and a toothpick stuck in the middle comes out clean. Keep the pans on a wire rack and let them cool down. Make the frosting in the meantime.

To make the icing:

1. Add 1 1/4 cups of powdered sugar and 2 tsp vanilla extract in the bowl of cheese cream. Beat for 3 to 4 minutes with the whisk attachment on medium speed until smooth. Slow the mixer down to low and slowly add the 3 cups of cold heavy cream. Keep beating for 4 minutes or until the mixture gets thick and smooth. Change the speed to medium and beat for 1 to 2 minutes or until the frosting is light, fluffy, and doubled in size. Put 1 cup of the frosting in a small bag with a zip top and put it aside.

Put the cake together:

1. Put 3 1/2 cups of Nilla Wafers in a big bag with a zip-top. Close the bag and gently crush the wafers into coarse crumbs using a rolling pin or the bottom of the frying pan. Peel and thinly slice 2 medium-ripe bananas with no spots on them.
2. Take the cakes out of their molds. Use a knife with a serrated edge to cut off the round tops of each cake. Put one cake layer, cut side down, on a cake stand or serving platter. Put 1 cup of the frosting on top and use an offset spatula to spread it into a thin layer from edge to edge. On top, put the sliced bananas and then an even layer of 1 cup of the crushed Nilla Wafers.
3. Place the last cake layer on top. Use the rest of the frosting to frost the top and sides of the cake. Use the rest of the crushed Nilla Wafers to cover the sides of the cake. Start at the bottom and work your way up, taking a handful of the crushed cookies and gently pressing them against the side of the cake so they stick to the frosting. Any pieces that don't stick and fall off can be pushed back into the frosting until the sides are completely covered.
4. Cut off one of the bottom corners of the frosting bag. Pipe small mounds of frosting around the top of the cake to make it look nice. Between each mound of frosting, put a whole Nilla Wafer.

50. CARAMEL BUNDT CAKE

Prep Time: 20 Minutes | Cook Time: 55 Minutes

Total Time: 1 Hour 15 Minutes | Serving: 10

Ingredients

- 2 tsp baking powder
- 250g unsalted butter at room temperature
- 1 cup of (250ml) buttermilk at room temperature
- 1 cup of (330g) dulce de leche (a thick caramel made from condensed milk)
- 1/2 tsp bicarbonate of soda
- 3 cups of (450g) plain flour
- 1 firmly packed cup of (250g) brown sugar
- 4 large eggs at room temperature
- 1 tsp vanilla bean paste

Caramel sauce:

- 2/3 cup of (165ml) pure (thin) cream
- 3/4 cup of (165g) caster sugar

Instructions

1. Set the oven temperature to 170°C and grease a 26cm bundt pan.
2. Use the stand mixer with a paddle connection, and blend butter and sugar on medium speed until the mixture is thick and pale.
3. Add the dulce de leche, vanilla, and eggs one at a time while the mixer runs and beats well after each addition.
4. Sift the flour, 1/2 tsp salt, baking powder, and baking soda into a different bowl.
5. Turn the speed down to low and add a third of the flour mixture and a third of the buttermilk to the bowl.
6. Alternate between flour and buttermilk until the mixture is smooth and well-blended.
7. Pour into a cake pan and cook for around 45 minutes or until a skewer inserted in the center comes out clean. After 10 minutes, take out the cake from the pan and put it on a wire rack to cool completely.
8. In the meantime, put sugar in a small-sized saucepan at medium heat to make the caramel sauce. Add 2 tbsp. Of water and stir until the sugar is gone.
9. Cook for 8 minutes, or until a dark caramel form, and then add cream and 1/2 tsp salt. Stir everything together, remove the heat, and let it cool completely.
10. To serve, pour caramel sauce over the cake.

51. CHEESECAKE

Prep Time: 20 Minutes | Cook Time: 1 Hour 15 Minutes | Cooling Time: 6 Hours

Total Time: 7 Hour 35 Minutes | Serving: 12

Ingredients

Graham Cracker Crust:

- 7 Tablespoons butter melted
- 1 ½ cups graham cracker crumbs (170g)
- 1 Tablespoon brown sugar (can substitute white)
- 2 Tablespoons sugar

Cheesecake:

- ⅛ teaspoon salt
- 1 ½ teaspoons vanilla extract
- 1 cup sugar (200g)
- ⅔ cups sour cream (160g)
- 4 large eggs room temperature, lightly beaten
- 32 oz cream cheese[2] softened to room temperature (910g)

Instructions

1. Preheat the oven to 325 degrees Fahrenheit (160 degrees Celsius).
2. First, make the Graham Cracker crust by mixing together the graham cracker crumbs, sugar, and brown sugar. Combine ingredients with a fork after adding melted butter.
3. Crumbles should be pressed firmly into the bottom and up the edges of a 9" Springform pan. Place aside.

Cheesecake:

1. Place the cream cheese in the bowl of a stand mixer and mix gently until it becomes smooth and creamy (be cautious not to over-beat, as it can incorporate too much air).
2. Blend in the sugar until a smooth mixture is achieved.
3. Add the sour cream, vanilla extract, and salt, mixing thoroughly until well combined. If using a stand mixer, remember to regularly scrape the sides and bottom of the bowl with a spatula to ensure even mixing of all ingredients.
4. While the mixer is on low speed, add the softly beaten eggs one at a time, gently swirling just until each egg is integrated. Once all the eggs are added, scrape the sides and bottom of the bowl with a spatula to ensure proper incorporation of all ingredients.
5. Transfer the cheesecake batter to the prepared springform pan. Keep the pan on a foil-lined cookie sheet to prevent leaks.
6. Bake for 75 minutes at 325°F (160°C) on the center rack of your oven. The edges will have expanded somewhat and may have just begun to turn a light golden brown, while the middle should spring back to the touch but remain Jello-jiggly. Don't overbake, or the texture will degrade, and we'll all suffer.

7. Take out from the oven and cool for 10 minutes on top of the oven3. After 10 minutes, gently release the crust from the inside of the springform pan with a knife (this will help prevent cracks as your cheesecake cools and shrinks). Do not remove the springform pan ring.
8. Allow the cheesecake to cool for another 1-2 hours, or until near room temperature, before replacing in the refrigerator and cooling overnight, or for at least 6 hours. I remove the springform pan ring shortly before serving and return it to the pan to store. Enjoy!

52. OATMEAL CAKE

Prep Time: 10 Minutes | Cook Time: 35 Minutes

Total Time: 45 Minutes | Serving: 16

Ingredients

Cake:

- ½ tsp salt
- ½ cup of butter
- 1 cup of granulated sugar
- 1 cup of quick cooking oats
- 1 ⅓ cups of all-purpose flour
- 1 tsp baking soda
- ½ tsp cinnamon
- 1 cup of packed brown sugar
- 2 eggs

Topping:

- 6 tbsp butter
- 1 cup of shredded sweetened coconut
- ¼ cup of evaporated milk
- ½ cup of packed brown sugar
- 1 tsp vanilla extract
- 1 cup of chopped pecans

Instructions

1. Get the oven ready at 350°F.
2. Spread butter on a 13"x9" pan. Pour 1 ⅓ cups of boiling water over quick oats and stir until well mixed. Set aside to cool.
3. Sift the flour, baking soda, salt, and cinnamon into a small bowl. Mix brown and white sugars with butter in a stand or large mixing bowl. After adding The eggs, beat for another minute on medium speed until everything is well mixed. Put the dry ingredients in the bowl of the mixer and mix for 1 minute. Add the oatmeal mixture two tbsp at a time and blend for another minute.
4. Pour into the pan that has been prepared, and bake for 35 minutes.

5. Start making the topping when there are 10 minutes left on the cake. Brown sugar, butter, and milk should be in a saucepan over medium heat. Continue cooking until the brown sugar completely dissolves and the mixture boils vigorously. Then turn off the heat and stir in the vanilla, coconut, and pecans. Once the cake is made, pour the topping over it and spread it out evenly. Put the cake under the broiler for one to three minutes or until the topping is golden brown.

53. CHOCOLATE ZUCCHINI CAKE

Prep Time: 20 Minutes | Cook Time: 30 Minutes

Total Time: 50 Minutes | Serving: 12

Ingredients

- 2 cups of all-purpose flour
- 1 cup of semi-sweet chocolate chips
- 2 cups of shredded zucchini
- 2 tsp vanilla extract
- 1 1/2 tsp baking soda
- 1 1/2 cups of sugar
- 1 large egg (optional)
- 1/2 cup of vegetable or canola oil
- 1/2 cup of cocoa powder
- 1 tsp salt

Instructions

1. Set oven temperature to 350 degrees F.
2. Oil, sugar, and vanilla are mixed in the bowl of a stand mixer along with a wire whip attached. (You could also use a large bowl and a hand mixer.)
3. Mix the flour, cocoa powder, baking soda, and salt separately.
4. Add Mixed flour to the oil and sugar mixture in three parts on medium speed. Mix well between each batch and scrape down the sides of the bowl.
5. (At this point, the batter will be dry and crumbly. When the zucchini is added, it will become more moist.)
6. Change the tool to the flat beater. Mix the zucchini in well while the mixer is on low speed.
7. Pour the batter into a 9-by-13-inch Pyrex or glass pan that has been cleaned.
8. Bake for 15 minutes.
9. Remove from oven. Put chocolate chips on top.
10. Bake 10 – 15 minutes more. If you put a toothpick or knife in the middle, it should come out clean. Do not overbake!
11. Put on a wire rack to cool. If desired, you have the option to sprinkle powdered sugar on top prior to serving.

54. CHERRY CAKE

Prep Time: 10 Minutes | Cook Time: 45 Minutes

Total Time: 55 Minutes | Serving: 24 Pieces

Ingredients

- 1 tsp almond extract
- 1 tsp vanilla extract
- 2 large eggs
- 21-ounce cherry pie filling
- 1 tsp baking powder
- 15-ounce white cake mix. You do not need the ingredients listed on the box

Frosting:

- 1/2 cup of softened unsalted butter
- 1/3 cup of canned cherry pie filling (as mentioned above)
- 2 1/4 cups of powdered sugar
- 1 tsp of almond extract
- 1 tsp of vanilla extract
- 16 ounces of softened cream cheese

Instructions

1. Preheat the oven to 325 degrees F. Lightly grease or spray a 13-by-9-inch baking pan to prepare it.
2. Put 1/3 cup of cherry pie filling aside so you can use it in frosting later.
3. Mix the dry cake mix, eggs, baking powder, extracts, and the rest of the cherry pie filling on low speed. Turn the speed up to medium and beat for about a minute until the mixture is creamy.
4. Empty the batter into the pan, ensuring an even layer using a spatula to smooth it out.
5. To test doneness, insert a wooden skewer into the center of the cake and bake for 45 minutes. When the cake is made, remove it from the oven and cool properlly in the pan on a wire rack.

Frosting made of cherry cream cheese:

1. Mix the cheese, cream, and butter at medium speed until smooth.
2. Turn the mixer to low and add the cherry pie filling and extracts. Once everything is mixed, beat it for a minute or two on medium until the cherries are broken into small pieces.
3. Turn the mixer to low and slowly add the powdered sugar until the mixture is well smooth and easy to spread. Keep it in the fridge until you're ready to use it.

Garnish:

1. It's up to you, but it's pretty! Put a maraschino cherry with a stem on each slice when you serve.

55. PEAR AND HAZELNUT TORTA CAPRESE

Prep Time: Minute | Cook Time: Minutes

Total Time: Minutes | Serving: 12

Ingredients

- 1 overripe pear, peeled, mashed or finely chopped
- 1/3 cup of (35g) cocoa, sifted, plus extra to serve
- 11/3 cups of (295g) caster sugar
- 150g unsalted butter
- 2 cups of (200g) hazelnut meal
- 200g dark chocolate, chopped
- 5 eggs

Instructions

1. Preheat the oven to 180°C. Grease a 20cm x 30cm lamington pan and line both the bottom and sides.
2. Put the butter and chocolate in a bowl that can handle the heat and set it over a pan of water just about to boil. Don't let the bowl touch the water as you stir the mixture until it is melted and smooth.
3. Just a little bit. Keep the sugar and eggs in the bowl of a stand mixer along with a whisk attachment, then Whisk on high speed for 5 minutes or until the mixture is thick and pale.
4. Mix in the hazelnut meal, pear, cocoa, chocolate mixture that has been melted, and a pinch of salt.
5. Spread into the ready pan and bake for 45 minutes until the top is cracked and crisp and the middle is soft. Cool to room temperature and sprinkle with more cocoa powder.

56. MALTED MILK CHEESECAKE

Prep Time: 30 Minutes | Cook Time: 60 Minutes

Total Time: 1 Hour 30 Minutes | Serving: 10

Ingredients

- 1 tbs cornflour
- 3 eggs
- 1 cup of (110g) malted milk powder
- 80g unsalted butter, melted, cooled
- 1/2 cup of (110g) caster sugar
- 300g shortbread biscuits
- 1kg cream cheese, at room temperature

Meringue:

- 4 eggwhites
- 1 cup of (220g) caster sugar
- Pinch of cream of tartar

Instructions

1. Preheat the oven to 150°C. Grease a 20 cm springform cake pan and line both sides with baking paper. Position the pan on a baking tray.
2. Put the cookies in a food blender and blend them until they are finely ground. Add the butter and thoroughly combine. Press the dough evenly into the pan's base. Refrigerate until ready for consumption.
3. Mix the cheese cream in a food processor until it becomes smooth.
4. Mix the sugar, corn flour, and eggs until they are all mixed together. Mix in the malted milk powder with a whisk.
5. Pour over the biscuit base. Put the cake on a baking sheet and bake it for an hour or until the middle is just set but still a little bit soft. Shut off the oven.
6. Cool the cake in the oven for 2 hours with the open door. Chill for at least 4 hours or overnight until firm.
7. In a heat-safe bowl, combine sugar, cream of tartar, and egg whites. To make the meringue, place the bowl over a pan of water that is barely simmering. Don't let the bowl of mixture touch the water as you stir until the sugar dissolves.
8. Whisk the meringue in a stand mixer on high speed for 8 minutes until stiff peaks form, and it has cooled.
9. Spread the meringue on top of the cheesecake. Just before serving, use a kitchen blowtorch to caramelize the top of the meringue.

COOKIES

57. CHOCOLATE CHIP COOKIES

Prep Time: 20 Minutes | Cook Time: 20 Minutes

Total Time: 40 Minutes | Serving: 20

Ingredients

- 2 large eggs, at room temperature
- 2 ½ cups of (315 grams) all-purpose flour
- 1 ½ tsp vanilla extract
- 1 cup of (200 grams) packed brown sugar
- 2 cups of chocolate chips
- 3/4 tsp fine sea salt
- 1 cup of (200 grams) granulated sugar
- 16 tbsp (230 grams) unsalted butter
- 1 ¼ tsp baking soda

Instructions

Make batter:

1. Put a rack in the middle of the bottom third of the oven. Preheat the oven to 350°F. To prepare two baking sheets, cover them with either a silicone mat or parchment paper.
2. Mix together the flour, salt, baking soda, and Set aside.
3. In the medium bowl of a stand mixer with a paddle attachment, put the butter, both sugars and vanilla. (Or use a hand-held mixer in a mixing bowl). On medium speed (speed 4 on our mixer), cream the butter and sugars when it becomes light and fluffy, about 3 to 5 minutes.
4. Scrape the bowl's sides and bottom, and then put the eggs in. Mix for 30 seconds on medium-low speed. The eggs won't be mixed in all the way.
5. Less the speed down, add the dry ingredients in thirds, beating for 1 to 2 minutes until they are just combined.
6. Sprinkle the chocolate chips in while the mixer is on low and mix just until they are all mixed in.

Bake cookies:

1. Drop 3 tbsp-sized mounds onto baking sheets or use a large cookie scoop. Leave 2 inches of space between the cookies so they can grow.
2. Bake the cookies for around 18 minutes, one sheet at a time, turning them once while they are baking. The edges of the cookies should be golden brown, but the middle should be light.After 2 minutes of cooling on the baking sheet, alter the cookies to a wire rack to finish cooling.
3. Keep cookies fresh by storing them in an airtight container. At room temperature, they'll last for three days, but if you refrigerate them, they can last up to a week.

58. SUGAR COOKIES

Prep Time: 15 Minutes | Cook Time: 10 Minutes

Total Time: 25 Minutes | Serving: 36 Cookies

Ingredients
- 2 tsp baking powder
- 2 tsp vanilla extract
- 3 cups of (456g) flour
- 1 cup of (222g) butter at room temperature
- 1 cup of (233g) granulated sugar
- 1 batch of Sugar Cookie Frosting
- 1 egg

Instructions
1. Turn the oven on to 350°.
2. For 3 minutes, mix the butter and sugar in the bowl of a stand mixer.
3. Scrape the sides, now add the vanilla and the egg. Mix until everything comes together.
4. Add the flour and baking powder to the bowl. Mix the dough slowly at first and then faster and faster until it comes together. It should feel like Play-Doh. If you need to, add a little flour or water to make it soft and easy to work with.
5. Turn out onto a surface dusted with flour. Roll it out with a rolling pin until it's about 1/4 inch thick. (While the cookies are baking, they won't get bigger or thinner. Roll out to the FINISHED thickness you want.)
6. Use cookie cutters to make the shapes you want. Move the cookies to a cookie sheet that has been lined with silicone.
7. Bake at 350° for 6–8 minutes, or until the centers are puffed up and no longer shiny. Take the cookies out BEFORE they start to turn brown. If they turn brown, the cookie won't be soft and chewy but dry and "cracker."
8. Frost with frosting made from sugar cookies, and enjoy!

59. GINGERBREAD COOKIES

Prep Time: 30 Minute | Cook Time: 10 Minutes | Additional Time: 30 Minute

Total Time: 1 Hour 10 Minutes | Serving: 48

Ingredients

- ½ tsp salt
- 1 cup shortening
- 1 ½ tsp ground cinnamon
- 1 cup brown sugar
- 1 ½ tsp ground cloves
- ¼ cup fancy or blackstrap molasses
- 1 ½ tsp ground ginger
- 2 ¾ cup all purpose flour
- ¼ cup hot water
- 2 tsp baking soda

Instructions

1. Cream together the shortening, sugar, molasses, and water with a KitchenAid stand mixer or an electric mixer.
2. Flour, baking soda, and spices go in next. Mix slowly until everything is mixed together and a soft dough forms.
3. Put dough in the fridge for at least two hours with plastic wrap on top.
4. Pre heat oven to 350 degrees F.
5. Use either parchment paper or wax paper to line baking sheets.
6. Flour the surface and roll out the dough to about 1/4" thick.
7. You can cut out cookies in the shape of a gingerbread man or other shapes.
8. Put on the cookie sheet that has been prepared and bake for 10 to 12 minutes.
9. Before decorating with the best gingerbread icing, let the cookies cool on a wire rack.

60. PEANUT BUTTER COOKIES

Prep Time: 5 Minutes | Cook Time: 10 Minutes

Total Time: 15 Minutes | Serving: 18

Ingredients

- 1/2 cup of sugar 100g
- 1 1/2 cup of all-purpose flour 180g
- 1 cup of peanut butter 250g
- 1/2 cup of butter unsalted
- 3/4 tsp baking powder 3g
- 1/2 cup of brown sugar 100g
- 1 egg large, room temp
- 1 tsp vanilla extract 5mL

Instructions

1. Set your oven temperature to 350 degrees Fahrenheit.
2. The flour and baking powder should be combined after being sifted.
3. In a stand mixer that has a paddle attachment, combine the butter and sugar. Add 1/4 to 1/2 tsp of sea salt, as desired.
4. The peanut butter should be thoroughly incorporated.
5. Mix the egg and vanilla extract, then add the flour mixture.
6. The dough should be placed into 1-inch balls, which you should then arrange on a parchment-lined baking sheet.
7. With a fork, press the cookies into a crisscross pattern.
8. Baking cookies takes about 10 minutes.
9. Cool the cookies well on the baking sheet before transferring them

61. OATMEAL COOKIES

Prep Time: 10 Minute | Cook Time: 10 Minutes | Chill Time: 2 Hour

Total Time: 20 Minutes | Serving: 12

Ingredients

- 1/2 cup of raisins or nuts, if you like and if you want to.
- 1 1/2 cups of whole, rolled, old-fashioned oats (not instant or quick cook).
- 1/4 cup of white sugar
- 1/2 cup of unsalted, room-temperature butter (1 stick)
- 1 large egg
- pinch salt, optional, and to taste
- 1/2 tsp baking soda
- 1/2 cup of light brown sugar, packed
- 1 heaping cup of semi-sweet chocolate chips
- 1 tbsp vanilla extract
- 1/2 to 1 tsp cinnamon, added to taste
- 3/4 cup of all-purpose flour

Instructions

1. Place the egg, butter, sugars, and vanilla in the bowl of a stand mixer provided with a paddle attachment, or use a large bowl and an electric mixer. Approximately four minutes at medium-high speed or until the mixture is smooth and creamy.
2. Stop mixing and scrape down the bowl's sides. Add the cinnamon, baking soda, salt, oats, and flour, if using, and mix on low speed for approximately one minute, or until just combined.
3. Add the chocolate chips, raisins, or nuts, if using, and beat on low speed for about 30 seconds or until just combined.
4. Use a large cookie scoop, a 1/4-cup of measure, or your hands to make 11 mounds of dough that are about the same size. Roll the mounds into balls and slightly flatten them. Tip: Put a few chocolate chips on top of each mound of dough in a smart way by taking chocolate chips from the bottom and putting them on top.
5. Put the mounds on a large plate or tray, cover with plastic wrap, and put in the fridge for at least 2 hours and up to 5 days. If you bake with dough that hasn't been chilled, the cookies will spread out and be thinner.
6. Set the oven to 350F and use a Silpat or cooking spray to line a baking sheet. Place mounds of dough at least 2 inches apart on a baking sheet. I bake 8 cookies per sheet.
7. For very soft cookies, bake for about 11 minutes or until the edges are set, and the tops are just set, even if the middle is slightly undercooked, pale, and shiny. Don't overbake. As cookies cool, they get firmer.
8. Allow the baking sheet to cool for 5 minutes before serving. I don't use a rack; I just let them cool on the baking sheet.

62. CHRISTMAS COOKIES

Prep Time: Minute | Cook Time: Minutes

Total Time: Minutes | Serving:

Ingredients

- 1 cup of softened butter
- 1 tsp nutmeg
- 1 tsp ground cloves
- ½ tsp salt
- 1 tsp ground ginger
- 1 large egg
- 1½ dark brown sugar
- 1 tsp baking powder
- 1 tsp ground cinnamon
- 3 cups of flour

Instructions

1. Attach the Sifter and Scale to your KitchenAid mixer.
2. Put a bowl there (not the bowl of your stand mixer) to catch the sifted ingredients.
3. Measure out the flour, baking powder, cloves, nutmeg, ginger, and cinnamon, and then use the attachment on speed 4 to sift them all together into the bowl.
4. Don't use the bowl.
5. Put the butter and dark brown sugar in the stand mixer bowl and attach it to the KitchenAid mixer.
6. Beat on speed 4 with the flat beater until the ingredients are well mixed and the color is light.
7. Turn the speed down to 2 and add the egg and salt. Mix until everything is well combined.
8. While the mixer is still going, slowly pour the ingredients from step 3 that have been sifted into the mixing bowl.
9. Mix until everything comes together and forms a dough.
10. Take the dough out of the bowl and roll it out until it's about 14 inches thick.
11. Put the dough between two layers of plastic wrap and put it in the fridge for at least 20 minutes.
12. Turn your oven on to 350°F.
13. Take the cookies out of the fridge, remove the top plastic wrap layer, and cut them into whatever shape you want.
14. Put your cookies on a cookie sheet covered with parchment paper and bake for around 12 minutes in an oven that has already been heated.
15. When the cookies are done baking, they will look dry, but when you touch them, they will feel soft.
16. Take the cookies out of the oven and put them on a rack to cool right away.
17. Use the recipe below to make royal ice that you can frost and decorate as you like.

63. SHORTBREAD COOKIES

Prep Time: 10 Minutes | Cook Time: 20 Minutes

Total Time: 30 Minutes | Serving: 3 Dozen

Ingredients

- 1 tsp (5ml) vanilla extract (optional but highly recommended)
- 1 3/4 cups of (225g) all-purpose flour
- Sprinkles (optional)
- 1 cup of (227g) unsalted butter, room temperature
- 1/2 cup of (65g) powdered sugar plus more for dusting

Instructions

1. Set the oven to 300F and put parchment paper on two baking sheets.
2. Using an electric mixer or stand mixer with a paddle attachment, now start beat the butter and powdered sugar for about 3 minutes or until the mixture is light and fluffy. If you want to, add the vanilla and beat for another minute.
3. Mix in half of the flour until it is almost all gone. Use the rest of the flour the same way.
4. Sprinkle a little powdered sugar on your hand and roll the dough into 1" balls, which are about 1 tbsp each. Use some powdered sugar on the tines of a small fork to slightly flatten the cookie dough. Add some sprinkles on top if desired.
5. Bake for 12 to 15 minutes, or until the edges just start to turn brown. It could take up to 25 minutes, depending on how big your cookies are. Let cool all the way down on the baking sheets.

64. GLUTEN FREE SUGAR COOKIES

Prep Time: 20 Minutes | Cook Time: 8 Minutes |

Total Time: 28 Minutes | Serving: 24

Ingredients

For the cookies:

- ¼ tsp kosher salt
- 2 cups of (280 g) all-purpose gluten-free flour will be a blend
- 8 tbsp (112 g) unsalted butter
- 1 (50 g (weighed out of shell)) egg at room temperature
- 3 tbsp (22 g) confectioners' sugar
- ½ cup of (100 g) granulated sugar
- ¾ tsp baking powder
- 1 tsp xanthan gum omit

For the frosting:

- ¼ cup of (2 fluid ounces) milk, at room temperature
- ⅛ tsp kosher salt
- 2 tsp meringue powder
- 10 tbsp (140 g) unsalted butter
- 1 tbsp pure vanilla extract
- 4 cups of (460 g) confectioners' sugar
- Seeds from one vanilla bean optional
- Sprinkles optional

Instructions

Make the cookies:

1. Set the oven's temperature to 350°F. Line baking sheets with parchment paper that hasn't been bleached and set them aside.
2. Put the flour, xanthan gum, baking powder, salt, granulated sugar, and confectioners' sugar in a large bowl and whisk them together until they are well mixed.
3. Add the butter and mix to moisten the dry ingredients with the butter. Press down on the butter with the back of the mixing spoon until the mixture looks sandy.
4. Mix in the egg and vanilla until all of the dry ingredients are moistened by the wet ingredients.
5. Knead the mixture along with clean, dry hands until it sticks together. It will be quite thick and stiff.

6. Put the dough on a clean, flat surface and roll it into a circle that is less than 1/3 inch thick. To prevent sticking, lightly flour the rolling pin.
7. Using a cookie cutter that is 2 1/2 inches in diameter (or any other shape you like), cut out shapes from the dough and put them about an inch apart on the baking sheets that have been prepared.
8. It can help to cut away the dough around the shapes and then pull the shapes off. Gather the scraps and roll them out again. Keep doing this until you've used all of the dough.
9. Keep the baking sheet in the middle of the oven that has already been heated and bake the cookies for about 8 minutes, depending on their size and shape, until the tops are just set. Some cookies may get a little brown around the edges.
10. Before they get too brown, take them out of the oven and let them cool on the baking sheet until they are set. Then, move them to a wire rack for cooling well.

Make the frosting:

1. Put the butter, milk, and vanilla in the bowl of your stand mixer that has a paddle attachment. Mix on medium speed until all thing is mixed well. Turn the mixer up to high and mix until the mixture is creamy.
2. Add the salt, the meringue powder, and about 3 1/2 cups of confectioners' sugar. Slowly stir until the sugar is mixed in. Turn the mixer up to high and beat the mixture until it is thick all over.
3. Add the vanilla seeds, if you want, and as much of the rest of the confectioners' sugar as you need to make the frosting thicker. Mix well.
4. Once the cookies are cool well, pipe or spoon a lot of frosting on top of each one and use a wide knife or offset spatula to spread it even layer. Scatter sprinkles, if desired.
5. Allow the cookies at room temperature for cooling until the frosting has slightly hardened. Keep any leftovers at room temperature in a glass container that won't let air in. Plain cookies will last longer if you freeze them.

65. CRUMBL COOKIES

Prep Time: 10 Minutes | Cook Time: 10 Minutes

Total Time: 20 Minutes | Serving: 12

Ingredients

- 1 tbsp cornstarch
- 1 tsp kosher salt
- 2 1/4 cups of milk chocolate chips, dough after baking
- 1 tsp baking soda
- 3 cups of all-purpose flour
- 2 large eggs, room temperature
- 1/2 cup of granulated sugar
- 1 1/4 cups of light brown sugar
- 2 tsp vanilla extract
- 1 cup of butter, room temperature

Instructions

1. Preheat the oven to 375°F. Line a spacious baking sheet with parchment paper. With the paddle attachment, beat the light brown sugar, granulated sugar, and butter on medium speed for three minutes in your stand mixer.
2. Mix the eggs, vanilla, baking soda, salt, and cornstarch for one minute, scraping the bowl as necessary.
3. Lower the speed of the mixer to low and add the flour. Mix until the flour is barely incorporated. Add chocolate chips and mix thoroughly.
4. Round up 1/3 cup of (4.2 ounces) of cookie dough and roll it into a ball. Break the ball of cookie dough in half, turn it over so the broken edge is facing up, and then press the two pieces back together to make a rough top. Spread the cookie dough out on the baking sheet, leaving 3 inches between each cookie. I make five cookies at once.
5. Bake for around 11 minutes, until the edges and top are slightly golden. Don't over-bake.
6. To make the cookies look like they came from a bakery, press more chocolate chips on top.
7. Place on a cookie sheet for cooling purposes for about 5 minutes, then keep a place on a wire rack to cool.

66. LEMON COOKIES

Prep Time: 25 Minutes | Cook Time: 12 Minutes | Chill Time: 30 Minutes

Total Time: 1 hour 7 minutes | Serving:

Ingredients

- 1/2 cup of (115 grams) unsalted butter will be soft
- Zest of one medium lemon
- 1/2 tsp baking soda
- 1 tbsp (15 ml) fresh lemon juice
- 1 large egg at room temperature
- 1 and 1/2 tsp lemon extract
- Optional: 2-3 drops of yellow food coloring
- 1 and 3/4 cup of (220 grams) all-purpose flour (spooned & leveled)
- 3/4 cup of (150 grams) granulated sugar
- 1/4 tsp salt

Instructions

1. Flour, baking soda, and salt should be combined and stirred together in a large bowl. Set aside.
2. Beating the butter and granulated sugar together for one to two minutes, or until the ingredients are thoroughly combined, can be done in the bowl of a stand mixer connected with the paddle attachment or a bowl with a hand mixer. After making sure that everything is thoroughly combined, add the egg and continue stirring.
3. Lemon peel, lemon juice, lemon extract, and yellow food coloring should all be mixed in together. When it becomes necessary, pause what you're doing and scrape the sides of the bowl.
4. Combine the liquid and dry components in a mixing bowl and stir until just combined.
5. Wrap the dough with plastic wrap properlly and chill it in the refrigerator for at least 30 minutes.
6. Set the oven temperature to 177 degrees Celsius (350 degrees Fahrenheit).Prepare two oversized baking sheets by lining them with silicone baking mats or parchment paper.
7. Bring out of the refrigerator the dough for the cookies. Using a cookie scoop equal to 1.5 tbsp, place cookie dough balls on baking sheets that have been previously prepped. Check to see that there is sufficient space between each one.
8. Bake the cookies for ten to twelve minutes or until the surfaces of the cookies are hard. After removing the cookies from the oven, place them on the baking sheets, where they will remain for five to ten minutes while they cool. After that, arrange the cookies in a single layer on a wire rack to finish cooling.

67. PUMPKIN COOKIES

Prep Time: Minute | Cook Time: Minutes | Total Time: Minutes | Serving:

Ingredients

Cookies:

- 1/4 tsp salt
- 1/2 cup of unsalted butter softened
- 1 large egg at room temperature
- 1 and 1/2 tsp lemon extract
- 3/4 cup of granulated sugar
- 1/2 tsp baking soda
- 1 and 3/4 cup of (220 grams) all-purpose flour (spooned & leveled)
- Zest of one medium lemon
- 1 tbsp (15 ml) fresh lemon juice

Frosting:

- 1/4 cup of milk
- 1/2 cup of packed brown sugar
- 4 cups of confectioners' sugar
- 1/2 cup of butter
- 1 tsp vanilla
- Extra ground cinnamon sprinkled on top, optional

Instructions

1. In a bowl, mix the dry ingredients like flour, baking powder, and salt. Set aside. After using a hand mixer for one to two minutes, cream the butter and granulated sugar together in a stand mixer equipped with a paddle attachment until the mixture is properlly light and fluffy.
2. Add the egg after stirring the other ingredients together.
3. Lemon peel, lemon juice, lemon extract, and yellow food coloring are combined in a bowl. When necessary, stop and scrape the bowl's sides.
4. Combine the liquid and dry ingredients until just combined.
5. Refrigerate for at least 30 minutes with a tight-fitting lid.
6. The oven temperature was set to 350 degrees Fahrenheit (177 degrees Celsius). Two large baking sheets should be covered with parchment paper or silicone baking mats.
7. Remove the cookie dough from the refrigerator. Using a 1.5-tbsp cookie scoop, place cookie dough balls on the prepared baking sheets. Ensure that there is space between each item.
8. Bake the cookies for 12 minutes or until the tops are firm. Remove the cookies from the oven and place them to cool for 10 minutes on the baking sheets. The cookies are then transferred to a wire rack to cool completely.
9. In a small saucepan, melt the butter and brown sugar together over low heat until they are smooth. Move to a medium-sized bowl. Stir in milk and vanilla. Add powdered sugar and beat until smooth. (I made twice as much frosting as I needed, but I still used it all. I think you should do the same.)
10. Spread frosting on the cookies when they are cool. If you want, you can add more cinnamon on top.

68. VEGAN CHOCOLATE CHIP COOKIES

Prep Time: 10 Minutes | Cook Time: 20 Minutes

Total Time: 30 Minutes | Serving: 24 Cookies

Ingredients

- 1 1/4 cups of brown sugar, lightly packed
- 2 tsp pure vanilla extract
- 1 1/4 cups of non-dairy chocolate chips
- 1/2 cup of vegan butter, slightly softened to room temperature
- 2.5 tbsp water
- 1 tbsp ground flaxseed
- 1 tsp baking soda
- 1/4 tsp salt
- 1 1/2 cups of all-purpose flour
- 2 tsp cornstarch

Instructions

1. Set the oven to 350 degrees F and put parchment paper or silicone mats on two cookie sheets.
2. Mix the ground flaxseed and water in a small bowl and set it aside to make your flax egg.
3. In a large bowl starting, beat the softened vegan butter and brown sugar with a hand mixer or a stand mixer along with a paddle attachment for 1 to 2 minutes or until creamy.
4. Mix in the vanilla extract and the flax egg.
5. Then, stop the mixer and add the flour. On top of the flour, sprinkle the cornstarch, baking soda, and salt. Mix on low speed until everything is evenly distributed throughout the mixture.
6. Either by hand or with a mixer, you may incorporate the chocolate chunks into the batter.
7. Roll about 1-2 tbsp of dough into balls. Place the dough on the pans that have been prepared, and bake for 10 minutes (or 12 minutes for bigger cookies) or until the edges are just barely golden. Do not overbake! They will have a light color and be puffy.
8. After 5 minutes, transfer the cookies to a cooling rack. As they cool, they will firm up and transform into the most delightful chewy cookies. Enjoy their scrumptious goodness!

69. ALMOND COOKIES

Prep Time: 15 Minutes | Cook Time: 15 Minutes | Total Time: 30 Minutes | Serving: 32 Cookies

Ingredients
- 2 egg yolks, slightly beaten
- 2 cups of all-purpose flour
- 1 cup of sliced almonds, plus more for topping
- 1½ tsp pure almond extract
- 1 cup of sugar
- 1 cup of (8 ounce) unsalted butter, softened

Instructions
1. Set the oven temperature to 350 degrees.
2. Mix the butter and sugar in an electric mixer at medium-low speed until the mixture is light and smooth. Mix the egg yolks and almond extract.
3. Pour the flour in slowly and scrape the sides of the bowl as needed until the dough is smooth. Add the sliced almonds and stir until they are just mixed in.
4. Take a tbsp of dough and roll it into a ball with your palms. Put the ball on a large, nonstick baking sheet that has not been greased. Keep doing this until all of the cookies are made. Make sure there is at least an inch between each cookie.
5. Use your hand or the back of a floured glass tumbler to flatten each cookie. Almond pieces should be pressed down on the top of each cookie.
6. Bake for 15 minutes, until the edges and bottoms are golden brown. Let the food cool down a bit before eating.

70. BUTTERSCOTCH COOKIES

Prep Time: 10 Minutes | Cook Time: 8 Minutes | Total Time: 18 Minutes | Serving: 36 cookie

Ingredients
- 1 tsp salt
- cups of butterscotch chips
- 1 cup of brown sugar
- 3 cups of all-purpose flour
- 1 tsp baking powder
- 1 cup of butter, softened
- 1 cup of sugar
- 2 eggs, large
- 1 tsp vanilla extract
- 1 tsp baking soda

Instructions
1. Turn oven on to 350°F.
2. Cream the sugar and butter together in a stand mixer or a big bowl.
3. Add the vanilla and eggs one by one, and beat until the mixture is fluffy.
4. Blend salt, flour, baking powder, and baking soda in a petite bowl.
5. Gradually incorporate the flour blend into the moist ingredients and stir until fully combined. Add the butterscotch chips and stir.
6. Put the dough on a cookie sheet that hasn't been greased and bake for 8 to 10 minutes.

71. BANANA COOKIES

Prep Time: 20 Minute | Cook Time: 10 Minutes

Total Time: 30 Minutes | Serving: 16

Ingredients
- ½ cup of white sugar
- 1 tsp vanilla extract
- ¼ tsp salt
- 1 egg yolk
- ¾ cup of dark chocolate chips
- ½ cup of butter (at room temp)
- 1 tsp cinnamon
- ¾ tsp baking soda
- ½ cup of light brown sugar
- ¾ cup of mashed ripe banana (approx 2 medium bananas)
- 2 cups of all-purpose flour

Instructions
1. In the bowl of a stand mixer, give the butter, and sugars whisk on medium speed for about 4 minutes or until the mixture is smooth.
2. Add the mashed banana, egg yolk, and vanilla, and beat again until everything is well mixed.
3. Mix the flour, salt, baking soda, and cinnamon separately.
4. Combine the flour mixture in the bowl of the stand mixer and mix until a sticky dough forms at low speed.
5. Mix for a short time after adding the chocolate chips.
6. Put the dough in the fridge for an hour or in the freezer for 30 minutes.
7. Set the oven to 350 F and put parchment paper on two baking sheets.
8. Take some of the mixtures in your hands and roll it into balls. The dough will stick together a lot. Put the cookie balls on the baking sheets and leave enough space between them so they can spread.
9. Bake for 10–12 minutes, or until the center is set and the edges just begin to brown.
10. The cookies should cool for about 15 minutes on the baking sheet before being transferred with a spatula to a wire rack to colplete cooling.

72. BROWNIE COOKIES

Prep Time: 45 Minutes | Cook Time: 13 Minutes

Total Time: 48 Minutes | Serving: 36 Cookies

Ingredients

- 1/2 tsp
- 12 ounces bittersweet chocolate chips 60-70% cacao
- 1 tbsp vanilla extract
- 1/2 cup of butter
- 1 cup of pecans chopped, optional
- 1/2 cup of mini semisweet chocolate chips
- 1/2 tsp salt
- 1/4 cup of unsweetened cocoa powder[1]
- 1/4 cup of brown sugar
- 3 large eggs
- 1 cup of granulated sugar
- 3/4 cup of all-purpose flour

Instructions

1. Stirring constantly, melt the bittersweet chocolate pieces and butter in a sturdy saucepan over low heat until the chocolate is melted well and the mixture becomes smooth.
2. Take the pot off the heat and set it aside.
3. Mix the eggs, sugars, vanilla, baking powder, and salt on high speed for 5 minutes or until the batter is thick and creamy. This step is essential, so make sure to beat the mixture for the full 5 minutes.
4. Slow down the mixer and mix in the melted chocolate until everything is well mixed.
5. Mix in the flour and add cocoa powder until they are just mixed in.
6. Add nuts and tiny chocolate chips if you want to. Mix by stirring. At this point, the batter should have the consistency of a thick cake batter.
7. Cover the mixture and put it in the fridge for 30 minutes.
8. Turn the oven on to 350 F. Use parchment paper to cover two baking sheets.
9. Using a 1.5-tbsp cookie scoop, drop the dough about two inches apart on the cookie sheets that have been prepared.
10. Bake cookies for 8-10 minutes. The sides of the cookie will look set, but the middle will still look a little wet. Don't bake the cookies for too long, or they won't be crackly and gooey.
11. As the cookies cool, placed on the baking sheet, the shiny, crackly top will form.

73. RED VELVET COOKIES

Prep Time: 20 Minute | Cook Time: 10 Minutes

Total Time: 30 Minutes | Serving: 12

Ingredients

- ⅓ cup of light brown sugar
- 1 large egg
- ½ tsp baking soda
- ½ cup of white sugar
- 1 tsp vanilla extract

- 1 cup of white chocolate chips
- ¼ tsp salt
- ½ cup of butter
- ¾ tsp baking powder
- 2 tbsp cocoa powder
- 1 ⅔ cups of all-purpose flour
- ¼ tsp red food coloring

Instructions

1. In the bowl of a stand mixer, start beating the butter and sugars on medium speed for about 4 minutes or until the mixture is smooth.
2. Add the egg yolk, vanilla, and mashed banana, and beat again until everything is well combined.
3. In a other bowl, mix flour, baking soda, salt, and cinnamon together.
4. The flour mixture should be added to the stand mixer bowl, and it should be blended on low speed until just combined into a sticky dough.
5. Shortly after adding the chocolate chips, continue mixing.
6. The dough should be refrigerated for an hour or frozen for 30 minutes.
7. Turn the oven on to 350 F and put parchment paper on two baking sheets.
8. Use your hands to roll handfuls of the mixture into balls. The dough will have a lot of stickiness. Position the cookie dough balls on the baking sheets, ensuring adequate room for expansion during the baking process.
9. Bake for 10–12 minutes, or until the center is set and the edges are just starting to turn brown.
10. The cookies should cool for 15 minutes on the baking sheet before being transferred to a wire rack.

74. STRAWBERRY COOKIES

Prep Time: 10 Minutes | Cook Time: 10 Minutes

Total Time: 20 Minutes | Serving:

Ingredients

- ¾ cup of frozen strawberries
- ⅔ cup of cold unsalted butter, cut into cubes
- ¾ cup of granulated sugar
- 2 cups of flour, all-purpose or gluten-free flour
- 1 tsp baking powder
- pinch sea salt
- ½ cup of powdered sugar
- 1 tsp milk

Instructions

1. First, warm oven to 350 degrees Fahrenheit. Put parchment paper in a baking dish.
2. Put frozen strawberries in the microwave for 60 to 90 seconds until they are soft and juicy again. In the microwave bowl, there should be a little bit of strawberry juice. Don't empty.
3. Put cold butter cubes and sugar in the bowl of a stand mixer. Beat on high for about 2 minutes or until everything is mixed well.
4. Then, add strawberries that have been frozen and their juices. Mix by beating.
5. Combine the flour, salt, and sea baking powder. Stir to integrate ingredients.
6. Utilize a cookie scoop to place dough spheres on a lined baking sheet.
7. Bake 10 minutes or until sides are set. Remove from oven.
8. Prepare the sauce once the cakes have cooled down. In a small basin, combine the confectioners' sugar and milk. Mix thoroughly until homogeneous.
9. Lastly, drizzle over cookies that have completely cooled, and serve!

75. APPLE COOKIES

Prep Time: 20 Minutes | Cook Time: 24 Minutes

Total Time: 44 Minutes | Serving: 24

Ingredients

- 2 tsp vanilla extract
- 1/2 tsp cinnamon
- 1/2 tsp salt
- 1 1/2 cups of granulated sugar
- 1/3 cup of apple butter
- 1/2 tsp baking powder
- 8 tbsp unsalted butter at room temperature
- 2 eggs
- 2 1/2 cups of all-purpose flour

For Rolling the Cookies:

- 1/4 cup of granulated sugar
- 1/2 tsp cinnamon

Instructions

1. Set the oven temperature to 350 degrees. Put parchment paper on baking sheets and set them aside.
2. Mix the flour, salt, cinnamon, and baking powder in a big bowl. Whisk until the mixture is smooth.
3. Beat the butter and apple butter together in a stand or a big bowl with a hand mixer. Add the granulated sugar and beat for about three minutes or until the mixture is fluffy. Scrape both sides and bottom part of the bowl. Add the vanilla and then one egg at a time, the eggs. Beat until everything is mixed in, stopping once to scrape down the sides.
4. After stopping the machine, add the flour mixture. Turn the mixer's speed down until the flour is mixed enough to keep it from flying around. Turn the mixer to high for just a few seconds until the flour is completely mixed in. Be careful not to beat too much.
5. Sugar and cinnamon should be mixed in a small bowl. Using a cookie scoop that holds 1 1/2 tbsp, scoop out pieces of dough and drop them into the cinnamon sugar mixture. Turn it over once, then roll it between your hands to make a ball. The dough will stick together. If you can't work with the dough because it's too sticky, put it in the fridge for 30 minutes.
6. Bake the cookies about two inches apart for 10 to 14 minutes, or until the sides start turning golden brown and the middle is no longer doughy looking. Allow the cookies to cool for two minutes on the baking sheet before gingerly transferring them to a cooling rack to cool completely. Put into an airtight container.

76. BLUEBERRY COOKIES

Prep Time: 10 Minute | Cook Time: 13 Minutes | Chilling Time: 30 Minute

Total Time: 53 Minutes | Serving: 12

Ingredients

- 70 grams white chocolate chips, chopped
- 135 grams of all-purpose flour, about 1 cup
- 1/8 tsp salt
- 76 grams unsalted vegan butter, softened
- 80 grams of frozen blueberries
- 90 grams granulated sugar
- 1/2 tsp baking powder

Instructions

1. Preheat the oven to 400 degrees Fahrenheit.
2. Mix the flour, baking powder, and salt in a mixing basin.
3. Thaw the frozen blueberries in the microwave or stovetop until mushy and jammy. This should take around 30 seconds in the microwave on high and about 2-3 minutes on the stovetop on medium.
4. After cooling the blueberries for 2-3 minutes, it's time to whip up the butter and sugar with an electric mixer or stand mixer. Beat them together until the mixture turns significantly lighter and fluffier. Then, cream the blueberries with the butter and sugar on high speed, mashing them into the mixture until they are pureéd and completely mixed with the butter and sugar. The result should boast a deep purple hue. Randomly fold the dry ingredients into the wet components to form a dough, and don't forget to add some white chocolate chips for extra deliciousness.
5. Because the dough will be very slack, chill it in the freezer for 30 minutes before shaping it into 12 balls.
6. Bake the cookies for 10-13 minutes or until the edges are slightly brown. Allow to cool for 5-10 minutes on a cooling rack before serving!

77. COCONUT COOKIES

Prep Time: 15 Minutes | Cook Time: 10 Minutes

Total Time: 25 Minutes | Serving: 12

Ingredients

- ¾ tsp baking soda
- 1 tsp vanilla extract
- 1 ½ cups of toasted desiccated coconut
- ⅓ cup of light brown sugar
- ½ cup of butter
- 1 ½ cups of all-purpose flour
- 1 large egg
- ⅓ cup of white sugar

Instructions

1. In the bowl of a stand mixer, whisk the butter and sugars on medium speed for about 4 minutes or until the mixture is smooth and fluffy.
2. Then beat again to mix in the egg and vanilla extract.
3. Mix the flour, baking soda, and dried coconut together in a separate bowl.
4. Add this to the bowl of the mixer and mix on low speed when it becomes a thick dough forms.
5. Put the dough in the fridge to chill for an hour or in the freezer for about 25 minutes.
6. Set the oven to 350 F and put parchment paper on two baking sheets.
7. Roll the dough into balls with your hands and put them on the baking sheets with enough space between them so they can spread. The dough should make enough cookies for 12.
8. Bake for 10–12 minutes, or until the edges just start to turn brown.
9. Allow the cookies to cool for roughly 15 minutes on the baking sheet before replacing them with a wire rack by using a spatula to achieve complete cooling.

78. GINGER COOKIES

Prep Time: 10 Minutes | Cook Time: 13 Minutes

Total Time: 23 Minutes | Serving: 30

Ingredients

For the Cookies:

- 1/4 cup of molasses dark
- 2 tsp baking soda
- 2 tsp ground ginger
- 1 tsp ground cinnamon
- 2 tsp vanilla extract
- 3/4 cup of brown sugar packed
- 3/4 cup of butter softened
- 1/2 tsp ground cloves
- 3/4 tsp salt
- 1/2 tsp cardamom
- 1 egg large
- 2 1/2 cups of all-purpose flour 300g

For Rolling:

- 1/4 cup of sugar Sanding or granulated
- 1/2 tsp cinnamon

Instructions

1. Turn the oven on to 350F. Mix the flour, baking soda, salt, ginger powder, and cloves together in a big bowl using a sifter. Mix them together and put them aside.
2. Mix the butter, sugar, and molasses together with a paddle tool on a stand mixer or with an electric mixer. Beat until the color lightens and it gets fluffy.
3. While the mixer is on low, add the egg and then add the vanilla. Scrape the bottom part of the bowl and mix again until all of the ingredients are mixed in.
4. Mix on low to medium-low until the flour mixture is just mixed in. One last time, scrape the bowl clean and use a spoon to fold in any flour that is left.
5. To make 1.5- to 2-inch balls, use a small ice cream scoop or a tbsp. Roll each one into a ball with your clean hands, then roll it in sugar or sand.
6. Put the balls about two inches apart on a baking sheet, place them with parchment paper, and bake at 350F for 12 to 13 minutes. When you take the cookies out of the oven, the sides will be done, but the middles will still be cooking.

79. BROWN BUTTER BROWN SUGAR COOKIES

Prep Time: 15 Minutes | Cook Time: 8 Minutes

Total Time: 23 Minutes | Serving: 36 Cookie

Ingredients

- 1 1/2 tsp baking powder
- 1 tsp salt
- 1 1/4 cups of brown sugar, packed
- 2 large eggs
- 3 cups of all-purpose flour, sifted
- 1 tbsp vanilla extract
- 1 1/2 cups of unsalted butter
- 1/4 cup of granulated sugar

Instructions

1. Put the butter in a small sauce pot and turn the heat to medium. Keep an eye on the butter as it melts and simmers, and stir it every so often. Turn off the heat when the bits of butter at the bottom of the pot have turned a dark teddy bear brown, and the butter itself is a light brown color. It should smell like nuts, not like smoke. Put the butter in the fridge until it becomes firm again.
2. Set your oven temperature to 350 degrees F. Put parchment paper on a few baking sheets. Scrape the hard brown butter into the bowl of a stand mixer, which has a whisk attachment. Make sure to get all the dark bits. They give a lot of taste. Add the brown sugar and start beating the mixture on high for about 5 minutes or until it is light and fluffy. It's fine if there are still a few chunks of brown sugar.
3. Clean out the bowl and turn the machine to low. Mix in the baking powder, salt, vanilla extract, and eggs. Once everything is thoroughly combined, gradually add the flour. When the mixture looks smooth, stop the machine.
4. Put the sugar on the table in a small bowl. To measure out the cookie dough, use a 1 1/2-tbsp cookie scoop. Roll the scoops into balls, and then roll each and every ball in the powdered sugar to coat it.
5. Put two inches of space between the cookies on the baking sheets. Use the bottom of a drinking glass to flatten two balls of dough into rounds that are 1/2 inch thick.
6. Bake for 8-10 minutes. The sides of the cookies should be golden, but the middle should still be a little soft. Let them cool on baking sheets.

80. CINNAMON COOKIES

Prep Time: 20 Minute | Cook Time: 10 Minutes

Total Time: 30 Minutes | Serving: 15

Ingredients

- ⅓ cup of (67 grams) brown sugar
- 2 tsp vanilla extract
- ⅓ cup of (67 grams) granulated sugar
- 1 ½ cups of (180 grams) all-purpose flour
- 1 egg
- pinch of salt
- ½ cup of (113 grams) butter
- 1 tsp baking powder
- 1 tsp ground cinnamon

Topping:

- 2 tbsp ground cinnamon
- ¼ cup of (50 grams) granulated sugar

Instructions

1. Put parchment paper on the baking pan and preheat the oven to 350°F (180°C). Place aside. Salt, cinnamon, baking powder, and flour should all be combined and properly mixed in a big bowl. Mix thoroughly, then pause.
2. For this task, you can either use an electric or manual mixer. Use a stand mixer that has a paddle attachment, a hand mixer, or an electric mixer to combine the butter and sugar in the bowl. For about 2 to 3 minutes, mix at medium speed until the mixture is light and creamy.
3. Beat this mixture after adding the egg and vanilla essence until the egg is completely integrated.
4. Gradually incorporate small portions of the flour mixture into the egg mixture until the dough just combines.
5. If the dough is too sticky to work with, put it in the fridge for 15 to 20 minutes with plastic wrap on top. But these cookies don't have to be put in the fridge.
6. Using an ice cream scoop, take a piece of the dough and roll it between your hands to make a ball. Set the balls 3 inches apart on the cookie sheet that has been ready.
7. Mix the white sugar and cinnamon together in a small bowl to make the topping.
8. Spread the cinnamon sugar mixture over the cookie dough balls that have already been made. Be generous! I think you can never have too much spice.
9. Bake for 12 to 15 minutes or until the bottoms have turned golden brown. Take them out and let them cool for a few minutes on the baking sheet. Then, move them to a wire rack to cool fully.

81. HAZELNUT AND APRICOT BISCOTTI

Prep Time: 20 Minute | Cook Time: 1 HOur 5 Minutes | Rest Time: 1 Hour 10

Total Time: 2 Hour 10 Minutes | Serving:

Ingredients

- 1 cup of toasted hazelnuts
- 1 ¼ cups of granulated sugar and more for sprinkling
- 1 tsp coarse salt
- 2 tsp baking powder
- 2 tsp anise seeds
- 2 ½ cups of all-purpose flour
- 3 large eggs plus 1 more, beaten, for brushing
- 1 cup of coarsely chopped dried apricots

Instructions

1. Turn the oven on to 350. Whisk the flour, sugar, baking powder, anise seeds, salt, and nuts together in the bowl of your electric mixer. (I used the tool for whisking.) After mixing the dough for about two minutes, add the dried apricots. Change your connection to the paddle. Add the eggs and beat for about 3 minutes or until the dough comes together.
2. Put parchment paper on a baking sheet. Cut the dough in half and shape each half into a ball. Place on parchment paper and keep flattening and fixing until each log is about 13 inches long,and some larger than 2 inches in width and a little under an inch in height.
3. Brush the logs with the whisked egg and sprinkle with fine sugar. For about 35 minutes, bake. Let the pans cool for 40 minutes on a wire rack. Turn the oven temperature down to 300 while they are cooling.
4. Using a knife with serrations, cut the meat into about 1/2-inch-thick pieces. Place them on the paper with the cut side facing up and bake for about 30 minutes. Let them cool for about 30 minutes on wire racks.
5. It will last about a month in a container that keeps out air.

82. ORANGE COOKIES

Prep Time: 15 Minutes | Cook Time: 30 Minutes

Total Time: 45 Minutes | Serving: 24

Ingredients

For the Cookies:

- 2 cups of plus 2 tbsp all-purpose flour 255g
- 1¼ tsp baking powder
- 1 large egg
- ½ tsp salt
- ½ cup of unsalted butter softened (113g)
- ¾ cup of granulated sugar 150g
- 1 tbsp orange zest, about 2 oranges
- ½ cup of fresh orange juice 120ml

For the Glaze:

- Zest of 1/2 orange
- 1 cup of confectioners' sugar 120g
- 1 tbsp unsalted butter melted
- 1 to 2 tbsp fresh orange juice

Instructions

For the Cookies:

1. Heat the oven to 375°F. Prepare two large baking pans by lining them with parchment paper.
2. Mix the flour, baking powder, and salt in a medium-sized mixing bowl.
3. In a spacious mixing bowl or the bowl of a stand mixer, attach with the paddle attachment, blend together the sugar, butter, and zest for approximately 3 minutes, or until the mixture becomes airy and light. Incorporate the egg until everything is thoroughly blended.
4. At a low speed, put the flour mixture and the orange juice alternately until fully mixed. Occasionally pause to scrape the bowl. Take 1 tbsp-sized portion of dough and place them on the baking sheet, maintaining a 2-inch separation between each.
5. Bake each sheet for 10 minutes or until the middles look dry and feel hard to the touch. After a few minutes, move the cookies to a wire rack to cool fully.

To make the Glaze:

1. Whisk the sugar, zest, juice, and melted butter in a small bowl until smooth. Spread the sauce on each cookie's top. Let the cookies sit for about 20 minutes or until the glaze is set.

ROLLS

83. CINNAMON ROLL

Prep Time: 20 Minutes | Cook Time: 20 Minutes

Total Time: 40 Minutes | Serving: 12

Ingredients

Dough:

- 2¾ cups of all-purpose flour 330g
- 1 package instant yeast or 2¼ tsp. (7g)
- ½ cup of water 118ml
- 1 large egg
- ¼ cup of granulated sugar 56g
- 1 tsp. salt 4g
- 2 tbsp. butter, unsalted or salted 30g
- ¼ cup of milk 59ml

Filling:

- 1 tbsp. ground cinnamon 15g
- ⅔ cup of brown sugar 149g
- 1 tsp. vanilla extract about 5 ml
- ¼ cup of butter, unsalted or salted 56g

Vanilla Glaze:

- 1 tsp. vanilla extract 5ml
- 2-3 tbsp. milk 30 to 45ml
- ¼ cup of butter 56g
- 1½ cups of powdered sugar confectioner sugar (180g)

Instructions

1. Put the milk and water in a small bowl and heat it until it's between 105 and 115 F (40 and 44 C). Add the yeast and a tsp of sugar. Set the mixture aside for 5 to 10 minutes until it gets foamy. This is how you know that the yeast is good and has been active.
2. Mix the salt and flour in a tiny bowl and set it aside. Then, heat the butter. I usually use the microwave for this. Add the melted butter (make sure it's not too hot) and the rest of the sugar to the yeast that has been active. Whisk together.
3. Put the yeast and water in a big bowl. Mix the egg into the yeast batter with a whisk. Once everything is mixed, add our flour a little at a time. When it gets thick, switch to a wooden spoon. Use a stand mixer instead. Add a little flour until you have a nice sticky dough. First, gently mix the dough in the bowl with some additional flour. This will assist in removing the dough from the sides of the bowl. Next, move the dough onto a lightly floured surface.
4. Knead the dough for 8 to 10 minutes, either by hand or with a dough hook on a standing machine. Add a bit extra flour if the dough becomes too sticky. Put the dough in a bowl that has been oiled or covered with cooking spray. The dough should be allowed to double in size after being left covered with a moist towel or plastic wrap for 1 hour.

5. Then, roll out the dough and spread melted butter on top. Then, mix the vanilla extract, brown sugar, and cinnamon. You can use white sugar if you don't have brown sugar. Sprinkle that over the butter, and then tightly roll up the dough.
6. Cut 12 rolls out of the dough with dental floss or a knife. Put the rolls in a 9x13-inch baking pan sprayed with cooking spray. Allow the cinnamon rolls to ascend for roughly 45 minutes to one hour, ensuring they are covered with either plastic wrap or a cloth.
7. Remove the plastic wrap or cloth and brush the tops of the rolls with butter. Bake the rolls in a 375 F/190 C oven warmed for 15 to 20 minutes or until golden brown. Let them cool down after they are done.
8. Make the sauce while the rolls cool down. Add the powdered sugar, melted butter, vanilla extract, and milk. Add another tbsp of milk if you want the glaze to be thinner. The cinnamon rolls are done when you put the glaze on top. Enjoy!

84. SPRING ROLL

Prep Time: Minute | Cook Time: Minutes |

Total Time: Minutes | Serving:

Ingredients
- 4 carrots
- 12 radishes
- 4 mini cucumbers
- 1/4 white cabbage
- 2 avocados
- 8 cooked shrimps
- 100 g cooked rice noodles
- 12 rice paper wrappers
- A handful of fresh mint
- 4 handful salad

Instructions
1. Peel the carrots and cut the tops off the radishes.
2. Insert the Adjustable Slicing Disc to the Food Processor Attachment and attach it to the stand mixer.
3. Put the stand mixer on speed 10 and slice the radishes and cucumber.
4. Insert the Reversible Shredding Disc and shred the cabbage and carrots on speed 4. Combine the carrots and cabbage in a large bowl.
5. Slice the avocado and get everything ready to start assembling the spring rolls.
6. Place the avocado, shrimp, rice noodles, cabbage and carrot, radishes, cucumber, salad, and mint in a row across the center. Leave about 5 cm uncovered on each side of the rice paper.
7. Fold the uncovered sides inward and tightly roll the wrapper.

85. PUMPKIN ROLL

Prep Time: 25 Minutes | Cook Time: 15 Minutes

Total Time: 40 Minutes | Serving: 8

Ingredients
Cake Ingredients:

- 3/4 cup of all-purpose flour
- 1/2 tsp ground nutmeg
- 1 cup of walnuts, finely chopped
- 2/3 cup of pure pumpkin puree
- 1 tsp lemon juice
- 3 eggs (room temperature)
- powdered sugar
- 2 tsp ground cinnamon
- 1 tsp ground ginger
- 1 cup of sugar
- 1 tsp baking powder
- 1/2 tsp salt

Filling Ingredients:

- 1/3 cup of butter, room temperature
- 1 package cream cheese, room temperature
- 1 1/2 tsp vanilla extract
- 1 1/2 cups of powdered sugar

Instructions

1. Let's start by confidently preheating the oven to 375°F (190°C). Then, generously spray a 15x10x1-inch baking pan with nonstick spray. After that, line the pan with parchment paper and spray it again with nonstick spray. This will guarantee that your food won't stick to the pan. With that taken care of, set the pan aside and proceed to the next step of your recipe. Mix the flour, cinnamon, baking powder, ginger, salt, and nutmeg together and set it away.
2. For 5 minutes, beat the eggs on high speed in a stand mixer. While mixing at medium speed, gradually pour in the sugar. Combine the pumpkin with the lemon juice. Slowly incorporate the flour mixture. Distribute the batter evenly in the baking dish. Sprinkle some walnuts on top.
3. Bake for 15 minutes until you can lightly touch the cake, and it bounces back. Loosen the cake from the pan's edges and turn it onto a clean kitchen towel with a light dusting of powdered sugar. Take off the paper. Starting from a short side, roll the towel and cake into a spiral and let them cool on a metal rack.
4. Using a stand mixer, blend the cream cheese and butter with vanilla extract on medium speed until the mixture is smooth. Beat in the powdered sugar slowly.
5. Take off the towel and unroll the cake. Spread the filling on top of the cake, leaving 1 inch bare. Roll the cake back up and cut off the ends. Wrap in plastic wrap and put in the fridge for at least 2 hour.

86. DINNER ROLL

Prep Time: 30 Minute | Cook Time: 15 Minutes

Total Time: 45 Minutes | Serving: 15

Ingredients

- 1/2 cup of milk
- 2 tbsp honey
- Extra melted butter for brushing on top
- 3 1/2 to 4 cups of all-purpose flour
- 1 tsp fine sea salt
- 1 cup of water
- 2 tbsp melted butter
- 1 tbsp active dry yeast*

Instructions

1. Get your oven and dish ready. Make sure the oven is at 400°F. Spray cooking spray on a 9-by-13-inch baking dish and set it away.
2. Warm up the drink. Stir the water and melted butter together in a bowl that can go in the microwave. Add the milk and honey, stirring until thoroughly combined. Stir the liquid after 1 minute in the microwave. Keep heating the mixture for 15 seconds in the microwave until it hits 110°F. It will feel warm, but not too hot. (*You can also heat the mixture in a saucepan over medium-low heat until it hits 110°F.)
3. Add yeast. Pour the liquid mixture into a stand mixer's big bowl. Spread the yeast out evenly on top, give it a quick stir with a fork to mix, and let the yeast work for 5 minutes until it is foamy.
4. Add dry ingredients. Add the salt and flour, about 3 1/2 cups of, but not all of the flour.
5. Mix. Mix the dry ingredients with the dough hook on medium-low speed until everything is mixed. Should the dough stick to the bowl's sides, gradually add 1/4 cup of flour each time until the dough easily detaches from the sides and has a slightly sticky feel to the touch. Mix for another 4–5 minutes on low speed or until the dough is smooth. Then, shape the dough into a ball and place it in a greased bowl.
6. Cover the bowl with either a damp towel or a paper towel to allow the dough to rise. Leave it for 15 minutes.
7. Get the rolls ready. Punch the dough down gently and cut it into 15 pieces of the same size. Make a ball out of each piece of dough, and put the balls in the oiled baking dish. Cover the dish again with a wet towel or paper towel, and give the dough balls to rise for another 15–20 minutes.
8. Bake. Remove the cover, then bake for 15 minutes, or until the rolls are cooked all the way through and the top is a light golden color.
9. Apply additional butter for brushing. Position the baking dish on a wire cooling rack and brush the surfaces of the rolls with melted butter.
10. Warm is best. Then serve hot and enjoy!

87. CRESCENT ROLL

Prep Time: 12 Minute | Cook Time: 12 Minutes | Rising Time: 2 Hour

Total Time: 2 Hour 32 Minutes | Serving: 32

Ingredients

- ½ cup of white sugar
- ½ cup of whole milk
- 2 eggs
- 4 cups of all-purpose flour
- 1 tbsp instant yeast
- 1 tsp salt
- ½ cup of butter, room temperature
- ½ cup of warm water (110 degrees F/45 degrees C)

Instructions

1. Start by mixing water and yeast in the bowl of your stand mixer, using the dough hook. Use a large basin if making this by hand. Allow it to sit for 5 minutes to dissolve.
2. In the meantime, mix the milk, butter pieces, sugar, and salt in a medium bowl that can go in the microwave. Microwave for about a minute. Stir everything until it all melts.
3. Pour the butter mixture into a big bowl or a mixer with a stand. Mix well; the liquid should be at room temperature. If not, give it a few minutes to sit. Whisk in eggs.
4. Slowly add 3 3/4 cups of flour when mixing the dough on low speed. Add just enough flour to make a soft dough.
5. If you are making the dough by hand, take it out and put it on a lightly floured surface. Knead the dough up to 8 minutes.
6. Put the dough in an oiled bowl and turn it once to cover it. Cover with a clean and healthy cloth and set in a warm place for Around 2 hours or until the dough doubles. Press down on the dough.
7. Divide the dough into two equal parts on a surface that has been lightly dusted with flour. Then, roll out the dough into 12-inch circles and cut them into 16 pieces. From the wide end, roll up the wedges to make a crescent shape.
8. Spread oil or butter on a baking sheet pan, and then place crescent rolls on it about 1/2 to 1" apart. Place a kitchen towel over it, allowing the dough to rise for around 30 minutes until it becomes puffy.
9. Preheat the oven to 400 degrees F and spread butter on the tops. Put in the oven and bake for about 12–14 minutes or until the top is golden brown.
10. Serve hot with the rest of the butter if you want.

88. SAUSAGE ROLL

Prep Time: 10 Minutes | Cook Time: 15 Minutes

Total Time: 25 Minutes | Serving: 30

Ingredients
- Sausage
- 1 tsp sugar
- 1 egg
- 2 tsp salt
- 1 cup of (240ml) boiled water
- 1 cup of (240ml) milk
- 725 grams = 25.57 ounces flour.
- ½ cup of (120ml) butter or oil

Instructions
1. Butter and boiling water are mixed in a KitchenAid Stand Mixer until the butter melts.
2. Then mix in the milk, egg, sugar, salt, and yeast.
3. Let sit for 2–5 minutes until the yeast starts to work.
4. Put in the flour.
5. About 5 minutes are needed to knead the dough.
6. Cover the dough and give it time to rise until it's about twice as big as it was before. (about an hour).
7. Make buns about the size of an egg by pressing the dough between your thumb and fingers. Two sheets will be full of dough.
8. The meat is rolled into the bun.
9. Let the meat rolls rise until they are about twice as big as they were before.
10. Start the oven on to 400 degrees and bake for 18–20 minutes.

89. JELLY ROLL

Prep Time: 25 Minutes | Cook Time: 30 Minutes

Total Time: 55 Minutes | Serving: 16

Ingredients

For the Cake:

- 4 1/2 ounces all-purpose flour, such as Gold Medal blue label
- 1/2 ounce vanilla extract
- 1/4 tsp baking soda
- 3/4 tsp baking powder
- 3 ounces pistachio oil, roasted hazelnut oil, melted ghee
- 4 large eggs, straight from the fridge
- 1/2 tsp (2g) Diamond Crystal kosher salt
- 7 ounces plain or toasted sugar

For the Filling:

- 1/2 recipe cranberry jam

For the Frosting (optional):

- 1/2 recipe apple cinnamon sugar
- 12 ounces heavy cream
- 1/4 tsp

Instructions

1. Getting Ready: Set the rack in the oven to the lower-middle position and heat the oven to 350°F (180°C). Line the bottom of an aluminum half-sheet pan with parchment paper, and spray or oil the pan.
2. In the bowl of a stand mixer which has been fitted with a whisk attachment, combine the eggs, sugar, salt, baking soda, and baking powder.
3. Mix on medium speed when the sugar has dissolved properly, and the mixture is homogenous, smooth, and runny, but small bubbles start forming all over, about 3 minutes.

4. Increase the speed to medium and whip the mixture until it is a pale yellow color, thick enough to fall off the whisk in ribbons, and full of small, foamy bubbles, which should take about 5 minutes. Lastly, turn the speed up to high and continue whipping until the mixture is very pale, about double in size; whisk the mixture until it thickens to the point where the whisk creates a vortex-like pattern behind it, which typically takes around 5 minutes. If you let the mixture run off the whisk and into the bowl, it should briefly pile up on itself before it evens out. Please keep in mind that all times are just estimates and can vary a lot depending on the power and capacity of your stand mixer and things like the distance between the bowl and the beaters (more on that here). In every case, the best way to tell if something is ready is to look at it and feel it.
5. Once the foamed eggs are thick and fluffy, turn the speed down to medium-high and slowly pour in the vanilla and oil or melted butter. Lower the speed to medium-low and add all of the sifted flour at once. When almost all the flour is mixed in, turn off the mixer and remove the whisk attachment. Holding the attachment by its top, whisk the batter a few times by hand to ensure all the flour is mixed in. With a flexible spatula, fold the batter once or twice from the bottom up. Then, scrape the batter into the pan and spread it evenly with an offset spatula. About 12 minutes later, they should be puffed and lightly browned from edge to center, firm to the touch but still puffed and soft enough that a gentle poke will leave a shallow impression.
6. As soon as you take the cake out of the oven, cover the half-sheet pan with two large strips of foil and crimp the foil around the edges of the pan with a kitchen towel or oven mitt. Let the cake cool to about 70°F (21°C). If it doesn't cool enough, the filling might melt, but if it cools too much, it might get too hard in the cold and break when rolled.
7. Use a butter knife to loosen the cake edges from the pan. Stir the cranberry jam well and spread it evenly on the cake. Note that the amount of other jams or jellies may vary significantly in weight and volume due to consistency and moisture content. Lift the cake's widest end by the parchment underneath and carefully fold it inward until it overlaps. Keep rolling the cake by lifting and moving it with the parchment paper. As you roll, the paper will naturally peel away.
8. After rolling the cake, put it on a large platter and serve it immediately, or cover it with plastic until it's time to eat. To create a basic frosting, combine the apple-cinnamon sugar, cream, and salt and whip them until the consistency is thick and firm enough to be spread easily. This can be kept in the fridge in an airtight container to cover the cake before serving. You can also finish the cake by dusting it with powdered sugar. If you don't frost the cake, it can stay at room temperature for about 24 hours. If you frost it with whipped cream, you'll need to cover it, put it in the fridge for up to 24 hours, and then take it out about an hour before serving.

90. EGG ROLL

Prep Time: 55 Minute | Cook Time: 15 Minutes

Total Time: 1 Hour 10 Minutes | Serving: 12

Ingredients

- 1/3 cup of Warm Water
- 2 Eggs
- 2 cups of All-Purpose Flour
- 3/4 tsp Salt

Instructions

1. Put 2 cups of all-purpose flour, 3/4 tsp of salt, 1/3 cup of water, and 2 eggs in the bowl of a stand mixer with a dough hook. Mix on low speed for 3 minutes or until the dough comes together.
2. Knead on low for 3–4 minutes more.
3. Put plastic wrap around the dough. Let rest for 45 minutes.
4. Divide dough into 4 equal parts. Wrap up any dough you aren't using right now. Make a square out of the dough.
5. Turn your dough through a pasta machine with the biggest hole. Fold each side into the middle, and then run it through again.
6. Change the setting on the pasta machine to the next smallest one and run the dough through it twice. Repeat, moving to narrower and narrower levels until you get to the smallest setting. When the dough is too long, divide it in half and keep going.
7. Trim dough into pieces.
8. You can put egg roll wraps in the fridge for later or use them right away. If you want to stack them, dust each side with flour so they don't stick.

91. YEAST ROLL

Prep Time: 20 Minute | Cook Time: 15 Minutes | Rising Time: 1 Hour 30 Minute

Total Time: 2 Hour 32 Minutes | Serving: 24

Ingredients

- 1 ½ cups of milk, warmed to 110°F to 115°F
- 1 large egg
- ¼ cup of granulated sugar
- 1 tsp kosher salt
- 2 tbsp rapid rise yeast
- 4 tbsp unsalted butter, Will be melted, not hot
- 4 ½ to 5 ½ cups of all-purpose flour

Instructions

1. Mix the 3 cups of flour, milk, yeast, egg, melted butter, and sugar in the bowl of a stand mixer.
2. Mix the ingredients with a dough hook on low speed for 2 minutes or until the dough starts to come together. Add more flour, a quarter to a half cup of at a time, until the dough just begins to pull away from the bowl. Whenever you need to, scrape the sides of the bowl.
3. Turn the speed up to medium and keep mixing for another 5–6 minutes. If the dough sticks to the bowl, keep adding flour a few tbsp at a time until the dough is smooth and springy.
4. Make the dough into a smooth ball and put it in a big, lightly greased bowl. Cover it with a clean and healthy kitchen towel and wait until it doubles in size, which will take anywhere from 30 to 50 minutes, depending on how warm the room is.
5. When the dough has doubled in size, you can soften it by punching it down. Cut the dough into about 24 pieces that are all the same size. If you have a cooking scale, the best way to make sure each piece of dough is the same size is to weigh it.
6. Roll the pieces into balls and put them in a greased 9-by-13-inch baking dish or a baking sheet with the same dimensions. Cover with a clean towel and give it time to rise until it's doubled in size, which takes about 30 to 55 Minutes. Set the oven temperature to 375°F.
7. Bake for around 15 minutes in an oven that has already been warm, or until golden brown.
8. Pour melted butter on top and serve hot. The best way to serve yeast rolls is in big plastic zip bags, which keep them fresh for about 3 days.

92. PEPPERONI ROLL

Prep Time: 30 Minutes | Cook Time: 1 Hour 15 Minutes

Total Time: 1 Hour 45 Minutes | Serving: 4

Ingredients

Dough:

- 1 tbsp kosher salt
- 1 tsp instant yeast
- 2 1/2 cups of flour

Pepperoni Roll:

- 1/4 cup of olive oil
- 1 pound sliced lunch meat
- 1 pound cheese
- 2 ounces Parmesan, grated

Instructions

1. To make the dough, combine the flour, salt, and yeast in the bowl of a stand mixer using a dough hook tool. Mix thoroughly, then incorporate 1 cup of water. Mix the dough on low speed until it forms a rough ball. Mix at a medium-low speed for about 10 minutes or until the dough makes a smooth, silky ball. Make the dough into a tight ball and place it in the bottom of the mixing bowl. To ensure the dough rises properly, cover it with plastic wrap and keep it in a warm area for approximately an hour until it has increased in size by approximately two-fold.
2. Set the oven to 375 degrees F before you start making the pepperoni roll. Oil a baking sheet with a lip.
3. Roll the dough into a 1/4-inch-thick square. If the dough doesn't stretch well, cover it and let it rest at room temperature for 30 minutes, then try again.
4. Cover the dough with the pepperoni slices, leaving a 1/2-inch edge. The mozzarella should go on top of the pepperoni. Fold the dough's outside sides in and roll it up like a jelly roll.
5. Place the roll seam-side down on the baking sheet. On the top of the roll, make six small cuts at an angle. Coat the bread with oil and then sprinkle it with Parmesan. Bake until golden, 25 to 30 minutes.

93. FRENCH BREAD ROLL

Prep Time: 2 Hour 25 Minutes | Cook Time: 20 Minutes

Total Time: Minutes | Serving: 12

Ingredients

- 1 ½ cups of warm water
- 3 12 to 4 cups of (497–569 grams) more
- 1 tsp of active dry yeast or instant yeast
- 2 tbsp of sugar or honey in granulated form
- 2 tbsp of neutral-tasting oil, such as canola, vegetable, or olive oil.
- 1 tsp salt

Instructions

1. Mix the warm water, instant yeast, sugar, oil, salt, and 2 cups of the flour in a spacious bowl or the bowl of a stand mixer with a dough hook.
2. Start mixing, and keep adding the rest of the flour little by little until the dough pulls away from the sides of the bowl. Start kneading the dough for 4-5 minutes (7-9 minutes by hand) in a stand mixer.
3. The dough should be smooth and soft, but it should still have a little bit of stickiness. Stop the mixer after a few minutes of kneading and take a small piece of the dough to see if it needs more flour. It might leave a little bit of glue on your fingers, but if you can roll it into a short ball without it sticking all over your hands, it's good to go. If not, add a little more flour at a time.
4. Put the dough in a bowl that has been lightly greased and cover it. Let the dough rise for 1–2 hours or until it has doubled.
5. Lightly punch down the dough, and then turn it out onto a lightly greased countertop.
6. Divide the dough into 12 pieces that are about 2.75 ounces each, and roll each piece into a ball.
7. Put the rolls in a 9x13-inch pan that has been lightly greased or on a large baking sheet with a rim that has been lined with parchment paper or lightly greased. About 1/2 to 1 inch in the middle of each roll.
8. To prevent the rolls from flattening as they rise, cover them with lightly greased plastic wrap. Take care not to pin the plastic wrap under the baking sheet. Let the plastic wrap hang over the sides of the pan gently so that the rolls are fully covered but not pressed down.
9. Let the rolls rise for about an hour or until they are very puffy and double in size.
10. Set the oven temperature to 400 degrees. Bake for 15–17 minutes, or until the top is lightly browned and the inside is done. As soon as it comes out of the oven, brush it with butter.

94. NUT ROLL

Prep Time: 1 Hour 30 Minute | Cook Time: 45 Minutes

Total Time: 2 Hour 15 Minutes | Serving: 2

Ingredients

Dough Ingredients:

- ¾ cup of whole milk
- ½ cup of Butter
- 1 tsp. Kosher salt
- 1 large egg
- 2 1/4 tsp instant dry yeast
- (softened)
- 4 cups of bread flour
- 3 tbsp. sugar
- ½ cup of sour cream

Walnut filling:

- 3 cups of walnuts
- (finely chopped)
- 1 tsp. Finely grated orange zest
- 1 cup of granulated sugar
- 2 large eggs
- ¼ cup of Butter
- ½ tsp cinnamon
- ¾ cup of brown sugar
- ((½ stick Butter,) cut into cubes)
- pinches ground clove

Instructions

To make nut roll dough, follow these steps:

1. Mix the milk, yeast, and sugar in the bowl of a stand mixer. Allow for the formation of bubbles. It should only take about ten minutes.
2. Combine the softened butter, sour cream, eggs, 4 cups of flour, and salt in a mixing bowl. Mix on low speed for 1-2 minutes, or until a dough forms.
3. Increase the mixer speed to medium and let the machine knead the dough for another 4 minutes or until it is smooth and elastic. The dough should have a soft texture and pull away from the sides of the bowl. Once ready, transfer the dough onto a lightly floured surface and sprinkle additional flour if it feels sticky. Then, gently knead the dough into a smooth ball and place it back into an oiled bowl. Cover with a towel and leave it in a heat place for 50-60 minutes or until it has doubled in size.

To make the walnut filling, follow these steps:

1. Heat the butter in a saucepan of medium size over medium heat until it melts.
2. Add the orange zest, spices, and sugars to the pan from the heat.
3. Combine the walnuts and one egg in a mixing bowl. Set aside the filling to cool completely.
4. To begin cooking, preheat your oven to 350°F and prepare a baking sheet by either lining it with parchment paper or using a nonstick spray.

How to Roll Out the Nut Roll Dough:

1. Roll one-half of the dough into a 14-inch thick rectangle, about 12-by-10 inches, on a floured surface with a rolling pin.
2. Take the dough and spread half of the filling on it, making sure to leave a 12-inch border at the bottom edge. Make sure that the longer side of the dough is facing you.
3. Roll the nut roll lengthwise to cover the filling like a jelly roll.
4. Pinch the edge to seal it, then place the roll on a baking sheet.
5. Repeat with the remaining filling and the second piece of dough, leaving at least 4 inches between the rolls on the baking sheet. Cover the loaves with a towel and set aside for 35 minutes or until slightly risen.
6. When ready to bake, start brushing the loaves with the egg wash and poke 5-6 holes through the roll with a chopstick before placing them in the oven.
7. 35-40 minutes, or until evenly golden brown.
8. Remove from the oven and place on a cooling rack to cool completely.
9. Rolls can be sliced and eaten once cooled, but they taste better the next day. Cut the rolls into 1-inch thick slices with a serrated knife.

95. CARAMEL ROLL

Prep Time: 60 Minutes | Cook Time: 30 Minutes

Total Time: 1 Hour 30 Minutes | Serving: 12

Ingredients

Caramel:

- 1 c. brown sugar packed
- ⅓ c. butter
- ¼ c. light corn syrup

Dough:

- 1 c. warm water
- ½ Tbsp salt
- 2 large eggs
- ½ c. sugar
- ¼ c. butter melted
- 3 Tbsp regular yeast
- 5-6 c. bread flour
- ¾ c. half and half

Filling:

- 6 Tbsp butter melted
- ⅔ c. white sugar
- ⅔ c. brown sugar packed
- 1 ½ Tbsp cinnamon

Instructions

1. Use nonstick spray to coat a 9-by-13-inch baking pan. Set aside
2. Bring brown sugar, light corn syrup, and butter to a boil in a small saucepan. Pour into the pan's bottom. Set aside.
3. Mix water, half-and-half, sugar, melted butter, and yeast in a stand mixer. Let sit for 15 minutes.
4. Add in salt and eggs. Mix until combined. Add 5–6 cups of bread flour until the dough comes together and doesn't stick to your hands. Knead the dough for 10 minutes in a stand mixer. Let it sit for 10 more minutes.
5. Mix together melted butter, brown sugar, sugar, and cinnamon to make the filling. Set aside.
6. Roll the dough into a 12x16-inch rectangle on a floured surface.
7. Spread the filling on top and start rolling from the long side. Slice into 12 big pieces. Place in a 9-by-13-inch pan with caramel sauce that has been set up.
8. Bake at 375 degrees for 30 minutes or until the top is golden brown and the whole thing is done.
9. Five minutes in the pan to cool. Flip the pan over on the serving platter. Serve right away.
10. Keep leftovers in a container that lets air in.

96. POTATO ROLL

Prep Time: 20 Minute | Cook Time: 10 Minutes | 2 Hour

Total Time: 2 Hour 30 Minutes | Serving: 10

Ingredients

- 1 cup of milk
- 4 tbsp unsalted butter
- 1 egg
- 1 1/2 tsp salt
- 4-5 cups of all-purpose flour
- 2 tbsp butter melted
- 2 1/4 tsp active dry yeast
- 1/2 cup of prepared mashed potatoes
- 1/4 cup of sugar
- 1/4 cup of warm water

Instructions

1. In the stand mixer's bowl, combine warm water and yeast, allowing it to dissolve.
2. Put the milk, mashed potatoes, and 4 tbsp of butter in a small bowl or measuring cup of that can go in the microwave.
3. Heat on high for one minute, stir, and then heat for another 30 to 60 seconds until the butter is melted well and the milk becomes warm but not hot.
4. Add the sugar, salt, egg, and milk mixtures to the yeast mixture.
5. Add two cups of flour and stir everything together. Mix in more flour, 1/4 cup of at a time, until the dough is soft and pulls away from the bowl.
6. Work the dough by kneading for approximately 8 minutes until it becomes smooth and stretchy. Form the dough into a ball, then put it in a greased bowl, cover it, and let it rise for about an hour or until it has doubled in size.
7. Once an hour has pass away, punch down the dough using your hands. Preheat the oven to 400°F. Take each of the 24 dough pieces and shape them into balls. Keep the dough balls on a baking sheet that will be coated with cooking spray or lined with parchment paper.
8. Cover the dough and let it rise for 30–60 minutes or until it bounces back when lightly touched.
9. 10–12 minutes, or until the top is golden brown. Use the last 2 tbsp of butter to paint the bread. Warm is best.

SE ROLL

Prep Time: 30 Minutes | Cook Time: 30 Minutes | Resting Time: 1 Hour 30

Total Time: 2 Hour 30 Minutes | Serving: 12

Ingredients

Rolls:

- ¼ cup of unsalted butter melted
- 2 tsp instant yeast
- ½ tsp sea salt
- 2 large eggs, at room temperature
- 1 cup of warm whole milk
- 3 ½ - 4 cups of all-purpose flour
- 1 tbsp sugar

Filling:

- 2 cups of sharp cheddar cheese, shredded
- ½ tsp garlic powder
- 1 tsp Italian seasoning
- ½ cup of unsalted butter, at room temperature

Instructions

1. Mix the milk, instant yeast, sugar, eggs, butter, 3 12 cups of flour, and salt in the bowl of a stand mixer. Mix the ingredients with a dough hook for about 4-5 minutes or until the flour is mixed in. If the dough feels too sticky, add flour gradually in one-tbsp portions. However, it's actually better if the dough remains slightly sticky. Leave the dough to rise for an hour at room temperature or until it has doubled in size.
2. Sprinkle some flour on your work surface. Take the dough out of the bowl and beat it down. The dough should be about 14 inches thick and about 12 by 16 inches. Not everything has to be just right. I use a 9x13-inch baking dish as a measuring tool. Spread the butter that has been softened all over the dough. Put the cheese and seasonings on top and press down to keep them in place.
3. Roll the dough into a log with the long side closest to you. Try to keep it tight all the way through. Cut 12 rolls about 1" thick with a sharp knife. Put the rolls in a 9x13 baking dish lined with parchment paper. Cover with plastic wrap and give time to rise for 20 to 30 minutes.
4. Turn oven on to 350°F. Bake the rolls for about half an hour or until the tops are golden brown and the centers are cooked.

98. CIABATTA ROLL

Prep Time: 25 Min | Cook Time: 20 Min | Resting Time: 1 Hr 15 Min | Total Time: 3 Hr | Ser: 12

Ingredients

Biga:

- 1 cup of all-purpose flour
- 3/4 cup of warm water
- Ciabatta Dough
- 3/4 tsp active dry yeast

biga:

- 2 cups of warm water
- 2 tsp salt
- 1 tsp active dry or instant yeast
- 4 cups of all-purpose flour

Instructions

Biga:

1. Mix the ingredients in the Instant Pot liner. Stir with a lot of force for 30 to 60 seconds.
2. Turn the Instant Pot to Yogurt LOW, cover it with the lid, and let the Biga sit for 45 minutes. At the end of 45 minutes, the Biga should be warm and bubbling.

Dough for Ciabatta:

1. Put the water, yeast, and Biga in the bowl of a stand mixer. To break up the Biga, stir it with a silicon spoon.
2. Add the flour and salt to the bowl, and use the dough hook to mix them. Start slowly and keep going until all of the flour is used. When all the flour is mixed in, increase the speed to 4–6. The dough will be thin and sticky. At about 10 minutes, the dough should stay on the hook and not stick to the sides of the bowl.
3. After the dough sticks to the dough hook, mix for another 5 minutes. The dough will be shiny and have a very smooth texture. The dough will fall to the bottom of the bowl when the mixer stops.
4. Spray the Instant Pot liner with nonstick spray after you clean it out. Put the dough in an Instant Pot that has been well greased. Put a top on it. Let the dough rise for 30 minutes on yogurt.
5. Gently transfer the dough from the Instant Pot onto a countertop dusted with flour.
6. Form the dough into a long rectangle and cut it into 12 equal pieces with a pizza cutter.
7. Use your fingers to make dents and make a square with the rolls. Let the rolls rest while you preheat the oven to 450°. Then, bake the rolls for 20 minutes.
8. Make dents in the rolls with your fingers and shape them into a square.
9. Let the rolls sit while you heat the oven to 450°.
10. Bake the rolls for 20 minutes or until they are golden brown.
11. Let the rolls cool down for the best sandwiches before cutting them up.

99. ORANGE ROLL

Prep Time: 25 Minutes | Cook Time: 25 Minutes

Total Time: 50 Minutes | Serving: 12

Ingredients

For The Rolls:

- ¼ cup of (½ stick) unsalted butter
- ½ cup of cold milk
- ½ cup of fresh orange juice
- 1 pound (3 ½ cups of) all-purpose flour
- 2 tsp instant or active dry yeast
- ⅓ cup of white granulated sugar
- ½ tsp salt
- zest of 1 large orange
- 1 large egg

For The Filling:

- ½ cup of white granulated sugar
- zest of 1 large orange
- 2 tbsp unsalted butter, melted

The Orange Icing:

- 1 ¼ cups of powdered sugar
- 6-8 tsp orange juice

Instructions

MAKING THE DOUGH:

1. In a small saucepan, melt the butter and milk over low heat. Stir or stir around to melt without getting too hot. Put the orange juice to the side and add it.
2. Mix flour, yeast, sugar, salt, and orange zest in the stand mixer bowl. Mix them well.
3. Pour the warm milk mixture and egg into the bowl and stir it quickly.
4. To make the dough look smooth and elastic, attach the dough hook with a stand mixer and mix it for about 6-7 minutes.
5. Put a little oil in a clean bowl and then put the dough in it. Flip it over so that the oil gets on both sides. Let the dough rest in a warm area for one hour or until it has doubled.

Make the filling:

1. Set aside 1 tsp of the zest for the topping, then add the remaining to the sugar. Press them with your fingers to get the oils out until they are all mixed in.
2. Mix in the butter that has been melted.

Putting the rolls together:

1. Turn the oven to 180C/350F/160C fan forced and use butter to grease a 9x13 inch baking tray.
2. On a little bit of floured surface, roll the dough into a large rectangle, about 12x14 inches.
3. Spread the filling slightly over the dough, leaving an inch of space on the longest side.
4. Roll up as tightly as possible from the longest side closest to you to the other side to make a long log. Next, take a sharp knife and evenly divide the log into 12 slices.
5. Place the rolls on the baking sheet with the cut side facing up. Give them 30 more minutes to rest and get up.

Baking:

1. Bake for 22 to 24 minutes, turning the tray halfway through, until the cookies are golden brown.

For the orange icing:

1. Mix the icing sugar and the zest and half of the orange juice. Slowly add more juice until the desired consistency is reached, and then pour it over the rolls.

100. GARLIC BUTTER PARMESAN ROLL

Prep Time: 2 Hours | Cook Time: 35 Minutes

Total Time: 2 Hour 35 Minutes | Serving: 9

Ingredients

For the dough:

- 1 envelope (2 1/4 tsp) dry yeast
- 2 cups of all-purpose flour
- 1/2 cup of whole milk, lightly warmed
- 2 tbsp granulated sugar
- 4 tbsp unsalted butter
- 1 tsp kosher salt
- 1 large egg, room temperature
- 1 large egg yolk, room temperature

For the filling:

- black pepper that has just been ground, kosher salt, 1/2 tsp
- 1 tbsp olive oil
- 4 tbsp unsalted butter,
- 1/4 cup of chopped parsley
- 2 cups of thick-cut shredded mozzarella cheese
- 4 garlic heads with the tops cut off to show the cloves

For the topping:

- 1 tbsp chopped parsley
- 1–2 tsp minced garlic
- 1 tbsp freshly grated parmesan cheese
- 2 tbsp butter, melted

Instructions

For the dough:

1. Be sure to warm the milk to about 110°F. I like to microwave my cold milk for 45 to 50 seconds, after which it should be warm (if it's too hot, set it aside until it cools down to the desired temperature of 110°F). Warm the milk and sugar in a stand mixer bowl, and then add the yeast on top. When using active dry yeast, allow the mixture to sit for 7–10 minutes without being disturbed. After that time, the mixture will bubble and smell good. *If using instant yeast, you can move on to the next step without waiting for the mixture to bloom.
2. Add the flour, salt, egg, egg yolk, and melted butter after that. In a stand mixer, attach the dough hook and knead the dough for up to 8 minutes on medium speed or until it starts to come together. Make sure the dough is smooth. Add a tbsp more flour only if necessary if your dough is sticking to the sides or bottom of the bowl. If a stand mixer is not an option, you can also knead the dough by hand for ten minutes on a lightly dusted surface.
3. Create a ball out of the dough and place it in a big bowl that has been lightly greased. To let the dough rise, place it in a warm environment until it doubles in size, which usually takes 1-2 hours, depending on the temperature. To cover the bowl, first tightly wrap it with plastic wrap. Then, place a clean kitchen towel or linen on top.
4. Let's roast the garlic for the filling while the dough is rising. Set the oven to 400°F. Each garlic bulbs's papery outer layer should be peeled off and thrown away. The garlic bulbs should be placed cut side up in a tiny baking dish covered with foil. The garlic bulbs should be coated with oil all over before being enclosed with foil. The garlic should be roasted for 30 to 40 minutes or until the cloves are golden brown and easily pressurized. Allow the garlic heads to cool down so that you can handle them without getting burned. After gently pressing the garlic cloves out of their skins with your hands or a small paring knife, set them aside.
5. When the dough has risen, punch it down and turn it out onto a work surface that has been lightly dusted with flour. Now that the dough has been rolled out into a roughly 13-by-8-inch rectangle let's make the filling.

For the filling:

1. Put the garlic cloves that have been roasted in a food processor or blender. Pulse the garlic cloves together until they resemble a paste. Keep a thin border around the edges as you spread the soft butter over the dough. I prefer to carry out this task with my hands (and, if necessary, disposable gloves). Spread the roasted garlic paste or mixture next, then add the parsley chiffonade, salt, and pepper. Finally, scatter the cheese shredded evenly over the dough and gently pat it into the mixture with your hand.

Rolling the dough:

1. Starting with the longest side and placing the seam side down, tightly roll up the dough into a log. Use your hands to gently stretch out the log while in the log position, if necessary. After that, pinch the seam to neatly tuck the edges as much as possible. Because they are not as full in size as the other sections, I like to trim off a little bit of the ends on both sides of the dough. This step is completely optional.

Cutting the dough:

1. Cut the log crosswise into 9 pieces using a large knife or unscented floss tied around your fingers.
2. The parchment paper should line a 9-by-9-inch baking dish or another comparable container (just in case any filling leaks out). The rolls should rise once more in a warm environment for one to two hours or until puffy. Put the rolls in the baking dish and seal it tightly with plastic wrap and a fresh kitchen towel or linen.

Baking the rolls:

1. Preheat the oven to 350 degrees Fahrenheit. Remove the towel and bake the rolls for 30-35 minutes or until lightly golden brown. Prepare the topping while the rolls bake.

For the topping:

1. parmesan cheese,Melted butter, chopped parsley, and minced garlic should all be combined in a small bowl. Set aside the topping after thoroughly mixing it.
2. When the rolls are done baking, brush them with the topping mixture right away. If desired, top the rolls with additional grated parmesan cheese. Enjoy while still warm!

BUNS

101. HAMBURGER BUNS

Prep Time: 20 Minutes | Cook Time: 15 Minutes | Additional Time:

3 Hour 10 mins

Total Times: 3 Hour 45 Minutes | Serving: 8

Ingredients

- 1 cup of warm water (105 degrees F/41 degrees C)
- 1 (.25 ounce) package active dry yeast (such as Fleischmann's ActiveDry Yeast®)
- 1 tsp sesame seeds, or as needed
- 3 tbsp white sugar
- 3 tbsp butter, melted
- 2 large eggs, divided
- 1 pound all-purpose flour, or as needed - divided
- 1 ¼ tsp salt
- 1 tbsp milk
- 1 tsp olive oil

Instructions

1. Put yeast in the bowl of a large stand mixer. Whisk in 1/2 cup of flour, warm water, and salt until smooth. Give the mixture 10-15 minutes to rest to get a foamy texture.
2. Mix 1 egg, melted butter, sugar, and salt into the yeast mixture well with a whisk. Add the rest of the flour, about 3 cups.
3. Attach a dough hook to the stand mixer and proceed to knead the dough at a slow speed for approximately 5 to 6 minutes until it reaches a soft and adhesive consistency. If necessary, scrape the sides. Use a silicone spatula to poke and prod the dough. If a lot of dough sticks to the spatula, add more flour.
4. Move the dough to a floured work surface. The dough will be sticky and stretchy but shouldn't stick to your fingers. Form the dough gently into a smooth, round shape and tuck any loose ends under.
5. First, clean the bowl of the stand mixer and add some olive oil. Next, place the dough inside the bowl and turn it over a few times to ensure that the oil coats the surface evenlyCover the bowl with a layer of aluminum foil and keep it in a warm spot for approximately 2 hours, or until the dough has increased in volume by twofold.
6. Use a parchment paper to cover a baking sheet.

7. Move the dough to a floured surface and pat it down to eliminate any air bubbles. Shape the dough into a 5x10-inch rectangle that is slightly rounded and about 1/2 inch thick.
8. If you need to, dust the dough with a little flour and cut it into eight pieces. As before, shape each piece round and tuck the ends under gently.
9. With your hands, gently pat and stretch the dough rounds into flat, 1/2-inch-thick discs. Set the buns about 1/2 inch apart on the baking sheet you just made. Dust buns with just a little bit of flour.To prepare, cover the baking sheet with a piece of plastic wrap, making sure not to seal it completely. Let the buns rise until they have doubled in size, which usually takes 1 hour.
10. Put in the oven and turn the temperature to 375F (190C).
11. Blend the last egg and milk together in a small bowl using a fork. To prevent the risen dough from deflating, gently brush the tops part of the buns with the egg wash.Sprinkle sesame seeds on each bun.
12. Bake in a preheated oven for 15 to 17 minutes or until the top is lightly browned. Where two buns touch, they will stick together a little. Let cool down all the way. To serve, rip the buns apart and cut them in half lengthwise.

102. HOT CROSS BUNS

Prep Time: 30 Minutes | Cook Time: 20 Minutes |

Total Times: 2 Hoir 45 Minutes | Serving: 12

Ingredients

For the buns:

- 300ml full-fat milk, plus 2 tbsp more
- 50g butter
- 500g strong bread flour
- 1tsp salt
- 75g caster sugar
- 1tbsp sunflower oil
- 7g sachet fast-action or easy-blend yeast
- 1 egg, beaten
- 75g sultanas
- 50g mixed peel
- zest 1 orange
- 1 apple, peeled, cored and finely chopped
- 1tsp ground cinnamon
- 1 tsp mixed spice

For the cross:

- 75g plain flour, plus extra for dusting

For the glaze:

- 3tbsp apricot jam

Instructions

1. Boil 300 mL whole milk, then remove from heat and add 50 g butter. Allow it to cool until it reaches the temperature of your hand. Combine 500g of strong bread flour, 1 tsp salt, 75g of caster sugar, and a 7g sachet of fast-action or easy-blend yeast in a mixing bowl. Make a well in the middle. Pour in the warm milk-butter mixture, then 1 beaten egg. Mix thoroughly with a wooden spoon, then bring everything together into a sticky dough with your hands.
2. Shift the dough to a lightly floured surface and knead it with one hand while stretching it with the heel of the other and folding it back on itself. Repeat for another 5 minutes, or until the dough is smooth and pliable. Put the dough in a lightly greased mixing bowl. Let it rise for 1 hour in a cozy spot. covered with oiled plastic wrap, or until it has doubled in size and can be indented with a finger.
3. Add 75g of sultanas, 50g of mixed peel, the zest of 1 orange, 1 finely chopped apple, ground cinnamon, and mixed spice while the dough is still in the bowl. Knead the dough to ensure that everything is evenly distributed. Give time to dough to rise for another hour, or until it has doubled in size. Cover with oiled plastic wrap once more to prevent the dough from crusting.
4. Cut the dough into 15 equal pieces, each weighing about 75 grams. Roll up each piece into a smooth ball on a floured work surface. Place the buns on one or two baking sheets lined with parchment paper, leaving enough space between them for the dough to expand. Wrap it in oiled cling film or a clean tea towel, but don't wrap it. Allow it to rise for another hour.
5. Preheat the oven to 200 degrees Celsius/180 degrees Celsius fan/gas 6. To make the cross glue, combine 75g plain flour and 5 tbsp water. Add the water one tbsp at a time until you have a thick paste. Fill a piping bag by nozzle with the mixture. Pipe a line along each row of buns, then do the same in the opposite direction to make a cross. Bake for 18-20 minutes, or until golden brown, on the middle shelf of the oven. If you have two trays, the bottom tray may take a minute or more than the top tray.
6. Melt 3 tsp apricot jam over low heat, then strain to remove any chunks. Brush the jam on top of the hot buns while they are still warm, then set aside to cool.

103. STEAMED BAO BUNS

Prep Time: 20 Minutes | Cook Time: 20 Minutes

Total Times: 40 Minutes | Serving: 12

Ingredients

- 4 cups of All-Purpose Flour
- 1 tsp Baking Powder
- 1 tsp Instant Dry Yeast
- 1 1/2 tbsp Caster Sugar
- 1/2 tsp Salt
- 1 pinch Caster Sugar
- 1 tbsp Rice Vinegar
- 1 tbsp Warm Water
- 3/4 cup of Water
- 1 tbsp Sunflower Oil
- 3 tbsp Milk
- Sunflower Oil (as needed for brushing the dough)

Instructions

1. Mix 4 cups of All-Purpose Flour, 1/2 tsp of Salt, and 1 1/2 tbsp of Caster Sugar in the bowl of a stand mixer with a dough hook.
2. Mix 1 tsp. of Instant Dry Yeast, 1 pinch of Caster Sugar, and 1 tsp.
3. Add the yeast mixture, 3 tbsp of milk, 1 tbsp of sunflower oil, 1 tbsp of rice vinegar, and 3/4 cup of water to the flour mixture.
4. Knead the dough until it is smooth, which should take about 10 minutes.
5. Put the dough in an oiled glass bowl, cover it with a new, damp tea towel, and let it rise in a warm place for about 2 hours.
6. The dough should have doubled in size.
7. Add 1 tsp of baking powder to the dough, put it back in the bowl of the stand mixer, and knead it for 5 minutes.
8. Roll the dough into a long, about 3 cm thick sausage.
9. Cut out pieces that are about 3cm wide. Should be about 16 to 18 pieces.
10. Wrap the dough properly with plastic wrap and keep it in the refrigerator for at least 30 minutes.
11. Use a rolling pin to make each ball about 3–4 mm thick and in the shape of an oval.
12. Brush a small amount of sunflower oil (as needed) on top of each oval of dough.
13. Stick a chopstick through the middle of the dough and rub more sunflower oil on it.
14. Fold the dough over the chopstick.
15. Then, slowly pull the chopstick out and place each bun on a clean baking sheet lined with a tea towel. Let rise in a warm or hot place for 1 hour and 30 minutes, or until they have doubled in size.
16. Heat up a large steamer by putting it over a medium-high flame. After 8 minutes of being steamed, the buns will puff up. Depending on how big your steamer is, you may need to do this in more than one step. Serve, and have fun!

104. CINNAMON STICKY BUNS

Prep Time: 45 Minutes | Cook Time: 30 Minutes Rise Time: 10 Hour

Total Times: 11 Hour 15 Minutes | Serving: 15

Ingredients

For the dough:

- 4 tbsp unsalted butter, at room temperature, plus more for greasing
- 3 large egg yolks
- 3/4 cup of milk
- Up to 1 tbsp finely grated orange zest, to taste
- 3 to 4 cups of all-purpose flour, divided, plus more for dusting
- 1 1/4 tsp salt
- 1/4 cup of warm water (105 to 115°F)
- 1/3 cup of sugar, divided
- 1 (1/4-ounce) package active dry yeast

For the filling:

- 1/2 cup of firmly packed light brown sugar
- 4 tbsp unsalted butter
- 1 tbsp ground cinnamon

For the topping:

- 3/4 cup of firmly packed light brown sugar
- 1 tbsp light corn syrup
- 1 1/2 cups of (6 ounces) coarsely chopped pecans
- 3 tbsp honey
- 4 tbsp unsalted butte

Instructions

1. To make the dough, mix warm water, yeast, and 1 tsp of sugar in the bowl of an electric mixer. Stir the mixture until the ingredients are dissolved, then let it sit for about 5 minutes until it becomes foamy.
2. Add milk, butter, remaining sugar, egg yolks, orange zest, salt and 3 cups of flour. Mix on low speed until everything is well-blended.
3. Switch to a dough hook and then, still on low speed, add more flour, a few tbsp at a time (up to 1 cup of more), until the dough is away from the sides of the bowl.
4. To get a dough that is smooth and just a little bit sticky, knead it for 5 minutes on medium speed. In case the dough is too wet, adding a small amount of flour should do the trick.
5. Form the dough into a ball and put it in a large bowl that has been greased. Turn the dough over in the bowl so that the butter covers it. Use plastic wrap to cover the bowl. ALet the dough rise in a warm place until it is twice as large., which typically takes an hour but may take up to two hours if the location is not entirely warm.

6. Punch down the dough after it has risen. Turn out onto a surface that has been lightly floured and let it sit for 20 minutes.
7. Brown sugar and cinnamon should be mixed together in a small bowl. In a separate bowl, melt butter and keep separate.
8. Roll out the dough into a size of 12" x 18" rectangle on a floured surface. Spread the cinnamon-sugar mixture on top of the melted butter.
9. Roll the dough into a tube, beginning with the long side. Place the seam side down and cut into 15 pieces across.
10. Mix brown sugar, butter, honey, and corn syrup in a 1-quart saucepan over low heat. Stir until the sugar and butter melt. Pour the mixture into a 9-by-13-inch pan that has been greased, and sprinkle pecans on top.
11. Pack them in so close they touch. Cover the buns with plastic wrap, leaving enough space for them to rise, and put them in the fridge overnight.
12. Take the rolls out of the fridge and let them sit at room temperature forabout 40 to 60 minutes while the oven heats up.
13. Set the oven temperature to 375°F. Bake buns until golden, 25 to 30 minutes.
14. Take the pan out of the oven and quickly (but carefully, so you don't burn your toes!) flip it over onto a serving tray or baking dish. Let the buns cool down a bit, then serve them hot.

105. HOT DOG BUNS

Prep Time: 40 Minutes | Cook Time: 30 Minutes | Proff Time: 10 Hour

Total Times: 11 Hour 10 Minutes | Serving: 12

Ingredients

- 17.6 ounce all purpose flour 4 US cups of, measured by spoon and level method
- ¾ cup of warm water
- 1 egg for the egg wash
- 1 1/2 tsp salt
- Extra oil to lightly oil the bowl
- 1 tbsp sugar
- 2 tbsp softened butter / oil
- ½ cup of warm milk
- 1 egg
- 2 tsp dry active yeast

Instructions

1. To start making the dough, first combine flour, yeast, salt and sugar in the bowl of your stand mixer. Whisk together the water, milk, and egg in a separate small bowl. Then, use either the paddle attachment on your stand mixer or a dough whisk to combine the dry ingredients.Combine the flour, yeast, sugar, and salt in the bowl of your stand mixer.
2. Whisk together the water, milk, and egg in a separate small bowl.

3. Combine the dry ingredients with a paddle attachment on your stand mixer or a dough whisk. Mix the water, milk, and egg mixture.
4. To make the dough, use the dough hook on your stand mixer and knead it. The dough should be quite wet and sticky. Knead the dough for 5 minutes until it comes together in a smooth ball.
5. Knead in the oil or butter for 5-10 minutes (I did it for about 8 minutes), or until the dough is shiny, smooth, and sticky.
6. Place the dough in a large, lightly greased mixing bowl. Make sure the top of the dough is lightly oiled as well.
7. Wrap the bowl with plastic wrap and place it in the refrigerator for 8 hours or up to 24 hours for optimal results.If you want to bake it the same day, let the dough rise in a warm place for 1 Hour , or until it doubled in size, and then cover it with plastic wrap.measure terms of size.
8. The day you plan to bake the bread rolls, remove the dough from the refrigerator and place it on a lightly floured work surface. Lightly dust the top of the dough, too. If the dough wasn't chilled, you may need to use more flour on your hands and work surface to keep the dough from sticking.

For the cutting method for hot dog buns:

1. Roll the dough out into a rectangle about 16 inches long and 4 to 5 inches wide. Cut the dough into 10 pieces and place them about 1.5 inches apart on a baking sheet lined with parchment paper.

For the shaping method for hot dog buns:

1. Divide the dough into 12 or 10 even pieces. I usually weigh the bread dough so I know how much each section should weigh.
2. Just knead each piece for a few seconds to make a smooth ball. Each piece of dough should be rolled out into a piece that is about 5 inches long and 4 inches wide. Then ROLL the dough TIGHTLY into a cylinder. Fold the edges in and pinch the edges and seams together to seal them. Place each piece about 2 inches apart on a baking sheet lined with parchment paper.

For burger buns:

1. Divide the dough into 8 portions (for larger buns) or 10 portions (for smaller buns) and shape them into smooth balls by rolling them in your hands. Arrange these balls on a baking tray lined with parchment paper, leaving about 3 inches of space between each.

For burger buns:

1. Cut the dough into 8 sections (for larger buns) or 10 sections (for smaller buns) and roll these portions in your hands to form smooth balls. Place them on the parchment paper lined baking tray, about 3 inches apart

106. BRIOCHE BUNS

Prep Time: 45 Minutes | Cook Time: 15 Minutes

Total Times: 1 Hour | Serving: 8

Ingredients

- 1 egg
- ¼ cup of warm milk, 105-115 degrees F, whole milk is best
- 1 ½ tsp salt
- 1 ½ cups of white whole wheat flour
- 1 tbsp instant (rapid-rise) yeast
- 2 cups of all purpose flour
- 2 tbsp granulated sugar
- 1 cup of warm water, 105-115 degrees F
- 2 tbsp unsalted butter, at room temperature, cut into 4 pieces

For the egg wash:

- 1 egg
- 1 tbsp milk

Instructions

1. On a baking sheet, place parchment paper or a silicone baking mat.
2. Warm milk, yeast, and sugar are combined in the bowl of a stand mixer. To blend, stir slowly. Observe for five minutes.
3. The bowl needs to be seasoned with salt and an egg. Use the paddle attachment to mix at low speed.
4. Add the two flours and blend them together on low speed. Then stir again after adding the butter pieces.
5. Make the dough for 8 minutes with the dough hook. It will be very soft and a little bit sticky.
6. Move the dough to a floured work surface and roll it into a ball with your hands a few times. Make 8 pieces out of the dough. Make each piece into a round ball and put it on the baking sheet that has been prepared.
7. Cover the balls of dough loosely with a clean dish towel and let them rest for 15 minutes.
8. While you wait, turn the oven on to 400°F.
9. In a small bowl, mix the egg and 1 tbsp of milk with a fork. Take off the towel and use the egg wash to paint the tops of the buns. The tops of hamburger buns should be golden after 13 to 15 minutes in the oven.

107. BURGER BUNS

Prep Time: 20 Minutes | Cook Time: 15 Minutes | Additional Time: 2 Hour

Total Times: 2 HOur 35 Minutes | Serving: 8

Ingredients

- ⅓ cup of (43 grams) all-purpose flour
- 2 ½ tbsp (31 grams) granulated sugar
- 3 cups of (382 grams) bread flour, approximately (do not substitute this)
- 1 ½ tsp fine salt
- 3 tbsp (43 grams) unsalted butter, at room temperature
- 3 tbsp (44 grams) warm whole milk, between 105° and 120°F
- 1 large egg, at room temperature, slighten beaten
- 1 cup of (237 grams) warm water, between 105° and 120°F
- 2 ¼ tsp (1 packet, 8 grams) instant yeast

For topping:

- 1 large egg beaten with 1 tbsp water
- Sesame seeds, optional

Instructions

1. Mix the milk, water, yeast1, sugar, and egg in the bowl of a stand mixer with a dough hook.
2. Mix the flour into the bowl until it's all mixed in. Add the butter and salt. Knead the dough on medium-low speed for up to 10 minutes, or until it comes together into a soft, sticky dough that is not too sticky to handle. If you add too much extra flour, the buns will be tough. Depending on the weather , you may need to add up to 1/4 cup of (32 grams) more flour. I promise, it's better to be sticky than thick.
3. Put the dough in a bowl that has been lightly greased. Cover with plastic wrap and give it time in a warm place until it has doubled in size, about 1–2 hours.
4. Put parchment paper on two baking sheets. Cut the dough into eight equal pieces. Roll up each of piece of dough gently into a ball, and place four balls 2 to 3 inches apart on a baking sheet. If your dough is too sticky to work with, lightly grease your hands with cooking spray or lightly dust the tops of each dough ball with flour before rolling. Cover with a clean towel and   rise again for 1 to 1 1/2 hours, or until it's puffy and almost doubled in size.
5. Get the oven ready at 400°F. Brush a the egg then wash on top of each bun. Sprinkle with sesame seeds. Bake the buns for about 15 minutes, until the tops are golden brown, turning them over halfway through. Place on a rack to finish cooling.
6. Serve immediately, or transfer to a container that will keep air out and freeze for up to one month. Let it thaw at room temperature before putting it in a 350°F oven until it's toasty or warm.

108. PRETZEL BUNS

Prep Time: 20 Minutes | Cook Time: 25 Minutes | Total Times: 45 Minutes | Serving: 10

Ingredients

Dough:

- 1 3/4 cups of (397g) water, warm
- 2 tbsp (28g) unsalted butter
- 3/4 tsp salt
- 4 1/2 cups of (540g) King Arthur Unbleached Bread Flour
- 1/4 cup of (28g) King Arthur Baker's Special Dry Milk or nonfat dry milk
- 2 tsp instant yeast

Topping:

- pretzel salt or coarse salt

Water bath:

- 1 tbsp (18g) salt
- 2 quarts (1814g) water
- 1/4 cup of (57g) baking soda

Instructions

1. Weigh your flour, or put it in a cup of gently with a spoon and then wipe off any extra. To prepare the dough, you can mix and knead the ingredients manually, use a mixer, or a bread machine until the dough is smooth and a little sticky. Using a stand mixer, it should take approximately 5 minutes.
2. Let the dough rise in a few greased bowl for about an hour, covered, until it has doubled in size.
3. Deflate the dough gently, and then place it on a lightly greased work surface.
4. Each piece of dough is about 100g, so di the dough into 10 pieces and roll each piece into a smooth ball. Use the palm of your hand to flatten each ball of dough until it's about 3" across.
5. Grease a baking sheet lightly, or line it with parchment paper and grease the paper. Put the balls on the baking sheet, cover it, and let them rest for 15 minutes.
6. Get the oven ready at 400°F.
7. Set up the water bath by bringing the water, baking soda, and salt to a boil in a large pot.Drop 5 balls of dough into the water bath at a time.
8. Turn the food over and cook for another 30 seconds. Put the buns back on the baking sheet with a slotted spoon.
9. Sprinkle coarse sea salt on the pretzel buns while they are still warm from the water. Cut a 1/2"-deep cross into the middle of each bun with sharp scissors or a knife. Boil, cut the tops off, and score the other 5 buns.
10. Bake the pretzel buns for 20 to 24 minutes, or until they are very dark brown. Take them out of the oven and put them on a rack to cool down.

109. POTATO BUNS

Prep Time: 35 Minutes | Cook Time: 15 Minutes | InActive Time: 1 Hour 10 Minute

Total Times: 2 Hour 1 Minutes | Serving: 9

Ingredients

- 2 tsp instant yeast
- 1 tbsp sesame seeds (optional)
- 2 large eggs
- 1 tsp table salt
- 2 tbsp unsalted butter
- 1 tbsp granulated sugar
- 2 ¼ cups of (12 ⅓ ounce) bread flour
- ½ pound russet potatoes, peeled and cut into 1-inch pieces

Instructions

1. In a small saucepan, cover the potatoes with water. Bring to a boil over high heat, then turn the heat down to medium-low and let the potatoes cook until they are soft all the way through about 8 to 10 minutes. Put 5 tbsp of the water from the potatoes in a bowl, then drain the potatoes and keep them back in the hot pot. Cook the potatoes over low heat while shaking them for about a minute to get rid of any water on the surface.
2. Process the potatoes with a food mill, ricer, or masher until they are very smooth, and add them to the pan. Take 1 cup of potatoes and put them in a medium bowl. Mix in the butter until it dissolves. Use a dish towel or aluminum foil to cover the bowl and keep the potatoes warm.
3. Mix the flour, sugar, yeast, and salt in the bowl of a stand mixer. Add the warm potatoes and use your hands to mix everything together. With the dough hook attachment, mix in 1 egg and the potato water you saved. Keep mixing on low speed until the dough is soft and a little sticky, about 8-10 minutes. Still warm is best for the dough.
4. Take the dough out and make a ball with it. Grease the bowl of the mixer lightly with oil, then put the dough back in the bowl and lightly coat it with oil. Cover the dough properly with plastic wrap and give it time to rise in a warm place for about 30–40 minutes, or until it has almost doubled in size. It will take less time in kitchens that are very warm.
5. Turn the dough out onto a slightly floured surface, pat it into an 8-inch square, and cut it into 9 equal pieces. Separate the pieces and cover them loosely with plastic wrap to place a skin from forming on top. Roll the dough rounds into tight balls, one at a time, and put them back on the work surface under the plastic wrap. Let them sit for 15 minutes.
6. Put parchment paper on two big baking sheets. Press each round of dough firmly into a 3 1/2-inch disk, pushing out large pockets of air. Place the disks in a single layer on the baking sheets and loosely cover with plastic wrap. Let the dough rise at room temperature for another 30–40 minutes or until it is almost twice as big. While the dough is rising, heat the oven to 425° F with the racks in the two middle spots.
7. Mix the last egg with a tbsp of water in a small bowl. Brush the egg wash lightly over the tops of the dough rounds and sprinkle with sesame seeds if you want to.

8. Bake the buns for 15–18 minutes, turning the pans halfway through from front to back and top to bottom until they are a deep golden brown. Move the pans to wire racks to cool for 5 minutes, then move the buns to the racks to cool completely before cutting.

110. RED BEAN BUNS

Prep Time: 1 HOur 20 Minutes | Cook Time: 20 Minutes

Total Times: 1 Hour 40 Minutes | Serving: 6

Ingredients

- a tiny pinch of salt
- 300 g all purpose flour
- 200 g red bean paste filling
- 1 tbsp. vegetable oil ,corn oil
- 150 ml warm water ,or 180ml to 185ml warm milk, the best temperature for liquid is around 35 degree C.
- 1.5 tsp. sugar tolerant instant yeast
- 40 g sugar

Instructions

1. Put all the dough ingredients into a stand mixer and knead for 6 to 8 minutes on low speed.
2. Shape the dough into a ball and place it in a warm location for around an hour or until it has doubled in size, taking into account the temperature of your surroundings.
3. Add about 2 tbsp of flour to the dough and knead it for 2 minutes at low speed in a stand mixer.
4. Then, take the dough out and cut it into 6 or 8 pieces. Make a round ball out of each piece. Press it so that the edges are thin and the middle is thicker. About 1.5 tbsp of red bean filling should go in the middle. Turn it over and shape it into a domed shape.
5. Put the buns on baking paper and then put them in a steamer. Cover the lid and let it sit for another 15–20 minutes at room temperature, which should be between 28°C and 30°C. When the water is cold, heat it in a pot for a few minutes until it is warm but not boiling. Put the steamer on top of the warm water and let it sit for 15 to 20 minutes.
6. Please begin heating up the fire and steaming the buns for an additional 20 minutes. Then, turn off the fire and let them sit for 5 minutes before eating.
7. If the buns have cooled, steam them again. No changes to make it better.

DOUGHNUTS

111. CAKE DOUGHNUTS

Prep Time: 20 Minute | Cook Time: 20 Minutes | Total Times: 50 Minutes | Serving: 12

Ingredients

Cake Donut Recipe:

- 2 tsp vanilla extract
- 2 large eggs room temperature
- 5 ounces granulated sugar
- ½ tsp salt
- ½ tsp nutmeg
- 15 ounces All-Purpose flour
- 2 tsp baking powder
- 32 ounces lard or oil for frying (4 cups)
- 1 tsp baking soda
- 6 ounces buttermilk room temperature
- 4 ounces unsalted butter softened but not melted

Classic Donut Glaze Recipe:

- 5 ounces powdered sugar
- 2 Tbsp milk or water

Chocolate Donut Glaze:

- 1 Tbsp corn syrup or glucose/honey
- 2 Tbsp butter
- 4 ounces chocolate chips
- 2 Tbsp heavy cream

Cinnamon Sugar:

- 1 cup of granulated sugar
- 2 Tbsp cinnamon

Instructions

For The Donuts:

1. Cream the softened butter and sugar in the bowl of your stand mixer with the paddle or whisk attachment on medium-high speed until the mixture is light in color and fluffy.
2. While mixing on low, add one egg, let it mix in, and then add the second egg. Use a medium-speed mixer to blend the ingredients together.
3. Incorporate the buttermilk and vanilla into the mixture, ensuring everything is well combined.
4. While the mixer is going on low speed, add the flour, salt, baking powder, baking soda, and nutmeg. Do not overmix. The dough will stick together.
5. Sprinkle a little flour on your work surface and move the sticky dough to it.
6. Lightly press the dough down until it's about an inch thick.
7. Fold the dough over itself three or four times until it's smooth.

8. To achieve a thickness of about 1/2 inch, use a rolling pin to flatten the dough. Let the dough sit for five to ten minutes while the oil heats up.
9. Turn on your FryDaddy or heat your oil to between 182°C and 190°C (360°F to 375°F). Set up a place for the oil to drain from the donuts by putting a cooling rack over a sheet pan.
10. Cut out the donuts with a donut cutter or ring cutter. The scraps can be pressed together and rolled out again to make as many donuts as possible. Just remember that the more you work the dough, the tougher the donuts will get.
11. Use your slotted spoon to slowly lower the donut into the hot oil. Fry the donut about 2 minutes, then flip it over and fry it for another minute.
12. Fry the donut holes for about a minute, stirring and pressing them down with a spoon until the outsides are golden brown.
13. Move the dough to a cooling rack over a sheet pan so the oil can drain away from the donuts.
14. Once your donuts are done, you can roll them in powdered sugar, cinnamon sugar, donut glaze, or chocolate glaze.
15. Donuts can be kept at room temperature for up to two days in a paper bag. They taste best when they are new. Do not refrigerate.

Classic Donut Glaze Recipe:

1. Pour the milk (or water) into a bowl and sift the powdered sugar into it. Whisk to mix. If you want it to be thicker or thinner, just add more powdered sugar or milk.

Chocolate Donut Glaze:

1. Add the heavy cream, corn syrup and butter to the chocolate chips in a medium-sized bowl. Stir until the chocolate is melted, then heat for 30 seconds and stir again. If you need to, microwave for another 15 seconds.

112. GLAZED YEAST DOUGHNUTS

Prep Time: 2 Hour | Cook Time: 30 Minutes

Total Times: 2 Hour 30 Minutes | Serving: 2 Dozen

Ingredients

For the Donuts:

- 1 ⅛ cup of whole milk - warm
- 2 ¼ tsp Instant Or Active Dry Yeast (one package)
- 1 ¼ sticks unsalted butter, a total of 10 tbsp (½ cup of plus 2 tbsp), melted
- 4 cups of all-purpose flour
- ¼ cup of sugar
- ½ tsp salt
- 2 whole large eggs lightly beaten
- Shortening/oil for frying

Glaze for hot yeast donuts:

- Dash of salt
- 2 tsp vanilla
- ½ cup of butter, melted
- 4 cups of powdered sugar
- Enough cream or milk to thin about 3 tbsp

Instructions

To make the dough:

1. Putting your finger in the milk should feel nice and warm (about 105 degrees). Fill a mixing bowl or the bowl of your stand mixer with milk. Stir the sugar to dissolve it. Add the yeast and mix everything. Give the yeast 5 minutes to rest.
2. Stir the beaten eggs and melted butter together in the bowl.
3. While the mixer runs slowly, sift the flour and salt into the bowl, then mix vigorously until a dough forms. Five minutes of mixing is enough to work the dough well. Turn off the mixer and let the dough sit for 10 minutes in the bowl.
4. After the dough has rested, put it in a bowl that has been lightly greased, cover it with plastic wrap, and put it in the fridge for at least 2 hours and up to overnight. The goal is to get the dough cold enough to be easy to work with and for the butter to harden.

To form the donuts:

1. Remove the dough from the fridge and roll it up on a floured surface to a thickness of approximately 1/2 to 1/3 of an inch. Use a donut cutter measuring three inches to cut out the doughnuts.
2. Put the cut donuts and holes on a baking sheet that has been lightly greased.
3. Do the same with the rest of the dough.
4. Cover the donuts and let them rise for about an hour until they are twice as big. The donuts will look very airy and full.

To fry the donuts:

1. In a cast iron skillet, heat a few inches of oil or shortening over medium heat until it reaches 350 to 375 degrees (use a thermometer!). Carefully fry the donuts for about 1 1/2 minutes per side until they turn golden brown. For the donut holes, it will only take about 30 seconds per side.
2. To remove the donuts from the hot oil, use a slotted spoon. Place them on a baking sheet lined with paper towels to absorb any excess oil. Allow them to cool slightly. Then, dip the warm donuts into the glaze, ensuring both sides are covered, enjoy

For the Glaze:

1. In a small bowl, melt the butter. Mix the vanilla in by stirring. Mix in the powdered sugar until a thick paste forms. Add milk, one tbsp at a time, to thin out the paste until the mixture is about as thick as school glue.

113. APPLE CIDER DOUGHNUTS

Prep Time: 20 Minutes | Cook Time: 5 Minutes

Total Times: 25 Minutes | Serving: 20

Ingredients

Apple Cider Donuts:

- 1 cup of apple cider
- ½ cup of granulated sugar
- ½ cup of firmly packed brown sugar
- 6 tbsp unsalted butter, softened
- 2 large eggs, room temperature
- ½ cup of buttermilk
- 1 tsp pure vanilla extract
- 4 ½ cups of all-purpose flour
- 1 tbsp baking powder
- 1 tsp baking soda
- 1 tsp kosher salt
- 2 tsp ground cinnamon
- ½ tsp ground nutmeg
- 1 medium apple, peeled, cored, and grated Macoun or Macintosh
- canola oil for frying

Cinnamon Sugar:

- 1 ½ cups of granulated sugar
- 2-3 tbsp ground cinnamon
- 1 tsp ground nutmeg

Instructions

Apple Cider Donuts:

1. Reduce the apple cider over low heat in a medium saucepan for about 30 minutes until you have about 3/4 cup. Put it away and let it cool to room temperature.
2. Put the flour, baking powder, salt, baking soda, and spices in a medium bowl and sift them together. Set the bowl aside. Using a stand mixer, cream the butter, white sugar, and brown sugar together in an
3. precious bowl.
4. Add the eggs one at a time and mix until they are all mixed in. Occasionally, use a rubber spatula to scrap the bowl's sides and bottom. Mix the condensed apple cider, the buttermilk, and the vanilla extract. Put in the flour mixture and mix.
5. Mix the grated apples into the batter in a gentle way.
6. Keep parchment paper on a baking sheet and set it aside.
7. Put the dough on a surface that has been dusted with flour. This dough can stick together. Fold the dough over with a plastic bench scraper and flour it before cutting out doughnuts.
8. Ensure that the dough is rolled out to a thickness of precisely 12 inches. Cut out the donuts with a doughnut cutter that has been lightly dusted with flour, then put them on the baking sheet set up.
9. Put several layers of paper towels on a baking sheet and set it aside.
10. Add about 3 inches of canola oil to a large, heavy-duty pot. Bring the temperature up to 375°F. Put four or five donuts into the oil, but don't crowd the pot. Cook for 1–2 minutes on each side until lightly golden brown.
11. Take the doughnuts out of the oil and drain them on paper towels. In a small bowl, mix all of the cinnamon sugar ingredients well. Sprinkle the cinnamon sugar on the donuts while they are still warm.

114. SWEET POTATO DOUGHNUTS

Prep Time: 45 Minutes | Cook Time: 2 Hour 45 Minutes

Total Times: 3 Hour 30 Minutes | Serving: 2 Dozen

Ingredients

Doughnuts:

- 1 1/4 tsp kosher salt
- 1/2 cup of whole milk
- 1/2 vanilla bean, seeds scraped
- 1/2 cup of light brown sugar
- 1 envelope instant dry yeast
- 1/4 tsp freshly ground nutmeg
- 3 tbsp unsalted butter
- 2 large egg yolks
- 1 tbsp dark rum
- 1 large egg
- 1 (12-ounce) sweet potato
- 1/2 cup of granulated sugar
- 3 1/4 cups of bread flour, plus more for rolling

Topping:

- 1 tsp cinnamon
- 4 tbsp unsalted butter, melted
- 1 cup of granulated sugar

Instructions

Make the doughnuts:

1. Pour holes all over the sweet potato with a fork, then cook it on high power for 8 to 10 minutes or until it's soft. Let the sweet potato cool, then peel it and puree it. You should have about 1 cup.
2. In a small pan over medium-low heat, start melting the butter until it smells nutty and has a light brown color, which takes about 4 minutes. Put the solids and browned butter in a small bowl and let it cool.
3. Put milk in the pan and heat it until it's just warm, about 105°F. Add warm milk to the bowl of a standing electric mixer equipped with a dough hook. Put in the yeast and let it sit for five minutes. On low speed, beat in the granulated sugar, light brown sugar, salt, vanilla

seeds, nutmeg, and rum. Mix the sweet potato puree, the browned butter and solids, the egg, and the egg yolks until everything is well mixed. With the mixer on low speed, add the bread flour step by step. Increase the speed to medium and beat for 1 to 2 minutes, or until the dough is evenly moist. Beat at moderately high speed for about 5 minutes or until a soft dough forms. Form the dough into a ball and place it in a bowl that has been greased. Cover the dough and let it rise for an hour in a draft-free area.

4. Punch the dough down, and then let it sit for 5 minutes. Roll out the dough on a flour spread surface until it is 1/2 inch thick. Make as many rounds as you can with a 2 3/4-inch round cutter. Use a smaller round cutter (1 inch) to cut out the center of each round. Place the doughnuts and holes on two baking sheets lined with parchment paper. Cover the doughnuts and holes loosely with plastic wrap and let them rise warmly for an hour.

5. Please set the oven temperature to 400°F and place the racks in both the upper and lower thirds of the oven. Bake the holes for 8–10 minutes and the doughnuts for 15–20 minutes, until they have risen and turned golden.

Make the topping:

1. Mix the sugar and cinnamon in a small bowl. Put half the hot doughnuts in a large bowl and drizzle with half the melted butter. Toss and turn the doughnuts to coat them. Sprinkle with half of the cinnamon sugar, toss, and turn until everything is evenly covered. Repeat with the rest of the doughnuts, cinnamon sugar, and butter. Put the doughnuts on a tray and serve.

115. MINI DOUGHNUTS

Prep Time: 10 Minutes | Cook Time: 20 Minutes

Total Times: 30 Minutes | Serving: 30 Mini

Ingredients

Donuts:

- 1/2 cup of buttermilk ((sub 1/2milk plus 1 tsp white vinegar blended))
- 1 egg (lightly beaten)
- 1/2 cup of granulated white sugar
- 1/2 tsp salt
- 1 1/4 cups of all purpose flour
- 1 1/4 tsp baking powder
- 1 1/2 Tbs butter (melted)

Glaze Chocolate:

- 1 cup of powdered sugar
- 1/4 cup of cocoa powder
- 3 Tbs milk
- 1 tsp vanilla extract

Pink/Raspberry:

- 2 tsp raspberry extract
- 2 Tbs milk
- 1 cup of powdered sugar
- 1-2 drop red food colorin

Instructions

Donuts:

1. Turn the oven on to 425.
2. Mix flour, sugar, baking powder, and salt in the bowl of your stand mixer.
3. Mix in the buttermilk, egg, and butter until they are JUST mixed in.
4. Pour half of the batter into each donut cup of using a piping or ziplock bag with the corner cut off. Don't worry too much about this, because the batter will rise a lot as it bakes, and you do want holes. (If you put too much in, the hole will close.)
5. Bake the donuts for 6 minutes, or until the top bounces back when touched.
6. Cool in the pan for 1–2 minutes, then move to a cooling rack.

Glaze (either flavor):

1. Mix all the ingredients until the sugar is gone. The mixture will run.
2. Dip the donuts in and let them sit on a cooling rack for 5–10 minutes.
3. Re-dip, add your chosen decorations, and let them dry.

116. CHOCOLATE DOUGHNUTS

Prep Time: 2 Hour | Cook Time: 2 Minutes

Total Times: 2 Hour 2 Minutes | Serving: 24

Ingredients

- ⅓ cup of warm water 95 to 105 degrees F
- 2-3 quarts Peanut or vegetable oil for frying
- 1 ½ tsp salt
- 1 ½ cups of milk
- ¼ cup of sugar
- 5 to 5.5 cups of all-purpose flour
- ⅓ cup of vegetable shortening or butter
- 2 eggs beaten
- 2 packages instant yeast about 4.5 tsp

Chocolate Doughnut Glaze:

4. 2 tsp vanilla extract
5. 2 cups of confectioners' sugar sifted
6. 1 tbsp light corn syrup
7. ½ cup of unsalted butter
8. ¼ cup of whole milk warmed
9. 4 ounces bittersweet chocolate chopped (I used semi-sweet chocolate chips)

Instructions

1. To make the dough, start by combining milk and shortening or butter in a medium-sized saucepan. Heat over medium heat until the shortening or butter is melted. Set it aside.
2. In a small bowl, dissolve the yeast in warm water for 5 minutes. Then, pour the yeast mixture into the large bowl of a stand mixer. Add the milk and shortening/butter mixture, making sure it has cooled to lukewarm. Add sugar, salt, eggs, and half of the flour.
3. Use the dough hook attachment and low speed to mix the ingredients until the flour is well mixed. Turn the speed up to medium and beat the mixture until all of the ingredients are well combined. Gradually add the remaining 5 cups of flour, mixing on low speed at first and then increasing to medium while beating well.
4. Allow the dough to knead for about 4 minutes, or until it becomes smooth and pulls away from the bowl. If the dough is too sticky, add the extra half cup of flour gradually.
5. To allow the dough to rise, coat a bowl with oil, place the dough inside, cover it, and let it sit for an hour or until it has doubled in size.
6. Move the dough to a well-oiled bowl, cover it, and rise for 1 hour or until doubled in size.

7. On a floured surface, roll out the dough to a thickness of 3/8 inch. Use a 2 1/2-inch doughnut cutter or pastry ring to cut out circles of dough. For the hole in the middle, use a 7/8-inch pastry ring. Place on a baking sheet that has been dusted with flour, lightly cover with a tea towel, and let rise for 30 minutes.
8. In a deep fryer or Dutch oven, heat the oil to 365 degrees F. Put 3 to 4 doughnuts at a time into the oil in a gentle way. Cook for 1 minute per side or until deep golden brown. Move to a cooling rack that has been set up in a baking pan. If you want to glaze it, let it cool for 15 to 20 minutes.
9. Mix butter, milk, corn syrup, and vanilla in a medium saucepan, then start heating over medium heat until the butter is melted. Turn down the heat, add the chocolate, and whisk it until it melts.
10. Turn off the heat, add the powdered sugar, and whisk until smooth. Put the mixture over a bowl of warm water, and immediately dip the doughnuts.
11. Give the glaze 30 minutes to set up before you serve it.

117. CINNAMON SUGAR DOUGHNUTS

Prep Time: 5 Minutes | Cook Time: 45 Minutes

Total Times: 50 Minutes | Serving: 8

Ingredients

Doughnut Dough:

- 2 Tbsp granulated sugar
- 1 large egg, at room temperature, lightly beaten
- ½ tsp salt
- 2 tsp active, dry yeast
- 425g all-purpose flour
- 50g Filippo Berio Extra Light Olive Oil
- 230g whole milk, lukewarm
- To fry - Filippo Berio Extra Light Olive Oil

Cinnamon Sugar:

- ½ tsp ground cardamom (optional)
- Pinch of salt
- 1 tbsp cinnamon (do less if you want these less spicy)
- 100g granulated sugar

Instructions

1. Mix the lukewarm milk, sugar, and yeast in the bowl of a stand mixer with a dough hook, and let it sit for 5–10 minutes or until foamy.
2. Mix on low run speed until the dough comes together after adding the flour, salt, egg, and oil. Mix for another 10–12 minutes until the dough is soft and smooth, and you can see light through a small piece (the window pane test).
3. Make a ball out of the dough and put it in a bowl. To chill the bowl, cover it tightly with plastic wrap and refrigerate for a minimum of three hours or a maximum of one day.
4. Turn the dough out onto a surface that has only a little flour on it. Roll out until it's about 1/2 inch (1.2 cm) thick. The dough should be about 12" (1.2cm) wide when rolled out. Cut out circles of dough with a circle cutter. I used a 3 14" process. Using a 1" circle cutter, make a hole in the middle of each circle.
5. Put each one on a square of parchment paper, then put the courts on a baking sheet with space between them. Put the doughnut holes on the sheet with the doughnuts so they can rise.
6. Press the scraps together, roll them out again, and cut out more doughnuts, or cut them up and let them rise with the doughnuts so you can fry them as snacks (this is my preferred method).
7. Cover the doughnuts and let them rise for another 35 to 45 minutes. If you lightly poke them with your finger, you should be able to make a small mark that springs back.
8. Start heating Filippo Berio Extra Light Olive Oil in a sizable heavy-bottomed pot (cast iron works great for this) or deep fryer while the doughnuts rise. 350°F/180°C should be the

temperature of the oil. Stack a baking sheet with parchment paper on top of a wire rack. Put the ingredients for the cinnamon sugar in a shallow bowl after thoroughly combining them.

9. Once the oil has reached the right temperature, test it with a few bits of dough or the most crooked doughnut you can. Slowly drop the doughnuts into the hot oil, two at a time. You can leave the parchment paper on if you want. It will come off when you put it in the oil, and you can fish it out with tongs. Cook for about 3 minutes, turning them over once until golden brown. With a slotted spoon, take the food out of the oil and put it on a cooling rack.
10. Give it 30 seconds to cool down before you toss in the sugar. Do the same thing with the other doughnuts. Put on a rack to cool.

118. JELLY DOUGHNUTS

Prep Time: 3 Hour | Cook Time: 3 Minute

Total Times: 3 Hour 3 Minutes | Serving: 12

Ingredients

Jelly Doughnuts:

- 3 large eggs room temperature
- sugar to coat doughnuts
- 2 ¼ tsp (1 packet) active dry yeast
- ¼ cup of lukewarm water
- 5 ½ cups of all-purpose flour
- 1 tsp salt
- 2 tbsp honey
- canola oil for frying
- 1 (18-ounce) jar Raspberry preserves or jelly (seedless jam or preserves)
- 1 ½ cups of whole milk warm
- ¼ cup of granulated sugar
- ½ cup of (1 stick) unsalted butter softened

Instructions

1. In the large bowl of a stand mixer, mix the yeast and warm water together. Add the sugar, honey, and eggs to the warm milk. Mix in the flour and salt with the dough hook attachment. Use a rubber spatula to scrape the bottom and sides of the bowl every so often. Cut the butter into small pieces and mix them into the dough. Several times, scrape the bowl. Beat the dough for about 5–7 minutes, or until it is smooth.
2. The dough needs to be kneaded for 5 or 6 minutes on a floured surface to become smooth. When you turn this dough out, it will be sticky. After kneading, size the dough into a round ball and put it back into the greased mixing bowl. Wrap loosely with plastic wrap and drape with a clean kitchen towel. Put in a warm place and let rise until it's doubled in size, which takes about an hour and a half.
3. Knead the dough for a minutes on a lightly floured surface. Turn the dough back into the greased bowl and let it rise for about an hour, or until it has doubled in size.
4. To begin, lightly flour a surface, and then roll out the dough until it is 1/4 inch thick. Then, use a 3 12-inch round doughnut cutter to cut out doughnut shapes. Every time you use the doughnut cutter, rub it in a lot of flour. Turn the doughnut cutter back and forth a bit and gently tap the doughnut out onto the counter.
5. Put the doughnuts in a single layer on a half-sheet pan that has been lined with parchment paper. You'll need to give them some space on the sheet pan so they can rise. (I usually put three doughnuts in each row, and you can fit about a dozen on each half-sheet pan.) Loosely cover the dish with plastic wrap and refrigerate it overnight. So, they can rise in the fridge, and when you wake up in the morning, you'll have done most of the work. Just start cooking them right away.

119. GLUTEN FREE DOUGHNUTS

Prep Time: 10 Minutes | Cook Time: 5 Minutes

Total Times: 15 Minutes | Serving: 12

Ingredients

Wet Ingredients:

- 2 eggs
- 1 cup of whole milk
- 1 cup of sour cream
- 1 tsp gluten-free vanilla extract
- 5 tbsp butter (softened) melted

Dry Ingredients:

- 1 1/2 tsp gluten-free baking powder
- Oil for deep frying
- 1 1/2 tsp salt
- 1 1/4 cup of cane sugar
- 2 tsp xanthan gum
- 6 cup of All-Purpose Gluten Free Flour Blend (OR 1 1/2 C white rice flour, 1 1/4 C potato starch, 1 1/4 C tapioca starch, 1 C brown rice flour and 1/2 C corn starch)
- 2 tsp baking soda

Glaze:

- 1/2 cup of powdered sugar
- 1 tbsp milk
- 1 tbsp butter melted

Instructions

1. Eggs and sugar are mixed in a bowl that stands on its own.
2. Mix well after adding the milk, sour cream, vanilla, and melted butter.
3. Mix flour(s), baking soda, baking powder, salt, and xanthan gum in another bowl.
4. Mix well as you slowly add the dry ingredients to the wet ones.
5. On a counter heavily dusted with gluten-free all-purpose or white rice flour, roll out the wet donut dough to a thickness of 2 inches. Use a lot of white rice or all-purpose flour to make the dough flexible and to dust the rolling pin.
6. Make donuts and donut holes from the dough.
7. In a deep fryer, heat the oil until it reaches about 375°F.
8. Fry the donuts for up to 3 minutes, making sure to flip them once. Put the finished donuts on a rack over a baking sheet that lined with paper towels to let the grease drain off.
9. Make an easy glaze by mixing together 1 cup of powdered sugar, 1 tbsp of melted butter, 2 to 3 tsp of milk, and 1/2 tsp of vanilla. You can also make a chocolate glaze, which we'll talk about below.
10. Glaze warm donuts, then set them on a wire baking rack to drip.

120. VEGAN DOUGHNUTS

Prep Time: 2 Hour 30 Minutes | Cook Time: 30 Minutes

Total Times: 3 Hour | Serving:

Ingredients

- ¼ tsp ground nutmeg
- 125 g vegan butter/margarine (room temperature, cubed)
- 250 ml lukewarm water (approx. 40°C)
- 1 packet instant yeast (7g / ¼ ounce / 2¼ tsp)
- zest of 1 lemon/orange (optional)
- ½ tsp vanilla extract
- 1 tbsp rum (optional)
- 80 g sugar
- 500 g all-purpose flour
- 1 tsp fine sea salt
- 1 litre sunflower oil (for frying)
- favourite jam for filling

Instructions

1. Combine lukewarm water, sugar, salt, instant yeast, lemon zest, rum, and vanilla extract in the bowl of a stand mixer. You can mix the ingredients using a fork or a whisk.
2. If you are using active dry yeast, prepare it by mixing it with a tsp of sugar and a cup of warm water. Wait a few minutes until the top becomes foamy, then add the remaining ingredients as directed.
3. First, attach the dough hook to the stand mixer and add the flour to the bowl. Next, knead the dough on low to medium speed for around 5 to 8 minutes or until it turns smooth, shiny, and no longer sticks to the sides of the bowl.
4. Next, gradually add the vegan butter, one cube at a time, while the mixer runs at medium-low speed. It may appear as if the ingredients are not coming together, but continue adding the butter until it forms a sticky dough.
5. Once all the butter is added, and the dough is mixed but still sticky, knead it on low to medium speed for a few more minutes until it becomes smooth and soft and begins to pull away from the sides.
6. To prevent the dough from sticking, move it to a large bowl lightly floured or greased. Cover the mixture with a clean tea towel or plastic wrap and give it time to rise in a warm place for around an hour until it doubles in size.

7. Once the dough is done, punch it to flatten it, move it to a clean, lightly floured surface, and knead it briefly. Weigh the dough, which should be approximately 950 g, and divide it into 17 pieces weighing 50–60 g each for smaller doughnuts or 12 pieces weighing about 80 g for larger doughnuts.
8. Roll the dough into smooth balls and set them on a baking sheet that slighlly dusted with flour. Let them rest and rise for another hour, or until they have doubled in size, covered with a clean dish towel . It all depends on how hot and humid the room is.
9. You could also use a circle cookie cutter to roll out the dough and cut out shapes.
10. Avoid excessively rising the doughnuts, as it may lead to hollowness inside and excessive oil absorption. Heat about 1.5 liters of oil in a heavy-bottomed pan to a temperature of 165 to 180 degrees Celsius (330F to 350F).
11. Fry 3–4 doughnuts until they turn golden, approximately 2–3 minutes per side. Place them on a plate covered with a paper towel. Allow them to cool completely before filling, then sprinkle sugar on top.

MEATBALLS

123. TURKEY MEATBALL

Prep Time: 20 Minutes | Cook Time: 30 Minutes

Total Times: 50 Minutes | Serving: 12

Ingredients

- 3 tbsp olive oil
- 1 tsp dried oregano
- 2 cloves garlic, minced
- 1 pound lean ground turkey
- 1/2 cup of gluten-free breadcrumbs
- 1 (28-ounce) jar pasta sauce of choice,
- 1 egg
- 1 tsp dried parsley
- 1 tsp sea salt
- 1/3 cup of yellow onion, finely chopped

Instructions

1. Put everything in a mixer with a paddle attachment and start mixing. Combine all ingredients and knead until meat forms small balls. Please note that if you don't have a mixer, mix the ingredients by hand in a bowl.
2. Roll the turkey meatball mixture into balls (mine were about 1 1/2 to 2 inches in diameter) and set them on a serving dish.
3. Olive oil (algae or cooking oil of choice) to generously coat the surface of a large (10-inch) cast-iron skillet heated over medium heat. Make sure the skillet is hot before adding the meatballs, and be careful to leave plenty of space between each one.
4. Prepare the meatballs for 1.5 minutes, flip them over, and cook for another 1.5 minutes. Turn the meatballs a few more times to get a good sear, but stop short of fully cooking them. Turn down the heat to medium.
5. Add the sauce to the pan very slowly (if the pan is too much hot, the sauce will splatter, so be careful). Cook the meatballs at a low boil for 20 minutes (or a slow simmer for an hour) covered in a skillet.
6. Use your preferred carb base, such as zoodles, rice, pasta, gluten-free noodles, etc., to top your meatballs.

121. SWEDISH MEATBALL

Prep Time: 30 Minutes | Cook Time: 20 Minutes | Total Times: 50 Minutes | Serving: 30

Ingredients

- 2 cups of (480 ml) chicken stock or low-sodium chicken soup from the store or made at home.
- 1/2 tsp apple cider vinegar
- 4 tsp (18g) kosher salt
- 3 tbsp (45g) flour
- 1 medium onion, minced, divided
- Minced flat-leaf parsley to garnish
- Canola or vegetable oil for frying
- 1 tsp (5ml) soy sauce
- Yukon Gold potatoes boiled in butter and lingonberry jam to serve
- 1/8 tsp ground allspice
- 5 tbsp (75g) unsalted butter, divided
- 12 ounces (340 grams) of ground pork that has about 25% fat
- 1/4 tsp of ground white pepper, plus more to season
- 1 pound. 4 ounce (560 g) of ground chuck beef (about 20% fat).
- 2 large egg

Instructions

1. Toss bread with milk in a medium bowl until well-coated. Wait around 10 minutes until the bread has softened and absorbed most of the milk.
2. While waiting, melt approximately 2 tbsp (30 grams) of butter in a skillet with medium heat. Add half of the onion (sliced) and cook, stirring every so often, for about 7 minutes, until the onion turns golden and is soft.
3. Mix ground beef, ground pork, soaked bread and any remaining milk, cooked onion, raw onion, 4 tsp salt, eggs, white pepper, and allspice in a stand mixer that fitted with the paddle attachment or in a food processor. Beat for 30 seconds to 1 minute, beginning on low speed and increasing to medium-high, until ingredients are well combined.
4. Prepare parchment paper on a baking sheet. To prevent the meatball mixture from sticking to your hands, wet your hands as needed and roll tbsp-sized portions into balls slightly smaller than golf balls. Bring to a baking sheet covered with foil.
5. Place a rack over a baking sheet and preheat the oven to 200°F (90°C). The oil in a large skillet should be heated to 350 degrees Fahrenheit (177 degrees Celsius). Fry the meatballs in batches, 2 minutes per batch, until browned all over, turning once. Put the meatballs on a rack after browning them, and bake them to keep them warm.
6. In a medium saucepan, melt the remaining 3 tbsp (45g) of butter over medium heat until it becomes foamy. Next, add the flour and cook for an additional 3 minutes, or until the raw flour smell disappears. Add the chicken stock and cook, constantly whisking, until the mixture thickens, about 3 minutes. Soy sauce and cider vinegar can be whisked in. Add salt and white pepper to taste.
7. Toss meatballs in the gravy and coat thoroughly. Meatballs should be heated through in a simmering sauce. Serve immediately as an appetizer on toothpicks or with buttered potatoes and lingonberry jam.

122. ITALIAN MEATBALL

Prep Time: 25 Minutes | Cook Time: 40 Minutes

Total Times: 1 Hour 5 Minutes | Serving: 25

Ingredients

- 5 cups of (1.2L) tomato sauce
- 1 tsp ground fennel seed
- 1/3 cup of (80ml) buttermilk, plus more as needed
- Freshly ground black pepper
- 4 large egg yolks
- 1/2 cup of loosely packed parsley leaves
- 8 medium cloves garlic
- 3 ounces (85g) fatty pancetta, finely minced
- 1 pound (455g) ground pork (at least 25% fat
- 1 tbsp Diamond Crystal kosher salt (12g); for table salt use half as much by volume or the same weight
- 1 pound (455g) ground beef (at least 25% fat
- 1 medium (8-ounce; 225g) yellow onion, minced
- 2 ounces (55g) Parmigiano-Reggiano, grated, plus more for serving
- 1 tsp dried oregano
- 3 ounces

Instructions

1. Spread gelatin over the top of the stock in a heat-safe measuring cup of and set the cup of aside for 5 minutes. (If you don't want to use stock and gelatin, skip to the next section.) Dissolve gelatin in stock in a microwave for 2 minutes while stirring once or twice. The stock should be poured into a large, heatproof bowl and chilled until firm, about 30 minutes.
2. Toss cubed bread with buttermilk in the bowl of a stand mixer. Ten minutes later, after standing and tossing occasionally, the bread should be completely soaked. Check for dry areas by squeezing the bread with your fingers or mashing it with a spoon; if any areas remain dry, add more buttermilk, 1 tbsp at a time, until the bread is evenly moistened.
3. Blend in some onion, pancetta, Parmigiano-Reggiano, garlic, parsley, egg yolks, oregano, fennel, salt, and pepper to the buttermilk and bread. If using gelled stock, chop it very finely and add it.
4. Insert the paddle into the mixer and place the bowl in the mixer stand. Beat the bread mixture on low speed, increasing to medium-high speed, and stopping to scrape down the sides as much as needed until everything is well combined. Beat in a third of the beef and pork until they are evenly distributed throughout the bread mixture at medium speed.

5. Take the bowl off the mixer and add the rest of the meat. Gently mix the meatball mixture with a clean hand, separating the ground meat with your fingers just until the ground beef and pork are evenly distributed, and no pockets of unincorporated meat remain.
6. The broiler should be preheated, and the oven rack should be in the highest position. To line a baking sheet with a lip, you can use aluminum foil. Make about 10 meatballs by rolling the mixture into balls the size of your hand and placing them on the baking sheet. Broil meatballs for about 7 minutes or until browned on top. (Browning times can differ greatly from one oven broiler to the next.)
7. Add meatballs to a pot of simmering tomato sauce. Simmer for about 10 minutes or until an instant-read thermometer reveals an internal temperature of 145°F (63°C) in the meatballs.
8. To serve, spoon additional sauce over meatballs and sprinkle with additional cheese.

124. BEEF MEATBALL

Prep Time: 25 Minutes | Cook Time: 5 Minutes

Total Times: 30 Minutes | Serving: 25

Ingredients

- Frying oil (used for frying the meatballs)
- Salt and pepper (to taste)
- 2 eggs
- 100g of the soft part of bread
- 1 tbsp chopped rosemary
- 200g of finely grated breadcrumbs
- 80g Parmesan cheese
- 400g lean beef
- 1 tbsp chopped chives

Instructions

1. Attach the food grinder to the Artisan Stand Mixer and use it to mince the meat. Meatballs made fresh on the spot are guaranteed to be of superior quality and could be tailored to your preferences by using a variety of meats (beef, veal, pork, chicken, etc.).
2. Mix the minced meat, Parmesan, parsley, chives, and eggs in a glass bowl. The last step is to mix in the squishy bread. Use a spoon made from wood to thoroughly combine the salt and pepper you've added. Roll the mixture between your palms to form round balls, then transfer to a plate with breadcrumbs and roll around until the balls are evenly coated. Put them on a clean plate and wrap the plate tightly with plastic.
3. Warm the oil in a wok and fry the meatballs for two to three minutes (the time will vary depending on their size). Drain on paper towels and serve immediately.

125. BBQ MEATBALL

Prep Time: Minutes | Cook Time: Minutes

Total Times: Minutes | Serving: 65

Ingredients
- 1/2 pound ground bacon
- 1/2 cup of Plowboys BBQ Yardbird Rub
- 2 eggs
- Eat Barbecue The Next Big Thing Barbecue Sauce
- 1 pound ground pork
- 1/3 cup of breadcrumbs
- 1/2 red bell pepper, roughly chopped
- 3 cloves garlic
- 1/4 large yellow onion, roughly chopped
- 1 pound ground beef
- 3 ounce Asiago cheese, grated

Instructions
1. You can either use a food processor to properly chop the bell pepper, onion, and garlic, or you can chop them by hand until they reach a paste-like consistency. Mix everything together in a stand mixer's bowl except the sauce. Mix on medium for about a minute with the paddle attachment. The finished product must be sticky and cohesive.
2. Prepare a 225°F temperature in your Yoder Smokers YS640 Pellet Smoker. Roll the meat into balls about 3/4 of an ounce in size. Cook on a Frogmat, which will prevent sticking. To smoke your food, set the temperature of the smoker to 225°F and smoke it for 1-1.5 hours. Make sure that the internal temperature of the food reaches 165°F by using an instant-read thermometer. Use a Maverick PT-75 instant-read thermometer to determine the exact temperature inside. Move to a cooking vessel. Put sauce on it right away.

126. LAMB MEATBALL

Prep Time: 60 Minutes | Cook Time: 1 Hour 30 Minutes

Total Times: 2 Hour 30 Minutes | Serving: 4

Ingredients

For the Meatballs:

- 1 tbsp extra virgin olive oil
- A meat grinder or meat grinder attachment of a stand mixer
- 2 1/2 pounds of lamb shoulder without any bones, cut into 1-inch pieces
- 2 1/2 tsp of Maldon sea salt or another granular sea salt
- 1/2 pound of fine bread crumbs (about 2 cups)

For the Sauce and Finishing:

- 1 large Spanish onion, finely chopped
- 5 garlic cloves, thinly sliced
- 1/2 Maldon sea salt or another granular sea salt
- 2 tsp of ground coriander seeds that have been toasted
- 1 1/2 tsp heated and ground cumin seeds
- 2 Dutch or other long, hot red chili peppers that have been cut with a sharp knife.
- 1 28-ounce can of peeled, drained, clipped, and hand-squished tomatoes
- About 1/2 cup of Greek-style yogurt made with whole milk
- 4 large eggs
- A handful or so of mint leaves
- A small handful of thin, small cilantro leaves
- Extra virgin olive oil

Instructions

1. Home meat grinding: I prefer freshly ground meat because it is more pliable and tender when making meatballs. Most pre-packaged ground meat from the supermarket is already over-mixed, sticky, and has the consistency of paste. A dedicated meat grinder or the grinding attachment for a stand mixer will do the trick. I always fry a tester meatball before shaping the rest to ensure the seasoning is just right (and to have a tasty snack on hand).
2. Place the lamb in a large mixing bowl, cover with plastic wrap, and place in the freezer for about an hour or until the edges become crunchy.
3. Mix the lamb thoroughly with the salt, and then toss it with the bread crumbs. Put the ingredients through a medium-sized die in a meat grinder of a stand mixer, and then transfer to a bowl. Repeat passing the mixture through a medium die.

4. Take a small amount of the mixture in your hand and roll it into a ball using firm but gentle pressure; each ball should be slightly larger than a golf ball. The outside of each meatball should be smooth, with no major cracks or crags, but this warning often causes cooks to be too timid when forming the balls. Pinch the ball together at the seams so it doesn't fall apart while cooking. Use the remaining ingredients and try again.
5. Swirl the oil around in an 8- to 9-quart Dutch oven with a lid and heat it over high heat. Cook the meatballs in batches until the grill is smoking, avoiding crowding the pan and turning them with tongs occasionally so they brown evenly and develop a shiny, dark crust. You must take care not to overcook them. Reduce the temperature slightly if you notice any black spots. Brown them until you're satisfied with the color, moving them to a plate as they're done. Each batch will take about 12-15 minutes to complete. Remove half of the fat still present in the pan.
6. Turn the heat down to medium-high and add the onion, garlic, and salt. Cook, stirring frequently, for a minimum of 5 minutes, or until the onion is soft and becomes browned and the garlic has a toasty aroma and is a deep golden brown. This is the base for the sauce. Stirring constantly, cook the spices for a minute after adding the coriander, cumin, and chilies.
7. When the bottom of the pot is beginning to get sticky from the tomatoes, turn the heat down to low and add the tomatoes.
8. After adding the water and bringing the sauce to a boil, lower the heat to a simmer and let it cook for another 5 minutes. Two cups of the sauce should be removed to a blender, processed until smooth and fluffy, then returned to the pot. (At this point, I always get nervous because the sauce seems so bland, but trust me, it will taste fantastic once you're done.)
9. Place the meatballs back into the pot along with any accumulated liquid, and stir gently to coat. Cook, covered, at a low simmer for about half an hour to let the flavors meld. Adjust the heat as needed.
10. Reduce the heat to low, add the yogurt in dollops, and break the eggs into the sauce in various places. Tear the mint leaves and cilantro into small pieces and sprinkle them in. Keep the heat at medium and cover the pot. I prefer my yolks a little runny, so I cook them for about 10 minutes after the whites have set. Right out of the pot or into shallow bowls, with enough eggs and yogurt for everyone.

127. COCKTAIL MEATBALL

Prep Time: 15 Minutes | Cook Time: 30 Minutes | Total Times: 45 Minutes | Serving: 8

Ingredients

- 2 cloves garlic, minced
- 1 large egg
- 1/2 cup of ketchup
- 2 tbsp water
- 3/4 cup of white sandwich bread, cubed
- 1 tsp baking powder
- 8 ounce ground pork
- 1/4 cup of heavy cream or milk
- 1/2 cup of dark brown sugar
- 1 tbsp shallots, grated
- 8 ounce 85/15 lean ground beef
- 1/8 tsp ground allspice
- 1/4 tsp ground black pepper
- 1 1/4 tsp salt
- Fresh parsley, finely chopped (to taste, for garnish)
- 1/2 tbsp Worcestershire sauce
- 1 1/2 tbsp apple cider vinegar

Instructions

1. Bring the oven to a temperature of 325 degrees F (160 degrees C).
2. To prepare for baking, generously coat a baking or cooling rack that is oven-safe with nonstick cooking spray. Then, place it on a baking sheet that has been lined with aluminum foil for effortless cleaning.
3. Mix the Egg (1) and the Heavy Cream (1/4 cup) in a medium bowl using a whisk. Mix in the 3/4 cup of White Sandwich Bread and mash it until there are no more significant pieces of bread. I am putting aside.
4. For about 2 mins on high speed, scraping the bowl as needed, combine the Ground Pork (8 ounces), garlic (one clove), ground allspice (1/8 tsp), ground black pepper (1/8 tsp), salt (3/4 tsp), and baking powder in a stand mixer fitted with the paddle attachment.
5. Beat the bread ingredients on high speed for 1 minute, scraping the bowl as needed, until they are thoroughly combined and smooth.
6. Mix the 8 ounces of 85/15 Lean Ground Beef on medium-low speed for 20 seconds, scraping the bowl until the beef is incorporated.
7. Form the meat mixture into tbsp-sized round meatballs, wet your hands (sticky and wet hands help; keep soaking them as you go), and set them on the prepared rack. To achieve perfect doneness, bake for 20 minutes.
8. Meanwhile, prepare the sauce by combining 1/2 cup of ketchup, 1/2 cup of dark brown sugar, 2 tbsp of water, 1 1/2 tbsp of apple cider vinegar, 1/2 tbsp of Worcestershire sauce, 1 tbsp of chopped shallots, 1 clove of minced garlic, 1/8 tsp of ground black pepper, and 1/2 tsp of salt in a large sauté pan. Slowly simmer for about 10 minutes, stirring occasionally, until thickened.
9. After the meatballs have baked, transfer them to the sauce and toss to coat.
10. Place the meatballs on a serving platter and drizzle the sauce before serving. Fresh parsley, to taste, can be used as a garnish. Eat while it's hot!

128. KETO MEATBALL

Prep Time: 10 Minutes | Cook Time: 20 Minutes

Total Times: 30 Minutes | Serving: 16

Ingredients

- 2 cloves fresh garlic, grated
- 2 pounds ground beef
- ¼ tsp pepper
- ½ cup of fresh parsley, chopped
- 1 tbsp Italian seasoning
- ¼ tsp salt
- ½ onion, grated
- 1 egg
- ½ cup of grated Parmesan cheese

Instructions

1. To start, turn the oven on and set it to 400 degrees Fahrenheit. Next, get a baking sheet ready by lining it with parchment paper or brushing it lightly with oil.
2. The ground beef, egg, Italian seasoning, salt, pepper, Parmesan cheese, garlic, onion, and herbs should all be mixed in a large bowl. Mix the ingredients by hand or in a mixer, and knead them together.
3. To make meatballs, scoop the mixture with an ice cream scoop. The scoop measures 16 meatballs and yields a quarter cup of the meatball mixture. Form the meat into a rough ball by scooping it into your hand.
4. Prepare a baking sheet for the meatballs.
5. Warm the oven to 400 degrees and cook the meatballs for 15 to 20 minutes.

129. GLUTEN-FREE MEATBALL

Prep Time: 15 Minutes | Cook Time: 45 Minutes

Total Times: 1 Hour | Serving: 6

Ingredients

- ¼ Cup of Coconut Flour
- 12 cup of fresh parsley You can use 1 tsp of dried parsley in its place.
- ½ Tsp Salt
- Fresh Basil, 12 cup. 1 tsp of dried basil can be used instead.
- 2 Pounds Ground Beef
- ½ Tsp Red Pepper Flakes
- 2 Eggs

Instructions

1. Put everything into a bowl to start. Mix by hand or with a heavy-duty mixer. The meat should not be overworked. Add the meat last to prevent the eggs and flour from flying out of a stand mixer.
2. Form into about 20 meatballs of medium size once the ingredients are combined. Make a loose ball with them by pressing gently.
3. Put the meatballs in a large baking dish and cover them with the sauce.
4. The meatballs need about 45 minutes in the oven at 350 degrees.
5. When the meatballs are finished cooking, take them out of the oven and serve them over your preferred gluten-free pasta. Enjoy!

130. VEGAN MEATBALL

Prep Time: 20 Minutes | Cook Time: 20 Minutes

Total Times: 40 Minutes | Serving: 30

Ingredients

- 1/2 tsp ground black pepper
- 1/4 cup of finely chopped yellow onion
- 2 cloves garlic, minced
- 1 tsp salt
- 1/2 cup of breadcrumbs I used panko
- (2) 12-ounce packages of Impossible ground beef
- 3 tbsp of chopped Italian flat leaf parsley (optional)
- 4 tbsp of just egg or flax eggs
- 1/4 cup of unsweetened soy milk

Instructions

1. Get the oven and pan ready by heating it to 425 degrees Fahrenheit and brushing an olive oil-coated rimmed baking sheet with the mixture. Use parchment paper if you prefer.
2. Put the breadcrumbs in a small bowl and pour the milk over them to make a breadcrum mixture. After soaking for 5 minutes, combine the breadcrumbs with the JUST Egg, garlic, salt, and pepper. Combine the ingredients thoroughly. Putting aside.
3. To prepare the meatballs, combine the ground Impossible beef and the finely chopped onion in a large bowl. Combine the two using a stand mixer fitted with the paddle attachment or a large wooden spoon. Mix in the fresh parsley and the bread crumbs from the small bowl. Combine all of the ingredients by mixing them thoroughly.
4. Shape the meatballs by scooping out a small amount of the mixture and rolling it into balls by hand or with a cookie scoop. They can be slightly less than perfectly spherical. You can adjust the size up or down somewhat. Mini meatballs are my favorite kind.
5. Put the meatballs on the pan and into the oven. Turn them over after 10 minutes and bake for another 10 minutes or until they reach the desired color and doneness.
6. Serving Suggestions: Grape jelly meatballs, Swedish meatballs, teriyaki sauce, or warm marinara sauce. Or wherever else strikes your fancy!

PASTA AND NOODLES

131. CHEESE TORTELLINI

Prep Time: 1 Hour Minutes | Cook Time: 15 Minutes

Total Times: 1 Hour 15 Minutes | Serving: 4

Ingredients

Pasta Dough:

- ¾ cup of water
- 3 tbsp mascarpone cheese
- 2 cups of all-purpose flour
- ½ tsp salt

Filling:

- ¼ cup of romano cheese shredded
- ¼ cup of asiago cheese shredded
- ½ cup of whole milk ricotta cheese
- ½ cup of mozzarella cheese shredded
- ¼ cup of mascarpone cheese
- 1 tsp Italian seasonin

Instructions

1. First, make the filling out of the cheese. Put all the cheeses in a medium bowl and mix them. Mix the Italian spice into the cheese filling until it is evenly distributed. Set aside.
2. Next, make the dough for the tortellini. Put the flour and salt in a bowl and make a well in the middle. Mix the mascarpone cheese and 12 cups of water with a fork or wooden spoon until loose ball forms.
3. Put the dough on the table and knead it for 5 minutes with your hands. If you need to, add more water. The dough should not be sticky and should be hard.
4. After preparing the dough, wrap it tightly in plastic wrap and give it time to rest for 30 minutes.
5. Get ready to roll out the dough, and put the rest of the water in a bowl that you will use to seal the tortellini.
6. To prepare for rolling the dough, sprinkle some flour over your work area and divide the dough in half. Cover one half with plastic wrap and focus on the other piece first.
7. Follow the directions on the package or roll the pasta until it is thin enough that you can see your fingers through it.
8. For a KitchenAid pasta attachment, start with the biggest setting (#1) and roll your dough through the rollers. Then, move the roller to the next smaller setting (#2) and put the dough through it again. Repeat until setting number 5 is reached.
9. Once the dough is thin enough to see through with your fingers, cut it into two rectangles of similar size. Cut the rectangles into pieces that are 2 inches by 2 inches. Put about 1 tsp of filling in the middle of each square of pasta.

10. Wet the edges of the tortellini with your finger dipped in water. To make a triangle, turn one corner of the tortellini over and fold it over to the other side. Use your fingers to firmly close them.
11. Again, wet your finger and press the two tips at the bottom together to make ravioli.
12. Once you've made all of the tortellini, bring a pot of water to a boil. Boil the tortellini for about two to three minutes or until they start to float. Strain out the hot water and toss the pasta in the sauce.

132. FRESH PASTA

Prep Time: 1 Hour 20 Minutes | Cook Time: 2 Minutes

Total Times: 1 Hour 22 Minutes | Serving: 8

Ingredients

- 4 (4) eggs
- 300 g (2.4 cups) plain flour
- 2 (2) egg yolks
- 1 tsp (1 tsp) salt
- 150 g (0.9 cups) semolina

Instructions

1. Put everything you need to make pasta into the bowl of your stand mixer. On the lowest setting, use the dough hook to mix all the ingredients together. Then knead for about five minutes, one or two settings faster, depending on your machine.
2. Leave the dough to rest for an hour with the bowl covered.
3. Cut it into quarters and flatten it with your hand or a rolling pin until it fits in the pasta attachment of your stand mixer.
4. Use the widest setting on the pasta maker. Go back through. Change the machine's thickness setting and go through it twice more.
5. If you are making tagliatelle, keep doing this until you get to the second-thinnest setting. Just cut the pasta in half if it gets too long to handle.
6. Roll it out and cut it into thin strips with a knife, or use a roller tagliatelle cutter to make thin slices.
7. Cook for about 2 minutes in a large pot of salted boiling water. Add the sauce you like best and serve.

133. SHRIMP PASTA

Prep Time: 35 Minutes | Cook Time: 15 Minutes

Total Times: 50 Minutes | Serving: 4

Ingredients

Pasta dough:

- 2 1/3 cups of (300g) all-purpose flour
- 3 eggs
- 1 tbsp (15ml) olive oil
- 1 tbsp (15ml) water

Shrimp scampi:

- 1 tbsp (15ml) olive oil
- 2 cloves garlic, minced or sliced
- 1 large shallot, diced (or 1/2 small onion)
- 1/2 pound (225g) shrimp, peeled and deveined
- 1/4 tsp chili flakes
- kosher or sea salt, to taste
- Fresh cracked black pepper, to taste
- 1/2 cup of (120ml) dry white wine
- 1/4 cup of (20ml) chunky tomato sauce, or chopped tomatoes
- about 1 Tbsp (15ml) fresh lemon juice, or to taste
- fresh chopped Italian parsley, for garnish

Instructions

Make the pasta:

1. Make a mound of flour on a work surface or in a stand mixer with a paddle attachment, and then make a well in the middle of the flour. Into the well, put the eggs, olive oil, and water. Mix the center of the eggs, olive oil, and water on low to medium speed or with a fork, adding the flour slowly as you go. After a couple of minutes, Turn the dough out onto a lightly floured surface when it starts to come together.
2. Knead the dough until it feels smooth, which should take about 5 minutes. If the dough starts to stick, sprinkle a little flour on it. Make a ball out of the dough, and then flatten it into a disc. Wrap the dough in plastic wrap and let it relax at room temperature for at least 30 minutes.
3. Make 4 pieces out of the dough. The first piece of dough should be shaped into an oval that is almost as wide as your pasta roller. Dust the work surface and the dough piece with flour. Run the dough that has been dusted through your pasta roller on the widest setting. Fold the dough in thirds, keeping the rectangle shape. Use your hands to make the dough thinner so it can go through the pasta roller without bunching up.

4. Dust the dough with flour once more. Set the pasta roller to the next-to-widest setting and run the dough through it again. By dusting the pasta roller with flour and rolling it through again and again, the settings got smaller, one setting at a time. As the dough gets thinner, you can feed it through the rollers by draping the dough sheets over the back of your hand.
5. When the dough is the right thickness (for this pasta, we usually roll it out to the third narrowest setting, #6 on the KitchenAid attachment), lay the dough sheet on a lightly floured surface. Cut the dough into the length of pasta you want. We usually make it about 1 foot long. Either use the fettuccine pasta cutter attachment to cut the dough into strips or use a wheel or knife to cut the dough into strands. Mix a little flour with the noodles and set them in a light pile. Roll and cut the other three pieces of dough the same way.
6. Cover the noodles with a dry towel and set them aside. Cook them within an hour or put them in the fridge for up to four hours. You can also put them in a zip-lock bag and freeze them for up to a month. Then, you can put the frozen pasta right into the boiling water.

Make the Shrimp Scampi:

1. While you make the shrimp scampi, start boiling a large pot of well-salted water for the pasta. Heat a large skillet over medium-high heat. First, add the olive oil, then the shrimp, garlic, and shallots. Season the shrimp with chili flakes, salt, and pepper. Sear the shrimp, making sure to stir them every now and then for about 2 to 3 minutes or until they are almost done.
2. Add the white wine and keep cooking until half of the wine is gone. Stir in the tomatoes or tomato sauce and cook for 1 minute or until everything is hot. Turn down the heat on the sauce and start to boil the pasta.
3. Bring the pasta to a boil, and then Add the pasta to the salted water that is already boiling. Boil the pasta for about a minute or until it is soft. Take the pasta out of the water with a spider strainer or tongs, and add it to the shrimp scampi. Mix the shrimp and sauce with the pasta.
4. Add fresh parsley and lemon juice, and serve on warm plates. Enjoy!

134. SALMON PASTA

Prep Time: 30 Minutes | Cook Time: 15 Minutes

Total Times: 45 Minutes | Serving: 4

Ingredients

- 300ml pouring cream
- Plenty of salt and freshly ground pepper to taste
- 2 cups of (300g) plain flour
- 30ml extra light olive oil
- 1 tbsp olive oil
- 2 spring onions, diced
- 3 eggs, lightly beaten
- good pinch salt
- finely grated rind of a large lemon
- 2 tsp fresh chopped dill (optional)
- 2 tbsp lemon juice
- Extra flour for dusting
- 350g smoked salmon, roughly torn or chopped
- 2 tbsp capers, drained

Instructions

1. Put the flat beater on the mixer stand. Put the flour, salt, eggs, oil, and lemon rind into the mixing bowl. Turn the mixer to high speed and mix until everything is mixed together. Please remove the flat beater and install the dough hook in its place. Knead the dough for 3-4 minutes or until it leaves a mark when touched. Cover the dough and let it sit for half an hour.
2. Knead the dough for about 30 seconds with hands that are lightly floured. Make 1 cm thick slices of meat.
3. Attach the pasta sheet roller to the stand mixer. Take a piece of the dough and pat it out to make it flat. Set the speed to 4. Put dough between the rollers. Fold the dough in half and put it back through. Repeat this step about three more times, each time making the roller setting less. (Total rolling should be about five times.
4. Put the pasta on a lightly floured work surface. Roll out the rest of the dough and do it again.
5. Tear the dough into big pieces and dust them lightly with flour.
6. To start cooking, fill a big pot with water and add some salt. Bring it to a boil. Cook the pasta for 3 minutes or until it is just tender. Drain the food and put it back in the pot. Set it aside to stay warm.
7. In a while, heat the oil in a large pan with a heavy bottom. For 1 minute, cook the green onions and capers. Mix in the dill, cream, lemon juice, salt, and pepper. Simmer for 2 minutes or until it gets a little bit thicker.
8. Mix the cream sauce with the salmon and pasta. Check the spices and add more pepper if you think it needs it. Serve right away.

135. VODKA PASTA

Prep Time: 15 Minutes | Cook Time: 15 Minutes

Total Times: 30 Minutes | Serving: 4

Ingredients

- 1,2 tbsp olive oil
- 2 cloves of garlic
- 320g Defrosted Toonish
- 0,6 dl vodka
- 320g tomato puree
- Salt and pepper to taste
- 1,2 chopped onions
- 1,2 dl Parmesan cheese, shredded
- 0,4 tsp white wine vinegar
- 240g crushed tomatoes
- 400g penne pasta
- Chili flakes to taste
- 0,4 dl full-fat cream
- 1,6 tbsp butter

Instructions

1. Peel onions and garlic and cut them up. To begin, heat some vegetable oil over medium heat. Add the onions and fry them until they're soft and golden, which typically takes about 2 minutes. After this, add the garlic and chili flakes and cook for an additional minute. Add tomato purée and keep cooking on low heat for another 10 minutes. Put in the crushed tomatoes and boil for 20 minutes.
2. Follow the directions on the box, but cook the pasta for 2 minutes less than suggested.
3. Then, add the vodka to the tomato sauce and use a stand mixer to make sure everything is smooth. Mix in the Toonish and Cream until they are warm. Add the vinegar, salt, and pepper.
4. Then add the pasta and 2 dl of the pasta water. Add parmesan cheese shreds and butter.
5. Add more Parmesan cheese and fresh basil leaves before serving.

136. MUSHROOM PASTA

Prep Time: 30 Minutes | Cook Time: 20 Minutes

Total Times: 50 Minutes | Serving: 2

Ingredients

For the pasta:

- 2 cups of AP flour
- 1-2 tsp water
- 1/2 tsp fine sea salt
- 2 whole eggs + 1 egg yolk (as fresh as possible), lightly whisked

For the sauce:

- 2 cloves garlic, minced
- 1 tsp fresh thyme, chopped
- 1 shallot, finely chopped
- Pinch of red pepper flakes

- 8 ounce cremini mushrooms, sliced
- Freshly cracked black pepper
- 1/2 cup of heavy cream
- 1/2 cup of dry white wine
- Fine sea salt
- 1/4 cup of grated pecorino, plus more for serving
- 1 tsp fresh rosemary, chopped
- 1 tbsp butter
- 2 tsp fresh chopped parsley, divided
- 1/2 cup of vegetable broth
- 1 tbsp olive oil

Instructions

1. To make pasta, sift the flour and salt into the bowl of the stand mixer. Put on the flat beater, turn the mixer to speed 2, and add the eggs slowly. After one minute of mixing, stop the machine and switch to the dough hook. Mix on low speed for two to three minutes, adding more water by the tspful if necessary, until the dough comes together in a ball and pulls away from the sides of the bowl. Rest the dough for 20 minutes.
2. Install the machine's bucatini and follow the machine's instructions, cutting and rolling the dough into walnut-sized balls and putting it through the tube at speed 10. Let the pasta sit while you make the sauce. If you're not going to use it right away, put it in a sealed container and store it in the fridge for up to two days.
3. To make the sauce, put the butter and olive oil in a big saucepan and heat them over medium-high heat. Once the butter is melted well, add the mushrooms, shallots, a pinch of salt, and the red pepper flakes in a single layer. Cook without stirring for 3 minutes, or until the mushrooms are golden brown. Turn the mushrooms over and cook for another 2 minutes, try to get a golden brown sear on both side . During the last half minute of cooking the mushrooms, mix in the garlic, thyme, and rosemary.
4. Add the white wine to the pan and scrape the bottom of the pan to get all the tasty mushroom bits. This will "deglaze" the pan and bring up all the tasty bits. Simmer until half of the wine is gone. While stirring softly, add the cream, vegetable broth, and a few turns of fresh black pepper. Bring to a boil for two to three minutes to let the sauce get a little bit thicker. Turn the heat down to low and add 1/4 cup of pecorino cheese, stirring gently until the cheese has melted. Mix in 1 tsp of chopped parsley and taste to see if it needs more salt or pepper. take out the pan from the heat and cover it to keep it warm.
5. To prepare the pasta, bring a large pot of salted water to a boil until it's al dente, which takes about 3 minutes for fresh bucatini or as long as the package says. Using a sliding spoon, add the pasta to the mushroom sauce and gently toss for 1 to 2 minutes, until the sauce thickens gradually and the pasta is covered. If the sauce look likes too thick, add a little pasta water.
6. Put the pasta on a plate and top with more grated pecorino, the last 1 tsp of fresh parsley, and fresh black pepper. Have fun right away.

137. EGG PASTA

Prep Time: 1 Hour 15 Minutes | Cook Time: 10 Minutes

Total Times: 1 Hour 25 Minutes | Serving: 1

Ingredients

- 3 1/2 cups of all-purpose unbleached flour, sifted (plus extra flour for preparing)
- 4 large eggs, beaten
- 1/2 tsp salt
- 2 Tbsp water

Instructions

1. Put eggs, water, flour, and salt in the bowl of a mixer. The bowl and flat beater are attached. Mix for 30 to 60 seconds at speed 2. If the dough is too dry, add more water by 1/2 Tbsp at a time.
2. Put the dough hook in place of the flat beater. Set the speed to 2 and knead the dough for 2 minutes. Take the dough out and knead it for 2 minutes by hand. Give it 20 to 30 minutes to rest.
3. Cut the dough into four pieces before you put the pasta sheet attachment on your food processor. Flatten one piece into the shape of a rectangle. both sides with flour. Remember not to overlook the remaining components. Connect the pasta sheet roller to your stand mixer and set it to level #1. Operate the stand mixer at speed 2, and pass the pasta dough through the pasta sheet roller. Fold the dough in half and put it through the machine again while you are on #1. I do this more than once.
4. Again, sprinkle a little flour on each side of the dough, change the setting to #2, and carry on the pasta dough through the sheet roller. I do this twice, and then I do #3 and #4 twice each. Don't use the #4 setting if you want the dough to be thicker.
5. Add flour to each side of your long sheet of pasta once more. Change the attachment to a spaghetti or fettuccine cutter and turn the machine on to speed 2. Run the pasta sheet through the cutter and hold it with your left hand as it goes through. Usually, it's very long, so I cut it and wrap it around my hand to make a nest. Let the pasta dry for a few minutes before putting it on the stove.
6. When you boil pasta, it only takes between 3 and 7 minutes.
7. I like to use the fettuccine cutter for this recipe.

138. CHINESE NOODLES

Prep Time: 10 Minutes | Cook Time: 60 Minutes

Total Times: 1 Hour 10 Minutes | Serving: 6

Ingredients

- 500 g high gluten flour bread flour
- 1/2 cup of cornstarch to prevent stickiness
- 50-100 grams flour to adjust the water and flour ratio
- 1 tsp
- salt
- 3 medium-size eggs
- 100 g water

Instructions

1. Mix the following things in the KitchenAid mixing bowl: 500 grams of high-gluten flour, 100 grams of water, and three medium-sized eggs. If you dislike eggs, leave them out and replace them with 240 grams of water. Last, put in a tsp of salt. Use your spatula to mix them up well.
2. Use the hook for making dough. Run it slowly for a total of 15–18 minutes. During the first 5 minutes of making dough, keep an eye on the dough and adjust the flour-to-water ratio by adding more flour or water. We want a dough with a low water-to-flour ratio, which means it should be pretty hard and not stick to your hands.
3. Cover the dough and let it rest for 30 minutes after the machine is done kneading.
4. Cut the dough into six equal parts. Make each piece roughly flat.
5. Set the thickness of the pasta roller attachment to its thickest point. Allow the piece of dough to go through the machine. Fold the sheets and run them through the roller repeatedly until they are in the shape of a rectangle.
6. Use some cornstarch to keep the sheets from sticking to each other.
7. Change the setting for thickness. Keep putting the sheets through the roller until you get the thickness you want.
8. Change the blade to make noodles from the sheets.
9. Add more cornstarch to the noodles, and you're done.

139. EGG NOODLES

Prep Time: 1 Hour | Cook Time: 4 Minutes

Total Times: 1 Hour 4 Minutes | Serving: 6

Ingredients

- 4 whole Eggs
- 1 tsp Olive Oil
- 1/2 tsp Salt
- 3 cups of All-Purpose Flour
- 1/4 cup of Water (Up To)

Instructions

1. Flour and salt should be put in a stand mixer.
2. Mix everything with a fork.
3. In the middle, make a well and add eggs and olive oil.
4. Use a fork to mix the eggs until the whites are completely mixed.
5. Turn the stand mixer to setting 2 or medium-low and use the dough hook. If, after 6 minutes of kneading, the dough is still very dry, you put a tbsp of water at a time. Kneading for at least a minute between each addition of water will help you avoid making a sticky mess by adding too much water. The dough will have a rough surface, but it will have pulled away from the bowl and formed a firm ball around the dough hook.
6. Knead the dough for 10 minutes more, or until it is smooth. This gives the gluten a chance to grow.
7. Cover the dough and let it sit for 35 minutes.
8. On a floured surface, cut the dough into four pieces. On a floured surface, roll out each piece of dough. Roll a piece of dough over the rolling pin and pull it until you get the thickness you want. Ensure there is enough flour under the sheet of dough so it doesn't stick to the work surface when cut. Then, cut the pasta to the size and thickness you want with a large, sharp knife.
9. Let it dry for at least an hour. I put mine on a few cookie sheets with some flour to keep them from sticking, since I use them the same day. If you want to use them later, you can hang them from hangers to dry overnight and use them then.
10. Pasta can be cooked in salted boiling water, stock, or soup. until tender, which should take about 4 minutes. Taste to see if it's done. Or, put it in the freezer until you're ready to use it.

140. RAMEN NOODLES

Prep Time: 30 Minutes | Cook Time: 2 Minutes | Resting Time: 1 Hour

Total Times: 1 Hour 32 Minutes | Serving: 12

Ingredients

- 3 cups of all-purpose flour 408g
- 2 large eggs beaten
- ½ cup of warm water
- 1 tsp fine sea salt
- 1 tsp baking soda

Instructions

1. Whisk together the flour, salt, and baking soda in the bowl of a stand mixer. Add warm water and eggs.
2. Put the bowl on the stand mixer and connect the dough hook. Mix on the slowest setting until all of the ingredients are wet. Add one or two clicks to the speed and mix until the dough comes together. Once a ball of dough has formed, keep kneading it for 5 minutes with the dough hook until it is smooth. Put the dough on a floured surface and shape it into a rectangle. Cover with plastic wrap and put in the fridge for at least an hour, but no longer than a night.
3. Sprinkle a lot of flour on a baking sheet with a rim.
4. Take the dough out of the fridge and cut it into six equal pieces. Place each piece on a floured work surface and loosely cover with plastic wrap. Flatten one piece into a rough rectangle about 1/2 inch thick with your palm. Rub the whole thing with flour. Start at the thickest setting (1) on a manual pasta machine and feed one end through. Move the dial to the next setting (2) and put the dough through the machine again. Repeat at the third and fourth places. (Cut the dough in half lengthwise before running it through the pasta cutter to shorten the noodles.)
5. Put on the attachment for cutting pasta, and lightly dust the blades with flour. Use the smallest cutter (ideally spaghetti-sized) to cut the dough. (Recipe Note #4) Coat and separate the noodles with flour, then put them on a baking sheet that has been prepared. Repeat with the other pieces of dough.
6. Cook noodles in water or broth for 1 to 2 minutes, or until they are done. The noodles can also be frozen. You can keep them straight from the freezer into boiling water, but they will take about 30 seconds longer to cook than when fresh.
7. Use noodles in the soups and stir-fries you like.

141. GARLIC NOODLES

Prep Time: 10 Minutes | Cook Time: 10 Minutes

Total Times: 20 Minutes | Serving: 2

Ingredients

Ingredients for sauce:

- 2 tsp of Worcestershire sauce
- 2 tsp of fish sauce
- ¼ tsp of sea same oil
- 1 Tbsp Oyster sauce
- Pinch of cayenne pepper
- 2 tsp soy sauce

Ingredients for Noodles:

- 1 Tbsp green onion, sliced
- 4 Tbsp of butter
- 6 ounces of spaghetti, cooked and warm
- 8 cloves of garlic
- ½ cup of reserved salted pasta water
- ¼ cup of grated parmigiano
- Pinch of red pepper flakes

Instructions

1. Mix the ingredients for the sauce, then set it aside.
2. On medium heat, melt butter in a pan. Just add the garlic and cook it for 30 seconds.
3. When you add the sauce, turn off the heat right away.
4. Put in the cooked spaghetti and toss it around to coat.
5. Add the cheese and mix everything together.
6. If the noodles look too dry, add some of the pasta water you saved.
7. Put noodles on a plate and sprinkle them with red pepper flakes and diced green onions.

142. RICE NOODLES

Prep Time: 35 Minutes | Cook Time: 15 Minutes

Total Times: 50 Minutes | Serving: 4

Ingredients

- 2 cups of rice flour, divided
- 1/4 tsp salt
- 1/2 cup of tapioca starch
- 1/2 Tbsp vegetable oil, for boiling noodles
- 1 tsp vegetable oil
- 1/2 Tbsp xanthan gum
- 2 1/4 cups of water

Instructions

Making the batter:

1. Add 1/2 cup of rice flour, water, salt,and vegetable oil to a medium saucepan. Mix with a whisk until the flour is gone and the mixture is smooth.
2. Stir the mixture continiouslly as you heat it over medium-high heat. (In about 2 to 3 minutes, the mixture should start to get thicker. Keep stirring and bring it to a slow boil.) Once the mixture starts to bubble, take out it from the heat and whisk it for one more minute to make sure it is smooth. Set the batter aside and let it cool for 15 to 20 minutes.
3. Combine the remaining 1 1/2 cups of rice flour, tapioca starch, and xanthan gum in a stand mixer. To blend the dry ingredients, mix them for 15 seconds on low speed.
4. Incorporate the batter you made earlier. Mix on low for 30 seconds, or until most of the ingredients are incorporated. Ensure to scrape the beater and the bowl's sides to eliminate any leftover dry ingredients. Mix the batter at medium speed for approximately 1 minute, or until it achieves a fluffy consistency.
5. Fill the potato ricer three-quarters of the way with small amounts of batter.
6. Bring a big pot of water to a rapid boil and stir in 1/2 tbsp of vegetable oil.
7. Fill a big colander or bowl with ice water and keep it close by. Put a salad spinner or a big colander in the sink.

Making the rice noodle:

1. To get the water moving, use a large spoon to swirl it around a few times. Holding the potato ricer over the boiling water, quickly and smoothly press down on the handle to force the batter into the water.
2. Dip the potato ricer into the water and swirl it around a few times to get the noodles out.
3. Mix the noodles slowly. When the noodles float to the top, scoop them up with a skimmer and put them in the cold water bath. Stir the noodles around for 30 seconds in the cold water. Drain the noodles and put them in the salad spinner.
4. Repeat the above steps with the rest of the batter. (The batter will fill the potato ricer three times.)
5. Rinse the starch off the noodles by swirling them in cold water for one minute and then letting them drain. Keep doing this until the water is no longer cloudy.
6. Use a salad spinner to get rid of any extra water.
7. If you want to serve it right away, put some rice noodles in each bowl. Make small mounds of noodles on a large plate if you want to serve them later.
8. The rice noodles are best when they are fresh out of the pot. Keep any leftovers in the fridge and eat them within 3–4 days

143. GARLIC SHRIMP ZUCCHINI NOODLES

Prep Time: 10 Minutes | Cook Time: 10 Minutes

Total Time: 20 Minutes | Serving: 4

Ingredients

- 2 medium zucchini
- 1 pound raw shrimp, shelled and deveined
- 2 Tablespoons butter (or olive oil)
- 3 cloves garlic, minced
- 3/4 cup parmesan cheese
- salt, to taste
- black pepper, to taste
- 1/4 teaspoon red chili flakes
- Lemon wedges, optional

Instructions

1. Use the vegetable spiralizer to cut the zucchini into long pieces that look like noodles. Put noodles to the side.
2. On medium-high heat, warm up a big pan. Melt the butter or olive oil, then add the shrimp and garlic. Cook the shrimp until its becomes pink and is done all the way through. If the heat is too high, the garlic could burn.
3. Add the zucchini noodles and cook for about 3 to 5 minutes, until they are soft. Zucchini noodles cook very quickly, so taste one strand as it cooks to decide how crunchy or "al-dente" you want the zucchini. Don't cook the zucchini noodles for too long or they will get too soft.
4. Take the pan off the heat, stir in the Parmesan cheese, and then squeeze some lemon juice over the shrimp and zucchini. Season with salt and pepper to your taste. If you want, add chili flakes and serve hot.

144. BASIC EGG NOODLES

Prep Time: 1 Hour | Cook Time: 4 Minutes

Total Time: 1 Hour 4 Minutes | Serving: 6

Ingredients

- 3 cups All-Purpose Flour
- 1/2 teaspoon Salt
- 4 whole Eggs
- 1 teaspoon Olive Oil
- 1/4 cup Water (Up To)

Instructions

1. Put the flour and salt in a stand mixer.
2. Mix together with a fork.
3. Make a well in the middle, and add eggs and olive oil.
4. Mix eggs with a fork until the whites are completely mixed in.
5. Attach the dough hook to a stand mixer and set it to 2 or medium-low speed. If the dough remains fairly dry after 6 minutes of kneading, you can incorporate 1 tablespoon of water at a time. Kneading for minimum a minute between additions will prevent you from adding excessive water, resulting in a sticky mess.
6. Cover and give time to dought dough rest for 35 minutes.
7. On a surface that has been dusted with flour, cut the dough into four pieces. Roll each piece of dough on a floured work surface. Roll a part of the dough over the rolling pin and pull it until the thickness you want is reached. Make sure the dough sheet has enough flour so that it won't stick to the work surface when it's cut. Then, use a large, sharp knife to cut the pasta to the desired thickness and size.
8. Allow to dry for 60 Minute. I put mine on a few cookie sheets with some flour to keep them from sticking because I use them the same day, but if you want, you can hang them from hangers and let them dry overnight so you can use them later, like my Granny did.
9. Pasta can be made in salted boiling water, stock, or soup. For about 4 minutes or until tender. Taste something to see if it's done. Or, you can put them in the freezer until you're ready to use them.

DIPS AND SAUCES

145. GUACAMOLE

Prep Time: 15 Minutes | Cook Time: 00 Minutes

Total Time: 15 Minutes | Serving: 6

Ingredients

- 3 avocados, cut into chunks
- 3 tbsp fresh cilantro, chopped
- 1/2 - 1 tsp coarse kosher salt, to taste
- 1/4 tsp ground cumin
- 1 medium clove garlic, minced
- 1/2 cup of finely chopped onion
- 2 Roma tomatoes, seeded and diced
- 1 lime juiced 2-3 tbsp
- 1-2 tbsp finely minced jalapeno optional

Instructions

1. In a small-sized bowl, stir together the lime juice, garlic, and onion. Lime juice's acidity will "tame" the garlic and onion.
2. Put the avocado and 1/2 tsp of salt in a stand mixer's bowl with a flat beater (paddle). Mix the ingredients on low speed until they are as smooth as you like.
3. Mix in the rest of the ingredients (including the mixture of lime, garlic, and onion). Add more salt to taste.
4. It can be made a few hours ahead of time. Keep it in the refrigerator with plastic wrap pressed all over the top to keep it from turning brown.

146. BUFFALO CHICKEN DIP

Prep Time: 30 Minutes | Cook Time: 40 Minutes | Total Time: 1 Hour 10 Minutes | Serving: 8

Ingredients

- 2 cups of shredded mozzarella cheese divided
- 3/4 cup of hot sauce(used Crystal)
- 1 8-ounce brick cream cheese, softened
- carrot, celery sticks, scoop chips suggestions
- 1 cup of blue cheese dressing
- 3 cups of shredded cooked chicken

Instructions

1. Set oven temperature to 350 degrees F.
2. Beat cream cheese in the stand mixer until smooth and creamy.
3. Add the hot sauce, blue cheese dressing, and 1 1/2 cups of mozzarella cheese. Mix on the slowest setting. Quit and clean the bowl. Mix until everything comes together.
4. Mix in the chicken by stirring.
5. Pour into a 2-quart baking dish, then sprinkle with the final 1/2 cup of cheese.
6. Bake for around 30–40 minutes or until bubbling and hot. Serve with celery and carrot sticks or chips.

147. MASHED POTATO

Prep Time: 20 Minutes | Cook Time: 20 Minutes | Total Time: 40 Minutes | Serving: 4

Ingredients

- 1 tbsp butter
- 4 tbsp Milk
- 8 large potatoes
- Salt/pepper/seasoning as required

Instructions

1. Peel and chop potatoes into equal-sized pieces.
2. Put the potatoes in a big pot of cold water, rinse them to remove extra starch, and drain.
3. Pour the boiling kettle into the potato pan. Put on a hob or stovetop and simmer until a fork can be stuck in and pulled out easily.
4. Drain the potatoes and set them aside. Make sure they're dry before moving on.
5. Put the potatoes in your stand mixer and attach the flat beater.
6. Beat the potatoes on low (speeds 1-2) for 1 minute or until there are no more visible lumps.
7. Change your flat beater for a wire whisk.
8. Mix on high for one to two minutes until smooth.
9. Mix on medium until the milk and butter are absorbed.
10. Salt, pepper, and any other seasonings you like can be added.
11. Eat and have fun!

148. TACO DIP

Prep Time: 10 Minutes | Cook Time: 00 Minutes

Total Time: 10 Minutes | Serving: 16

Ingredients

- 3 avocados, cut into chunks
- 3 tbsp fresh cilantro, chopped
- 1/2 - 1 tsp coarse kosher salt, to taste
- 1/4 tsp ground cumin
- 1 medium clove garlic, minced
- 1/2 cup of finely chopped onion
- 2 Roma tomatoes, seeded and diced
- 1 lime juiced 2-3 tbsp
- 1-2 tbsp finely minced jalapeno optional

Instructions

1. Combine the sour cream, cream cheese, and taco seasoning in a medium bowl. To make the mixture smoother, you can use a stand mixer.
2. Spread this mixture into a pie plate or round serving dish with a diameter of 9 inches. Shredded lettuce goes on top of the sour cream and cream cheese mix; sprinkle shredded lettuce, cheddar cheese, tomatoes, and black olives. Serve with chips made of corn.

149. MARGARITA DIP

Prep Time: 10 Minutes | Cook Time: 00 Minutes

Total Time: 10 Minutes | Serving: 16

Ingredients

- 2 tbsp fresh orange juice
- 2 tbsp lime juice
- ½ cup of powdered sugar
- 1 8-ounce block of room-temperature cream cheese
- Tostitos Sopapilla chips
- 4 tbsp unsalted butter
- ½ cup of heavy whipping cream
- ¼ tsp salt
- ¼ tsp vanilla extract
- Zest of one lime finely chopped
- 3 tbsp tequila optional

Instructions

1. Mix all of the ingredients for the dip in a bowl the day before you want to serve it. Whip the dip with a stand mixer until it is fluffy and light.
2. Put the dip in a bowl and put a lid on it. Keep overnight in the refrigerator.
3. Serve with Tostitos Sopapilla or Tostitos Cantina chips the next day.

150. BACON JALAPENO CHEESE DIP

Prep Time: 10 Minutes | Cook Time: 5 Minutes

Total Time: 15 Minutes | Serving: 6-8

Ingredients

- ¼ cup of crumbled bacon cooked crisp & drained
- 2-4 jalapenos, chopped, seeded & roasted
- 8 ounce cream cheese, softened
- ranch seasoning to taste
- ½ cup of cheddar cheese, grated

Instructions

1. To make this dip hot, heat the broiler to 500 degrees.
2. Add your bacon and jalapeno to a pan to get crispy; the flavors can mix. Take the food off the heat and put it on a paper towel to soak up the grease.
3. Cream cheese and shredded cheese should be put in the stand mixer. Mix slowly. Use a spatula to push the sides down.
4. Add ranch seasoning to the mix. Work on high to mix the cheeses and make a texture like whipped cream.
5. Add bacon & jalapenos. Mix with a spatula.
6. Move to an oven-safe dish and broil until the desired crispness is reached. If you want to serve it cold, put it in the fridge. You can also make a ball after a few hours.

151. CREAM CHEESE FRUIT DIP

Prep Time: 5 Minutes | Cook Time: 00 Minutes

Total Time: 5 Minutes | Serving: 1

Ingredients

- ¼ cup of powdered sugar
- 4 ounce cream cheese, room temperature
- 1 tsp. vanilla extract
- Serve with fresh fruit, graham crackers, and cookies

Instructions

1. Put all of the ingredients into the bowl of a stand mixer.
2. Mix or blend until everything is combined and smooth. Serve with anything you like, like fresh fruit and crackers.

152. CHOCOLATE CHIP COOKIE DOUGH DIP

Prep Time: 5 Minutes | Cook Time: 00 Minutes

Total Time: 5 Minutes | Serving: 10

Ingredients

- 1/3 cup of packed light brown sugar
- 1/2 cup of powdered sugar
- 1 1/2 tsp vanilla extract
- 1 8-ounce block of room-temperature cream cheese
- 1 cup of mini chocolate chips
- temperature
- honey graham crackers, animal crackers, chocolate graham crackers

Instructions

1. First, mix softened butter and cream cheese on medium speed with a stand mixer in a medium-sized bowl until the mixture is smooth.
2. Now, mix together the brown sugar, vanilla extract, and powdered sugar while the mixer is on low speed. Mix until everything is well blended.
3. Add mini chocolate chips and stir.
4. Serve with graham crackers to dip!

153. SPINACH ARTICHOKE DIP

Prep Time: 10 Minutes | Cook Time: 20 Minutes | Total Time: 30 Minutes | Serving: 8-10

Ingredients

- 1 cup of fresh spinach, Chopped
- 1/2 cup of Shredded Parmesan and Romano Cheese
- 1/2 tsp pepper
- 1 cup of marinated artichoke hearts, chopped
- 2 tsp fresh thyme
- 1 Brick Cream Cheese
- 1 tsp salt
- 1/2 cup of Mayonnaise
- 1/2 cup of Sour Cream

Instructions

1. Heat your oven to 325 degrees.
2. Put the cream cheese, mayonnaise, and sour cream in the bowl of an electric mixer with a paddle attachment. Salt, pepper, and fresh thyme should be added while the mixer is on low speed.
3. Chop the spinach and artichoke hearts as you mix.
4. Stop the mixer and use a spoon or rubber scraper to mix the spinach, artichoke hearts, and shredded cheese.
5. Pour into a dish that can go in the oven and bake for about 20 minutes to warm everything up.

154. CRAB DIP

Prep Time: 10 Minutes | Cook Time: 25 Minutes

Total Time: 35 Minutes | Serving: 8

Ingredients

- 1/2 cup of (120g) sour cream
- 1 and 3/4 tsp Old Bay seasoning
- 8 ounces (226g) full-fat brick cream cheese, softened to room temperature
- 1 tsp lemon juice
- 2 tsp Worcestershire sauce
- 1/2 tsp ground mustard
- 1 pound fresh lump crab meat
- 1/4 cup of (60g) mayonnaise
- 1 and 1/4 cups of (155g) shredded cheddar cheese divided
- Optional: 2 dashes of hot sauce (or to taste)

Instructions

1. Set oven temperature to 375°F (191°C).
2. In a big mixing bowl with a paddle attachment, combine the cream cheese on medium-high speed for around 1 minute until it is smooth and creamy.
3. Mix in the mayonnaise, sour cream, 1 cup of cheddar cheese, ground mustard, lemon juice, Old Bay seasoning, Worcestershire sauce, and hot sauce (if using). Beat on medium to high speed until everything is mixed. Mix in the lump crab meat gently with a spoon or rubber spatula. If you used hot sauce, taste it, and then, if you want, add more hot sauce.
4. Move to a 9-inch baking pan, pie dish, or skillet that can go in the oven. Put the last 1/4 cup of cheddar cheese on top.
5. Bake for 25 minutes or until the edges are hot and bubbling.
6. Warm is best.
7. Cover leftovers and put them in the fridge for up to 5 days. Reheat in the microwave or oven to 350°F (177°C) until warm.

155. BEAN DIP

Prep Time: 10 Minutes | Cook Time: 15 Minutes

Total Time: 25 Minutes | Serving: 12

Ingredients

- ¼ cup of jalapenos chopped, optional
- 4 ounce mild green chiles diced and drained
- ½ cup of sour cream
- ½ package taco seasoning
- 4 ounces of cream cheese softened
- 3 cups of cheddar cheese divided
- 16 ounces of refried beans canned
- 2 green onions divided

Instructions

1. Turn oven on to 375°F.
2. Cut green onions so that the white and green parts are separate. Set aside the green part.
3. Mix the cream cheese, refried beans, taco seasoning, and sour cream with the stand mixer until they are fluffy.
4. Add the whites of the onions, the jalapenos, the chiles, and 2 cups of cheddar cheese.
5. Spread in an 8x8-inch or 2-quart baking dish.
6. Add the rest of the cheese on top, and make for 20–25 minutes, or until hot and the cheese is melted.
7. As a finishing touch, sprinkle the remaining green onions on top. Serve with chips made of corn.

156. CORN DIP

Prep Time: 5 Minutes | Cook Time: 20 Minutes

Total Time: 25 Minutes | Serving: 8-10

Ingredients

- 2 cups of shredded pepper jack cheese divided
- 2 cloves garlic minced
- 1 jalapeno pepper chopped
- 4 ounces low-fat feta cheese
- 1/2 cup of sour cream
- 30 ounces canned corn, fully drained and rinsed
- 2 tbsp Frank's red hot sauce or your favorite wing sauce
- 2 tbsp juice from one lime
- 1/2 cup of fresh cilantro chopped
- 16 ounces 2 blocks low-fat cream cheese, softened
- 2 tbsp red onion chopped
- Favorite chips for dipping

Instructions

1. Turn the oven on to 350F.
2. Mix the 1 cup of the shredded chees, cream cheese, sour cream, garlic, hot sauce, and lime juice, and 1 in a stand mixer. Mix until everything is well mixed.
3. Put the cream cheese mixture in a large bowl and put the remaining one cup of cheese, the corn, feta, pepper, onion, and cilantro. Stir to combine.
4. Put the mixture into a baking dish that has been set up. If you want, you can add more cheese.
5. Bake for around 15-20 minutes or until the cheese is bubbly and hot. Add more cilantro, feta, and hot sauce to the top.Eat with chips and have a good time!

157. FRENCH DIP

Prep Time: 15 Minutes | Cook Time: 15 Minutes

Total Time: 30 Minutes | Serving: 32

Ingredients

- 2 cans of crescent roll dough
- 4 tbsp unsalted butter, melted
- parsley for garnish, optional
- 3 cups of cold water
- 8 ounce block of softened cream cheese, room temperature
- 1-ounce package au jus gravy
- 1 tbsp onion soup mix, divided use
- ½ pound sliced roast beef, 1/2 inch diced
- 4 ounces sliced provolone cheese, 1/2 inch diced

Instructions

1. Set the oven temperature to 375°F. Put parchment paper on two sheet trays and set them aside.
2. Mix the roast beef, cream cheese, provolone, and 1/2 tbsp of the onion soup in a big bowl using the stand mixer.
3. Unroll one piece of crescent dough at a time and cut it into triangles.
4. Cut each triangle in half, making two long triangles.
5. Put 1 heaping tsp of the filling on the bottom, wider part of the crescent roll.
6. Start with the widest part of the dough and roll it over the filling to make a crescent shape. Put it on the sheet tray that has been set up.
7. Repeat with the rest of the filling and dough, putting them on the sheet trays so they don't touch each other.
8. Now, mix the melted butter and the rest of the onion soup mix in a small bowl with a whisk.Brush the butter mixture all over the crescent dough out in the open.
9. Bake for 11 to 13 minutes or until the top is golden.
10. While the puffs are in the oven, mix the au jus gravy with the water according to the directions on the back of the package.
11. If you want, you can top the puffs with fresh parsley and serve them right away.

158. SWEET CREAM CHEESE DIP

Prep Time: 15 Minutes | Cook Time: 00 Minutes

Total Time: 15 Minutes | Serving: 6

Ingredients

- 2 tbsp heavy cream half and half or whole milk can be liked
- 1 cup of powdered sugar whisked to remove lumps
- 1/2 tsp vanilla extract optional
- 3 tbsp unsalted butter softened
- 4 ounce softened cream cheese at room temperature
- pinch of kosher salt

Instructions

1. First, put cream cheese and butter in a bowl and mix them. Then, combine cream cheese and butter on medium speed in a stand mixer until smooth and fluffy.
2. Blend in the powdered sugar, vanilla, and salt until mixed.
3. Add heavy cream and beat for around 2 minutes until smooth.
4. Store in the fridge in a container that won't let air in, or use right away.
5. You can also heat dip in the microwave for a warm glaze.

159. 7 LAYER DIP

Prep Time: 20 Minutes | Cook Time: 10 Minutes

Total Time: 30 Minutes | Serving: 16

Ingredients

- 4 tbsp taco seasoning, divided
- 8 ounces sour cream
- 1 medium white onion, diced (use yellow, green or purple onion)
- 2 Roma tomatoes, diced
- 4 ounces cream cheese, softened
- 16 ounces of refried beans
- 1 pound ground beef, cooked
- 1 ½ cups of shredded Mexican cheese
- 1 ½ cups of shredded lettuce, washed

Instructions

1. On the stovetop, cook one pound of ground beef on medium heat until it is no longer pink. Mix 3 to 4 tbsp of water and 2 tbsp of taco seasoning. Mix things up. Set to side.
2. Put 1/3 cup of water or milk in a small glass bowl. Stir it in the microwave for 45 to 60 seconds, or heat it in a medium pot on low heat on the stove. As the first layer, spread refried beans on the bottom of a 9x13 glass dish.
3. On top of the seasoned beef, spread more seasoned beef.
4. Warm up 4 ounces of cream cheese for 15 to 25 seconds in a bowl that can go in the microwave. Put in 8 ounces of sour cream. Mix the two cheeses with a hand-held mixer until the mixture is light and creamy. Mix in 2 tsp of taco seasoning. Mix things up. Spread a layer over the beef that has been seasoned.
5. Spread out 1 1/2 cups of shreds of cheese over the refried beans.
6. Spread out 2 cups of torn lettuce.
7. Choose what you want to put on the next layers. In the pictures above, the next layers are diced tomatoes, white onion, and purple onion.
8. Refrigerate for at least 60 minutes before serving.

160. BEER CHEESE DIP

Prep Time: 10 Minutes | Cook Time: 00 Minutes

Total Time: 10 Minutes | Serving: 4-6

Ingredients

- Loaf of crusty bread
- 16 ounce cream cheese
- 3 to 6 ounce of beer (1/4 to 1/2 a bottle)
- One 14 ounce container of spreadable cheddar cheese

Instructions

1. Put cream cheese in a stand mixer with a flat beater attachment and mix slowly to medium speed.
2. Slowly add cheddar cheese that can be spread, and keep mixing.
3. Add up to half a beer or more until the consistency is right.
4. Make a hole in the loaf of bread and save the extra to dip. Cut more bread because that's not enough.
5. Put cheese in the hole in the bread.

161. CHICKEN WING DIP

Prep Time: 10 Minutes | Cook Time: 20 Minutes | Total Time: 30 Minutes | Serving: 12

Ingredients

- 2 cups of (8 ounces) shredded sharp cheddar
- 2 cups of diced cooked chicken
- ½ cup of blue cheese dressing
- 1 (8-ounce) package of room-temperature cream cheese
- ½ cup of Buffalo wing sauce
- ¼ cup of crumbled blue cheese, optional

Instructions

1. Put the rack in the middle of the oven and heat it to 350°F.
2. Now, beat the cream cheese until it is smooth in a large bowl. Mix in the wing sauce, bleu cheese dressing, diced chicken, 1 cup of shredded cheese, and blue cheese crumbles (if using). Spread in a 1-quart shallow baking dish and top with the rest of the shredded cheese.
3. Bake for 20 to 25 minutes, or until the cheese is bubbly. Serve warm with whatever you want to dip.

162. CREAM CHEESE SALSA DIP

Prep Time: 10 Minutes | Cook Time: 00 Minutes | Total Time: 10 Minutes | Serving: 10-12

Ingredients

- 8 ounce container sour cream
- 8ounce block cream cheese, softened
- 15.5 ounce jar medium spice salsa
- 2 1/2 cups of shreds of sharp Cheddar cheese
- 1/2 cup of diced white onions

Instructions

1. First, Leave the cream cheese on the counter for 30 minutes to soften it. Doing this will help it mix well with the sour cream. Put the softened cream cheese and 8ounce of sour cream in a medium bowl. Blend until smooth with the stand mixer. It's fine if there are a few lumps, but you want it to be mostly smooth. If you have one, you can also use a stand mixer.
2. Pour the cream cheese and sour cream mixture into your serving dish and spread it to cover the whole bottom. You want the edge of the dish to be higher than the dip, like the pie plate in the picture. It will keep the liquid from the salsa from running off the plate and onto your table when it separates. Next, pour the whole jar of salsa on top and spread it out to cover the cream cheese and sour cream mixture. Next, put all the Cheddar cheese shreds on the salsa. Dice the onions and sprinkle them on top.
3. Serve with the chips you like and enjoy!

163. FRENCH ONION DIP

Prep Time: 5 Minutes | Additional Time: 1 Hour | Total Time: 1 Hour 5 Minutes | Serving: 12

Ingredients

- 8 ounces block-style cream cheese, softened
- 1-ounce onion soup mix, (1 packet)
- 1/2 cup of sour cream

Instructions

1. First, mix the sour cream and onion soup in the stand mixer until they are well-mixed and creamy. Put the cream cheese and mix until everything is smooth and well combined.
2. Serve right away with crisp crackers, fresh vegetables, or pretzels. Any leftovers can be kept in the fridge for around 5 days.

164. PULLED PORK DIP

Prep Time: 15 Minutes | Cook Time: 30 Minutes

Total Time: 45 Minutes | Serving: 8-10

Ingredients

- 1 cup of shredded mozzarella
- 1/2 cup of sour cream
- 1/4 cup of your favorite BBQ sauce
- 1 jalapeno, minced
- 8 ounce block cream cheese, room temperature
- 1 cup of shredded cheddar cheese
- 2 cups of leftover pulled pork
- 2 cloves garlic, minced

Instructions

1. Turn the oven on to 350f.
2. Put pulled pork in the bowl of your stand mixer with a paddle beater. Using a medium-high speed, beat the pork to break it into smaller pieces.
3. Mix in softened cream cheese, sour cream, BBQ sauce, shredded cheddar, and garlic. Beat well until everything is mixed together, scraping the sides of the bowl as needed.
4. Move the pulled pork dip to a 10" cast iron skillet or 9" by 9" baking dish, and jalapenos and mozzarella cheese go on top.
5. Bake at 350F for around 25–30 minutes, or until the dip is hot and the edges begin to brown.
6. If you want, broil the dip at 450 degrees for 2 to 3 minutes or until the mozzarella has melted and bubbled.
7. Take out of the oven and serve with pita chips, tortilla chips, crackers, sliced baguette, or vegetables!

165. APPLESAUCE

Prep Time: 5 Minutes | Cook Time: 15 Minutes

Total Time: 20 Minutes | Serving: 4-6

Ingredients

- 0,7 kg apples
- 83,3 ml water

Instructions

1. Wash and cut the apples into fourths.
2. Put the apples and water in a big pot and cook until they are soft and mushy.
3. Attach the Strainer for Vegetables and Fruit to the stand mixer. Pull the strainer through the apples.
4. Eat immediately or store in the refrigerator a container that keeps air out.

166. MAYONNAISE

Prep Time: 12 Minutes | Cook Time: 00 Minutes

Total Time: 12 Minutes | Serving: 1

Ingredients

- 240 ml Sunflower Oil
- 1 tsp Salt
- 1 tbsp Dijon Mustard
- 1 Egg
- 1 tbsp white wine vinegar

Instructions

1. Put a whole egg in a stand mixer with a whisk attachment and turn the power up. Let it break the egg up until it starts to foam. Turn the speed back up to high after adding the Dijon mustard. Add the salt and vinegar. Let the machine run for a minute or two to mix in a lot of air.
2. Add the oil slowly, and I mean slow. Keep the mixer going fast, and add just a drop at a time at first. Slowly, please! Once the mixture gets thicker, add more oil to make a very fine stream. If you go too fast, the emulsion will break, so the slower you go, the better.
3. Let the machine run until the consistency you want is reached. Stop the machine and put your homemade mayonnaise in a container that can be sealed again. It will last a week in the fridge.

167. RAW CRANBERRY SAUCE

Prep Time: 5 Minutes | Cook Time: 1 Hour

Total Time: 1 Hour 5 Minutes | Serving: 6-8

Ingredients

- 2 tsp grated orange zest, preferably organic
- 12 ounce fresh cranberries, rinsed and patted dry
- 12 ounce (about 1 2/3 cups of) granulated sugar

Instructions

1. First, using the stand mixer with a paddle attachment, mix the cranberries, sugar, and zest at a very low speed for at least an hour or until the cranberries break down.
2. Cover the citrus cranberry sauce and put it in the fridge for at least two hours and up to two days.

168. HOLLANDAISE SAUCE

Prep Time: 10 Minutes | Cook Time: 00 Minutes

Total Time: 10 Minutes | Serving: 4-6

Ingredients

- 1 TBSP lemon or lime juice
- 8 TBSP of butter (1/2 cup of or whole cube)
- 3 egg yolks
- A couple of dashes of cayenne pepper (Tabasco or Frank's Red Hot works too)
- Optional: ½ tsp mustard

Instructions

1. First, put the eggs, lemon juice, and cayenne pepper into the bowl of the stand mixer. Blend for around 2 minutes on medium speed.
2. While this is being mixed, melt the butter in the microwave or stove until it is completely hot. Putting the butter in the mixer while it's still hot is important.
3. Then, turn the mixer or blender to high speed and mix or blend for about 4-5 minutes until the hollandaise has a nice creamy texture.
4. Then put it right into your favorite dish, recipe, or vegetable (like asparagus) and serve it immediately.

169. TOMATO SAUCE

Prep Time: 30 Minutes | Cook Time: 3 Hours

Total Time: 3 Hours 30 Minutes | Serving: 36 ounce

Ingredients

- 2-3 olive oil
- 40 ripe plum tomatoes, cut into large chunks
- ¼ large yellow onion, diced
- 1 large sprig fresh basil
- 2 cloves fresh garlic, minced
- Maldon sea salt flakes

Instructions

1. Chop your plum tomatoes into big pieces to start getting them ready.
2. Put about a tbsp of olive oil in a big stockpot on the stove over medium-high heat. Add the tomato chunks and stir them every so often.
3. Cook the tomatoes for about 10 to 12 minutes or until they are soft and have given off their water. While the tomatoes are cooking, heat the oven to 225°F and put tin foil on a baking sheet with a rim.
4. Using the vegetable strainer for the stand mixer
5. Use a vegetable mill on cooked tomatoes. Keep the juice, but throw away the skin and seeds.
6. The liquid from the cooked plum tomatoes should be split into three parts:
7. Part 1 is the part with the tomato paste. Pour about 2 cups of, or one-third of your liquid, onto the baking sheet you've lined. If your baking sheet is too big and the sauce is spread too thin, you can make it smaller by folding up the edges of the tin foil. Makes sure that the paste cooks evenly and doesn't catch on fire.
8. Take the baking sheet in the oven, check on it every 15 to 20 minutes, and stir the food. The puree will start to become a paste.
9. Just take 1 cup of the liquid from the cooked tomato puree and put it aside.
10. Add diced onion and minced garlic to a stockpot with about a tbsp of olive oil and heat it over medium-low heat. Stir and cook for 1-2 minutes, until the food smells good. Add the rest of the cooked tomato purée to this pot and let it simmer. The sauce will start to thicken and reduce.
11. When the sauce has thickened, remove the heat and add a sprig of basil. Let it sit for 5–10 minutes, then throw it away.
12. When the tomato paste has thickened and the purée on the stove has reduced and finished steeping, they are ready to be mixed. Mix tomato paste into the sauce in the stock pot.

FROSTINGS

170. CHOCOLATE BUTTERCREAM FROSTING

Prep Time: 10 Minutes | Cook Time: 00 Minutes

Total Time: 10 Minutes | Serving: 16

Ingredients

- 2 tsp vanilla
- 1 ½ cups of butter, softened 3 sticks
- Pinch of salt
- 1 cup of unsweetened cocoa powder
- 4-6 tbsp heavy cream or whole milk
- 4-5 cups of powdered sugar

Instructions

1. In the bowl of a stand mixer with the whisk attachment or with a hand mixer, mix the butter and cocoa powder until they are smooth.
2. Mix in half of the powdered sugar while mixing at a medium speed. Take the rest of the powdered sugar, the vanilla, and the salt. Mix well, scraping the bowl as needed.
3. Now, add heavy cream or milk, 1–2 tbsp at a time, mixing well after each addition until the frosting is the right consistency for spreading or piping but still holds its shape.

171. VANILLA BUTTERCREAM FROSTING

Prep Time: 25 Minutes | Cook Time: 00 Minutes | Total Time: 25 Minutes | Serving: 24

Ingredients

- 1 tsp pure vanilla extract
- 1 cup of unsalted butter, softened
- 4 cups of powdered sugar or 16 ounces
- ¼ cup of heavy whipping cream or 3 tbsp milk

Instructions

1. With the stand mixer on medium speed, beat softened butter. Beat for 3 minutes or until the mixture is smooth and creamy.
2. While the mixer is on low, add the powdered sugar, cream, and vanilla extract. Turn up the speed to high and keep beating for 3 minutes. Note: You can add more cream if the frosting is too thick. Just add a tbsp at a time and mix well until the consistency is right for you.
3. Now, the cake is ready to be filled and iced. Or you can decorate cupcakes with it. You'll have enough frosting for a two-layer cake with a diameter of 8 inches or 24 cupcakes.

172. BUTTERCREAM FROSTING

Prep Time: 15 Minutes | Cook Time: 00 Minutes | Total Time: 15 Minutes | Serving: 2

Ingredients

Plain Buttercream:

- 3 Cups of Powdered Sugar
- 2 Sticks Salted Butte

For Maple Buttercream:

- Additional 1/2 Cup of Powdered Sugar
- 6 Tb Pure Maple Syrup

Instructions

1. Whip the butter for 30 seconds in a stand mixer with a whisk attachment.
2. Take 1 cup of powdered sugar at a time. Mix slowly, increase to medium/high, and scrape the sides between each addition. Each time you add sugar, mix for 30 seconds.
3. Stop and scrape down the sides. (3 cups of for plain frosting or 3.5 cups of for maple buttercream.) If you want to, add the maple syrup now.
4. (Add 1-2 tsp of vanilla paste or extract for vanilla buttercream frosting.)
5. Mix for 3 to 4 minutes on medium or high speed. The frosting will be fluffy and smooth.
6. Put your cake in the fridge for 5 minutes before you frost it.
7. Refrigerate any leftover frosting in a container that won't let air in.

173. CREAM CHEESE FROSTING

Prep Time: 30 Minutes | Cook Time: 00 Minutes | Total Time: 30 Minutes | Serving: 3

Ingredients

- 8 ounces Cream Cheese, softened
- 1 cup of butter, softened
- 1 tbsp vanilla extract
- 2-4 Tbsp Milk or Heavy Cream
- 4 cups of powdered sugar

Instructions

1. Put the butter that has been softened into the stand mixer's bowl that has a whisk attachment.
2. Beat the butter for one to two minutes.
3. Beat for 1 minute after adding the softened cream cheese.
4. Combine the powdered sugar one cup of at a time, beating between each addition.
5. Add the vanilla extract and whip the frosting for 2 to 3 minutes until it is light and fluffy.
6. If your frosting is too thick, mix milk or 1 tbsp of cream at a time until you get the right consistency.
7. Serve with your favorite baked goods, such as cupcakes, cinnamon rolls, cakes, and cookies.

174. PEANUT BUTTER FROSTING

Prep Time: 10 Minutes | Cook Time: 00 Minutes

Total Time: 10 Minutes | Serving:

Ingredients

- 1/4 cup of heavy whipping cream
- 4 1/2 cups of powdered sugar
- 1 tsp pure vanilla extract
- 3/4 cup of creamy peanut butter (no stir)
- 1 cup of (2 sticks) unsalted butter, softened

Instructions

1. Put the butter and peanut butter in the stand mixer's bowl with a paddle attachment. Mix on a medium-low speed until everything is mixed. A few small bits of butter are fine.
2. Now, add 2 1/2 cups of powdered sugar and mix on low until most of it is mixed.
3. Take the vanilla extract and the rest of the sugar. Mix in half the whipped cream.
4. On low speed, beat until the sugar is mixed in. Clean out the bowl, then add the rest of the whipped cream.
5. Slowly increase the speed to medium-high once the cream has been mixed in. Two minutes of beating. The frosting will be soft and fluffy.

175. WHITE FROSTING

Prep Time: 10 Minutes | Cook Time: 3 Minutes

Total Time: 20 Minutes | Serving: 5

Ingredients

- 1 2/3 cup of granulated sugar
- 1 tsp vanilla
- 5 large egg whites
- 1/2 tsp cream of tartar

Instructions

1. Clean your mixer's bowl and whisk with lemon juice or vinegar.
2. Now, combine the egg whites, cream of tartar, and sugar in the stand mixer's bowl.
3. Place the bowl over a pot with 1 to 2 inches of simmering water and stir the mixture constantly with a whisk until it is hot, no longer grainy to the touch, and a candy thermometer reads 160F. It should take about 2 to 3 minutes.
4. Put the bowl on your stand mixer and whip on medium-high for about 5 to 7 minutes or until the meringue is stiff.
5. While the meringue is being whipped, slowly pour in the vanilla. Taste and add more flavoring if desired

176. COOKIE FROSTING

Prep Time: 5 Minutes | Cook Time: 00 Minutes

Total Time: 5 Minutes | Serving: 12

Ingredients
- 1 tsp vanilla extract
- 4 ounces cream cheese (softened)
- ½ cup of unsalted butter (softened)
- ¼ tsp almond extract
- 1 ¼ cups of powdered sugar

Instructions
1. In a large bowl, beat the butter and cream cheese with a stand mixer (with the paddle attachment) at medium speed for around 2-3 minutes or until the mixture is light and smooth.
2. Add the vanilla extract, almond extract, and powdered sugar slowly while the mixer is on medium speed. Once everything is mixed in, turn the mixer to high speed and beat for around 2 minutes until the mixture is light and fluffy.
3. Spread or pipe frosting on cooled cookies, then sprinkle with sugar.

177. WHIPPED CREAM FROSTING

Prep Time: 10 Minutes | Cook Time: 00 Minutes

Total Time: 10 Minutes | Serving: 20

Ingredients
- ½ tsp almond extract
- 1 (8-ounce) package of softened low-fat cream cheese
- 1 tsp vanilla extract
- 2 cups of heavy cream
- ½ cup of white sugar

Instructions
1. First, combine cream cheese, sugar, almond, and vanilla extracts in a stand mixer's bowl. Mix until smooth with the whisk attachment on medium speed.
2. Slowly pour in heavy cream while the mixer is running. Stop every so often and scrape the bottom of the bowl. Whip cream continuously until a stiff peak forms.

178. CARAMEL BUTTERCREAM FROSTING

Prep Time: 10 Minutes | Cook Time: 00 Minutes

Total Time: 10 Minutes | Serving: 24

Ingredients

- 1-2 tbsp heavy cream
- 4 cups of powdered sugar
- 1 tsp vanilla extract
- 1/3 cup of caramel topping
- 1 cup of butter, softened
- pinch of salt

Instructions

1. Using the paddle attached to the stand mixer, combine the butter until soft and fluffy.
2. Mix in the vanilla, caramel topping, and salt until all mixed in.
3. Mix in the powdered sugar slowly.
4. Add as much cream as you want. Mix on medium-high speed for at least 2 minutes or until the mixture is light and fluffy.
5. Add a little more cream or powdered sugar to change the final texture.

179. LEMON BUTTERCREAM FROSTING

Prep Time: 5 Minutes | Cook Time: 10 Minutes

Total Time: 15 Minutes | Serving: 12

Ingredients

- ¼ cup of shortening
- 3 cups of powdered sugar
- ¾ cup of unsalted butter softened
- 2 lemons
- ½ tsp of lemon extract, optional

Instructions

1. Then, set the lemon zest aside. Get two tbsp of juice from one of the lemons. Save the rest of the lemon for something else.
2. Mix the butter and shortening at medium speed in the bowl of a stand mixer until the mixture is light and fluffy. Add the lemon zest, lemon juice (and lemon extract, if you're using it), and a pinch of salt. Blend well.
3. Add 1/2 cup of powdered sugar at a time and beat until the mixture is light and fluffy.
4. Now, add more powdered sugar to make it thicker. If you need to, add more lemon juice to soften the texture.

180. STRAWBERRY FROSTING

Prep Time: 10 Minutes | Cook Time: 00 Minutes

Total Time: 10 Minutes | Serving: 3

Ingredients

- 4 cups of (480g) confectioners sugar
- 1/4 cup of (60ml) of heavy cream or whole milk, at room temperature
- salt, to taste
- 1 tsp pure vanilla extract
- 1 cup of (230g) of unsalted butter, softened to room temperature
- 1 cup of (about 25g) freeze-dried strawberries

Instructions

1. Use a blender or food processor to turn the freeze-dried strawberries into a fine powder. About 1/2 cup of should be enough. A fine mesh sieve can be used to separate bigger seeds or pieces if they aren't getting small enough. Set aside.
2. In a big bowl, beat the butter at medium-high speed for about 2 minutes with a paddle-equipped stand mixer. Add confectioners' sugar, strawberry powder, heavy cream or milk, and vanilla. After 30 seconds on low speed, switch to high speed and beat for 2 minutes. Taste it. Add 1–2 more tbsp of heavy cream or milk if you want to thin it out. If the frosting is too sweet, take a pinch of salt.
3. Use it immediately, or put a tight lid on it and store it in the fridge for up to a week or in the freezer for up to 3 months. After freezing the frosting, let it thaw in the refrigerator for a few hours, then beat it at medium speed for a few seconds to make it creamy again. If necessary, thin out the frosting once more after defrosting or chilling by beating in a little heavy cream or milk.

181. VEGAN BUTTERCREAM FROSTING

Prep Time: 5 Minutes | Cook Time: 00 Minutes

Total Time: 5 Minutes | Serving: 7

Ingredients

- 1 tsp. vanilla extract
- 8 cups of (1120 g) powdered sugar, sifted
- 2-3 tbsp dairy-free milk
- 2 cups of (432 g) of vegan butter, room temperature

Instructions

1. Cream the vegan butter in the stand mixer's bowl with a whisk attachment until it is light and fluffy. It will start to get lighter. It should take about two to three minutes.
2. Combine 1 cup of powdered sugar at a time, mixing well after each addition. Start slowly and speed it up as the powdered sugar is mixed into the vegan butter. At this point, the mix should be smooth but thick. Add a tbsp of dairy-free milk if the powdered sugar isn't mixing in.
3. Add the vanilla extract and the last two tbsp of dairy-free milk, and beat again until fluffy and light.
4. Use on your cake, cupcakes, or macarons! This amount of frosting is enough to cover an 8-inch or 6-inch cake generously, with extra for decorating.
5. If you have any leftovers, put them in an airtight container in the refrigerator for around 5 days or in the freezer for up to 3 months. When you're ready to use the buttercream again, let it return to room temperature and mix it lightly for 2 to 3 minutes.

182. COOL WHIP FROSTING

Prep Time: 5 Minutes | Cook Time: 00 Minutes

Total Time: 5 Minutes | Serving: 6

Ingredients

- ½ cup of (1 stick) butter, softened
- 8 ounces cream cheese, softened
- 1 tbsp of pure vanilla extract
- 6 cups of powdered sugar
- 8 ounce cool whip, cold but not frozen

Instructions

1. First, add the cream cheese, softened butter, and vanilla to a stand mixer's bowl with a paddle attachment. At medium speed, beat until the mixture is light and fluffy, which takes about 2 minutes.
2. While the mixer is on low speed, carefully add the powdered sugar. When all powdered sugar is mixed in, scrape down the sides of the bowl, and then return the mixer to medium speed and combine until the mixture is fluffy around 1 minute.
3. Then, add the cool whip and mix at medium speed until everything is combined, around 30 seconds.
4. Put the frosting in a piping bag and use it immediately.

183. FROSTING RECIPE WITHOUT BUTTER

Prep Time: 10 Minutes | Cook Time: 00 Minutes | Total Time: 10 Minutes | Serving: 4

Ingredients

- ½ tsp Kosher salt
- 2 tbsp vanilla extract
- 2 tbsp heavy cream
- 1 pound (450 g) Powdered sugar
- ½ tsp lemon juice
- 2 tbsp cornstarch (or tapioca starch)
- 1 pound (450 g) Cream cheese

Instructions

1. Mix cream cheese, lemon juice, cornstarch, salt, and heavy cream for one minute with the paddle attachment on medium speed in the bowl of a stand mixer.
2. Add powdered sugar gradually, one cup of at a time, until you've used all of it. Then, add the vanilla extract and whip for another 1 to 2 minutes on medium-high until the mixture is smooth, light, and fluffy.
3. Change the consistency by adding a few tbsp of powdered sugar or a few tbsp of heavy cream.

184. COCONUT FROSTING RECIPE

Prep Time: 10 Minutes | Cook Time: 00 Minutes

Total Time: 10 Minutes | Serving:

Ingredients

- 3 ½ cups of powdered sugar
- 2 tbsp of coconut cream
- Pinch of fine sea salt
- 1 tsp pure vanilla extract
- 1 cup of butter, softened
- ½ tsp coconut extract

Instructions

1. First, combine the butter in a stand mixer's bowl with a paddle attachment until smooth.
2. Now, add 1/2 of the powdered sugar and a pinch of sea salt. Beat on low speed until most of the sugar is mixed in. Take the rest of the powdered sugar and mix on low until everything is mixed. Beat for 3 minutes with a medium speed.
3. Stop the mixer and clean the bowl with a spatula. Add the vanilla extract, coconut extract, and coconut cream, and beat for another minute on low. Raise the speed to medium once the cream and extracts are mixed in.
4. Use for cakes, cupcakes, or any other baked goods you like.

185. CHOCOLATE CREAM CHEESE FROSTING

Prep Time: 5 Minutes | Cook Time: 00 Minutes | Total Time: 5 Minutes | Serving: 2

Ingredients

- 1 1/2 – 3 cups of powdered sugar, or erythritol for keto
- 8-ounce cream cheese or vegan cream cheese
- 1/2 cup of cocoa powder
- 1 1/2 tsp pure vanilla extract
- 1/4 cup of butter or vegan butter
- 2 – 4 tbsp milk of choice
- 2 ounce melted chocolate (Optional)

Instructions

1. Let the butter spread and cream cheese come to room temperature. Mix everything together in a stand mixer. If it's too thick, add more milk of choice very slowly. If the mixture is too thin, add more powdered sugar. Cover and store frosting in the refrigerator for up to a week.

186. CHOCOLATE FUDGE FROSTING

Prep Time: 15 Minutes | Cook Time: 00 Minutes | Total Time: 15 Minutes | Serving: 8

Ingredients

- ½ cup of corn syrup
- ¼ cup of coffee
- ½ tsp salt
- 2 cups of semisweet chocolate
- 2 cups of unsalted butter softened
- 2 cups of powdered sugar
- 1 tsp vanilla extract
- 1 cup of cocoa powder

Instructions

1. Combine the chocolate chips, coffee, vanilla, and corn syrup in a bowl that can go in the microwave.
2. Use the microwave to melt all of the chocolate together. Heat it for 30 seconds and stir, then heat it for 10 seconds at a time and stir until it is smooth and fully melted. Let the chocolate mix cool, but don't let it get too hard.
3. Mix the butter, sugar, cocoa powder, and salt in the stand mixer's bowl on high speed for around 1 minute until the mixture is light and fluffy.
4. Mix the chocolate mixture that has cooled down with the butter mixture until smooth.
5. Depending on the temperature, you will want the frosting to be a different consistency. If it is too stiff, stir it in the microwave for a few seconds. If it is too soft, put it in the fridge for a few minutes to firm up.
6. You can use the frosting immediately to cover a cake or put it in a piping bag to decorate.
7. It was kept at room temperature for 3 days with plastic wrap on top. If you want to keep it longer, put it in a container that won't let air in and put it in the fridge or freezer.

DOUGHS

187. SALT DOUGH

Prep Time: 15 Minutes | Cook Time: 60-90 Minutes | Total Time: 75-105 Minutes | Serving: 4

Ingredients

- 1 ½ cups of Water
- 4 cups of flour
- 1 cup of table salt

Instructions

1. First, heat the oven to 250°F (120°C) on the regular setting, not the fan-forced setting.
2. Put flour and salt in a large bowl or the bowl of your stand mixer. Mix it up nicely.
3. Make a well and pour the lukewarm water into the dry ingredients.
4. Stand mixer: Knead the dough for around 5 minutes on speed 3 with the hook attachment of the stand mixer. It's ready when the dough forms a ball and doesn't stick to the bowl's sides or bottom. If it does, sprinkle more flour on top until the dough is soft and smooth.

Rolling salt dough:

1. Cut the big ball of dough into four smaller balls. Small amounts are easier to roll.
2. Next, roll the dough between 2 pieces of parchment paper to prevent the rolling pin from leaving marks on the dough. It was more likely to happen with wooden rolling pins. You don't need the paper if you have a glass or silicone rolling pin.
3. Now, roll the dough out to around 1/4-1/2 inch thick. The longer it takes to bake, the thicker the dough is, but for handprints, it's better to have thicker dough so that the handprint shows up.
4. Use a cookie cutter to cut out round pieces of dough, and then use those pieces to make handprints, fossils of dinosaurs, or whatever else you want.

Drying salt dough:

1. Before putting thick ornaments or handprints in the oven, let them dry at room temperature overnight or for 3–4 days. Make sure the room is not too damp, or the dough will soften.
2. You can bake your creations immediately if they are small (less than 2 inches in diameter) and not too thick (1/4 inch thick).

Oven baking:

1. Place your creation on a baking sheet lined with parchment paper and bake for about 90 minutes, checking every 20 minutes after 60 minutes to see how drying is going. The dough should turn white, get hard around the edges, and then in the middle.

188. PIZZA DOUGH

Prep Time: 15 Minutes | Proving Time: 1 Hour | Total Time: 1 Hour 15 Minutes | Serving: 2

Ingredients

- 115 grams (4 ounces / ½ cup) plain flour / all-purpose flour
- 300 grams/ml (1 ¼ cups of) warm water
- 250 grams (8.8 ounce / 1½ cups of + 1 tbsp) bread flour
- 1 level tsp salt
- 1 level tsp instant dry yeast

Instructions

1. Put the yeast, water, flour, and salt in a stand mixer's bowl.
2. Now, start the stand mixer on low speed for around 30 seconds with the dough hook in place. Then, turn it to medium speed and knead for about 8 to 10 minutes. It's ready when the dough looks smooth and doesn't stick to the sides of the bowl.
3. Split the dough in half and roll each half into a ball. Put the balls of dough into bowls with olive oil. Olive oil the surface of the dough by rolling it in it.
4. Cover the bowls with plastic wrap in a tight way. Put the dough bowls in a warm place and let them rise until they are twice as big. It can take from one to three hours.
5. Roll out the dough. After the dough has risen, stretch it, put it on baking sheets or pizza pans, and top it with whatever you want.
6. Bake in a hot oven at 430–480°F (220-250°C) for 10–15 minutes, or until done.

189. COOKIE DOUGH

Prep Time: 15 Minutes | Cook Time: 00 Minutes | Total Time: 15 Minutes | Serving: 3

Ingredients

- 1 tsp salt
- 1 cup of unsalted, room-temperature butter
- 2 cups of all-purpose flour
- ¼ cup of granulated sugar
- 2 ½ tsp vanilla extract
- 1 cup of miniature chocolate chips
- 2 tbsp milk plus more if needed
- 1 cup of brown sugar

Instructions

1. Put your flour in a bowl that can go in the microwave and heat it on high for 50 to 60 seconds or until the temperature inside the bowl reaches 166°F.
2. Cream the brown sugar, white sugar, and butter in a large bowl with the stand mixer. Beat for around 1 minute or until the mixture is white and fluffy. Put the vanilla and salt and beat until mixed in.
3. Mix in flour that has been heated until it is just mixed. Add milk a tbsp at a time, beating after each addition, until the dough starts to come together. Use a rubber spatula to mix in the small chocolate chips

190. PASTA DOUGH

Prep Time: 1 Hour 20 Minutes | Cook Time: 5 Minutes

Total Time: 1 Hour 25 Minutes | Serving: 8

Ingredients

- 2 (2) egg yolks
- 1 tsp (1 tsp) salt
- 300 g (2.4 cups of) plain flour
- 4 (4) eggs
- 150 g (0.9 cups of) semolina

Instructions

1. Put everything that goes into the pasta into the bowl of the stand mixer. Use the dough hook to mix all the elements on the lowest setting. Then knead for about five minutes, one or two sets faster, depending on your machine.
2. Leave the dough to rest for an hour with the bowl covered.
3. Cut it into quarters and flatten it with your hand or a rolling pin until it fits in the pasta attachment of your stand mixer.
4. Use the widest setting on the pasta maker. Go back through. Change the machine's thickness setting and go through it twice more.
5. Keep doing this until you get to the second-thinnest setting. Just cut the pasta in half if it gets too long to handle.
6. Roll it out and cut it into thin strips with a knife, or use a roller tagliatelle cutter to make thin slices.
7. Cook for about 2 minutes in a large pot of salted boiling water. Add the sauce you like best and serve.

191. PUFF PASTRY DOUGH

Prep Time: 30 Minutes | Chill Time: 4 Hours

Total Time: 4 Hours 30 Minutes | Serving: 1

Ingredients

- ½ cup of water (ice cold)
- 1 cup of salted butter (cut into small cubes)
- 2 cups of flour
- ½ tsp salt

Instructions

1. Put flour and salt in a stand mixer's bowl. Put things together.
2. Add butter. Use the paddle to mix everything. Mix until the ingredients are lumpy and the butter is spread out over the flour.
3. Mix in cold water. Mix the ingredients just until they come together. Still, the mix will be crumbly.
4. Pour the mix onto the counter. Mix the dough by hand until it forms a ball.
5. Flour the rolling pin and the surface lightly. Roll out the dough into a rectangle about 8 inches by 12 inches. Keep edges straight. If the edges get rough, push them back towards the center to make them straight again. As needed, add more flour to the counter and the rolling pin.
6. Turn the dough a quarter turn so that the long side faces you. Fold the dough over 2/3 of the way, starting on the left side, like you would fold a letter. Fold the right side of the dough over.
7. Rolling and folding should be done two more times.

192. BREAD DOUGH

Prep Time: 15 Minutes | Cook Time: 25-30 Minutes

Total Time: 1 Hour, 30-45 Minutes | Serving: 1 Loaf

Ingredients

- 2 tbsp melted butter
- 1/2 tsp salt
- 450g (3 cups of) plain bread flour
- 2 tsp caster sugar
- 250ml (1 cup) warm milk
- 1 tbsp (12g/2 sachets) dried yeast

Instructions

1. Mix flour, salt, yeast, and sugar in the bowl of a stand mixer. In the middle, dig a well. Add milk and butter. To make a smooth dough, remove it from the stand mixer and knead it for 10 minutes on a lightly floured surface.
2. Coat a big bowl with olive oil to grease it. Warp the dough with a damp tea towel and put it in the bowl. Put the dough in a warm, draft-free area to rise for around 45 minutes to 1 hour or until almost doubled size.
3. Use your fist to press down the middle of the dough. Turn out onto a lightly floured surface. Knead the dough for 2 minutes or until it is stretchy and back to its original size.

193. BISCUIT DOUGH

Prep Time: 10 Minutes | Cook Time: 30 Minutes | Total Time: 40 Minutes | Serving: 24

Ingredients

- 1 tbsp milk
- 125g butter, softened
- 1 tsp baking powder
- 1 egg, at room temperature
- 1/2 cup of caster sugar
- 1/2 tsp vanilla extract
- 2 cups of plain flour

Instructions

1. Turn oven on to 180°C. Line 2 baking trays with baking paper.
2. Using the stand mixer's bowl, beat the butter, sugar, and vanilla until the mixture is pale and creamy. Mix well after adding the egg. Dust the butter mixture with flour and baking powder. Stir in the milk until everything is just mixed.
3. Roll one heaping tbsp of the mixture at a time into balls. Put on baking sheets that have been covered with baking paper. Use the heel of your hand to flatten biscuits slightly.
4. Bake for around 15-18 minutes, turning the trays after 10 minutes, or until they are lightly golden. Let the cookies cool for 5 minutes on the trays. Move to wire racks to finish cooling. Serve.

194. PRETZEL DOUGH

Prep Time: 15 Minutes | Cook Time: 30 Minutes

Total Time: 45 Minutes | Serving: 10

Ingredients

- 5 to 5½ cups of (625 to 688 grams) all-purpose flour, divided
- ½ cups of warm milk (105°F to 110°F)
- 1 tbsp (9 grams) kosher salt
- 1 ½ cups of warm dark beer (120°F)
- 1 tbsp (14 grams) firmly packed dark brown sugar
- 2 tsp (6 grams) active dry yeast
- 2 tbsp (17 grams) malt powder

Instructions

1. Stir together warm beer, brown sugar, and yeast in the bowl of a stand mixer that has a dough hook attachment. Let the mixture sit for about 10 minutes or until it becomes foamy.
2. Add 625 grams (6 cups of) of flour, warm milk, malt powder, and salt, and beat until everything is mixed. Turn the mixer speed up to medium to high and knead the dough for approximately 5-6 minutes until it is smooth and elastic. If the dough is too sticky, add the last 1/2 cup of (63 grams) of flour.
3. Spray cooking spray into a big bowl. Turn the dough over in the bowl to grease the top. Cover and let rise in a warm place (75°F) with no drafts for about 1 hour or until doubled in size.

195. DONUT DOUGH

Prep Time: 2 Hours Minutes | Cook Time: 35 Minutes | Rest Time: 14 Hours

Total Time: 16 Hours 35 Minutes | Serving: 21

Ingredients

- 4 eggs - at room temperature
- 570 grams all-purpose flour - about 4 cups of
- 4-6 cups of vegetable oil or canola oil for frying
- 1 1/2 tsp salt
- granulated or powdered sugar for coating
- 60 grams granulated sugar - equals 1/3 cup of minus1 1/4 tsp
- 125 grams unsalted butter - softened to room temperature and cut into 1 tbsp-sized piece (about 9 T of butter)
- 2 1/2 tsp active dry yeast
- 150 grams water - warmed to 100°F

Instructions

1. First, Attach the yeast and water to the stand mixer's bowl with a paddle attachment. Let the yeast sit for 10 minutes or until it starts to foam. Add the salt, flour, sugar, and eggs. Mix in the middle. When the dough begins to unite and form a ball (about 3–4 minutes), switch to the dough hook and mix for 5–8 minutes. The dough should start to pull away from the bowl's sides. The dough will stick together a lot! My dough didn't clean the bowl completely.
2. Stop the mixer and give the dough 5 minutes to rest.
3. Turn the mixer back at to medium speed and place the butter, 2 tbsp at a time. Once the butter is added, mix for 5 minutes at medium-high speed or until the dough is smooth, shiny, and stretches when pulled. Again, the dough will stick to everything. If it's too sticky, add a few tbsp of flour and continue mixing for a few more minutes. But don't put in too much flour. This dough is sticky because that's how it's made.
4. Put the dough in a big bowl that has been lightly greased. Warp the bowl with plastic wrap and set it somewhere warm for 1 to 2 hours or until doubled in size.
5. Once the dough has doubled in size, take off the plastic wrap and punch it down with your fist. Then, cover it again and put the bowl in the fridge overnight to chill.
6. The next day, take the bowl out of the fridge. Cut the dough into pieces that are 50 grams each. About 21 balls will be made.
7. Put parchment paper on two baking sheets. Flour the parchment paper a lot.

196. SWEET DOUGH

Prep Time: 30 Minutes | Cook Time: 30 Minutes

Total Time: 1 Hour | Serving: 2

Ingredients

- 1 tsp kosher salt
- 2 large eggs, at room temperature
- 2 3/4 cups of unbleached all-purpose flour
- 2/3 cup of whole milk
- 1 3/4 tsp of dry yeast (from one 1/4-ounce envelope)
- 5 tbsp sugar, divided
- 1/2 cup of unsalted butter (1 stick), make into 1-inch pieces at room temperature, plus 1/2 tbsp melted butter

Instructions

1. Heat milk in a small-sized saucepan on medium heat or the microwave until a thermometer reads 110°F -115°F (43°C to 46°C). Now, pour the milk into a 2-cup of measuring cup of and mix in 1 tbsp sugar. Add yeast to the milk and mix with a whisk. Let sit for about 5 minutes, or until the yeast is foamy. Put the eggs and whisk until the mixture is smooth.
2. Mix the last 4 tbsp of sugar, the flour, and the salt in the stand mixer's bowl with a dough hook. Add milk mixture. While the mixer is running, add 1/2 cup of butter at room temperature, one piece at a time, mixing well after each addition. Mix for 1 minute on medium speed. Knead medium-high speed for around 5 minutes or until the dough is nicely smooth and soft.
3. Spread some melted butter inside a medium bowl and put the dough in it. Spread the rest of the melted butter on top of the dough and cover with plastic wrap. Cover with plastic and put in the fridge.
4. Let the dough rise in a warm place without drafts for 1–1 1/2 hours, or 2–2 1/2 hours if the dough has been in the refrigerator.

197. TAMALE DOUGH

Prep Time: 20 Minutes | Cook Time: Minutes | Total Time: 20 Minutes | Serving: 12

Ingredients

- 4 cups of masa harina
- 3 3/4 cups of warm chicken stock or water, divided evenly
- 1 tsp baking powder
- 1/2 tbsp salt
- 1 1/2 cups of vegetable shortening or lard at room temperature

Instructions

Whip the lard:

1. Put the shortening or lard in a large mixing bowl. Knead it with your hands until it gets light and airy, which should take about 20 minutes. Instead, you can beat it on medium speed for roughly 8 minutes in a stand mixer with a paddle attachment.
2. It will go from being yellowish to white.

Add the dry ingredients:

1. Mixing by hand while breaking up the big clumps of dough with your fingers. Add the masa harina, baking powder, and salt to the whipped lard. It will be a crumbly mixture that looks like wet sand.
2. Use a rubber spatula to repeatedly scrape the bottom and sides of the bowl while using a stand mixer to incorporate any dry ingredients that might adhere to the bowl.

Add the liquid:

1. Add 3 1/2 cups of chicken stock gradually while blending the mixture for 10 minutes on medium speed with the stand mixer.

Test the masa:

1. Drop a masa ball the size of a quarter into a glass of ice water. The masa is prepared if it floats. If it sinks, add the final 1/4 cup of chicken stock, knead for 5 minutes, and then repeat the test. Keep mixing and testing until the ball floats to the top of the glass. The masa will be sticky, wet, and spreadable.
2. Ready to prepare tamales. Up to 4 hours at room temperature and up to 48 hours in the refrigerator are the maximum storage times for masa. It won't grow mold due to the cold temperature, and the tightly sealed container will prevent drying out. Over the next 48 hours, it will sour.
3. If you want to make a lot of tamales, make the masa the day before you intend to assemble your tamales and the filling up to 2 days in advance. Keep the masa covered with a fresh kitchen towel while making it to prevent it from drying out.

198. DUMPLING DOUGH

Prep Time: 15 Minutes | Chill Time: 10 Minutes

Total Time: 25 Minutes | Serving: 24

Ingredients

- 1/2 tsp salt, 2.5 milliliters
- 2 cups of all-purpose flour, 240g
- 3/4 cup of water (110–120°F) 175 ml

Instructions

1. Mix the ingredients in a large bowl with a large wooden spoon until all the water is absorbed. Before you knead the dough, the ingredients won't work well together. The dumpling dough will only look like "shaggy dough" until you knead it.
2. Take the stand mixer with a dough hook. Put the wet and dry ingredients into the bowl of the stand mixer. Set the mixer to a low speed, like 2 or 3, and mix for 2 to 3 minutes. Take the dough out of the mixer and knead it by hand for a few minutes until it comes together into a single lump.
3. Put the dough in a large bowl.
4. Cover the big bowl with plastic wrap, and then let the dough rest for around 1 hour in its container. After an hour, put the dough on a large baking mat or cutting board. Before you pour the dough out, sprinkle a little flour on the cutting board or baking mat to keep it from sticking when you roll it out. Sprinkle a little flour on the dough so it doesn't stick together.
5. Roll the dough out until it's about 1/16 of an inch thick. You can cut the dough in half if it's too big for your cutting board or dough mat. Before rolling out the other half of the dough, you roll out one half and make the dumpling wrappers.
6. After rolling out the dough, use a 3-inch or 4-inch cookie cutter to cut out perfectly round dumpling wrappers.

199. DANISH DOUGH

Prep Time: 30 Minutes | Cook Time: 30 Minutes

Total Time: 60 Minutes | Serving: 2

Ingredients

- 2 large egg yolks at room temperature
- 1 tsp salt
- 2 1/4 tsp instant yeast
- 3/4 cup of whole milk, warm (100–110 F)
- 4 tbsp (1/2 stick, 57g) unsalted butter, room temperature
- 2.5 cups of (355 g) of all-purpose flour
- 1 large egg at room temperature
- 1 tsp pure vanilla extract
- 2 tbsp sugar
- 12 tbsp (1 1/2 sticks, 170g) unsalted butter, cold, cut in 1/2-inch pieces

Instructions

1. Butter up a big bowl.
2. Mix the milk, egg, egg yolks, vanilla, and salt in a large measuring cup.
3. Mix the flour, yeast, sugar, and salt on low in the bowl of a stand mixer with a paddle. Include the softened butter, put it in at room temperature, and blend on low until you completely integrate the butter into the flour, ensuring no pieces are visible. Add the cold butter and mix on low until you break up the butter into 1/2-inch slices. Mix on low until everything comes together after adding the milk mixture. The dough will have pieces of butter, which will be very sticky. Put the dough in the pre-prepared bowl and store it in the refrigerator for up to three days.
4. The following day, put the dough on a well-floured surface to work on. Knead the dough 10–12 times until it forms a ball. Cover the top with a thin layer of flour and a tea towel, and let it sit until it's room temperature. Roll the dough into a 16-by-20-inch rectangle. Pat the dough into a 6-inch square. If the dough is sticking, sprinkle more flour on the surface. Dust off any extra flour on the dough, and then use a bench scraper to fold the short ends of the dough into the middle, like a business letter. The first turn is here.
5. Turn the dough over so the seam is on the bottom, and roll it into an 8-by-16-inch rectangle. Like a business letter, fold the short ends over the middle. Repeat the steps until you've done them four times.
6. On the last turn, gently press the layers with the rolling pin. Wrap the dough tightly in plastic wrap and put it in the refrigerator for at least an hour or two days.

200. PIE DOUGH

Prep Time: 1 Hour 15 Minutes | Chill Time: 2 Days

Total Time: 1 Hour 15 Minutes | Serving: 2

Ingredients

- 1 tsp kosher salt
- 1/4 cup of cold water
- 1 1/2 cups of (192g) all-purpose flour
- 1 tbsp granulated sugar
- 12 tbsp (1 1/2 sticks) unsalted butter

Instructions

1. Cut the butter into pieces. Aim for 10 from the whole stick and 5 from the half stick so that each piece is smaller than 1 tbsp. Put the cut butter in the freezer for a few minutes while you work on the dry ingredients.
2. Now, combine the sugar, flour, and salt in the mixing container of a stand mixer with a paddle attachment. Just blend for a few seconds, and then turn off.
3. Put the pieces of butter into the dry ingredients. Mix on the lowest setting for 5 to 10 seconds, pulsing on and off to keep the flour from flying out of the bowl, and then turn off. At this step, it's better to undermix than overmix. You want each piece of butter covered in flour and slightly smashed by the paddle, but most of the pieces should be about the same size as when you started.
4. Set the mixer to the slowest speed possible, and slowly pour in the around 1/4 cup of cold water. Once everything is in, let the mixer run for a few more seconds, then turn it off and check on the dough. The final result should be a very rough dough that stays together when squeezed, with some dough starting to stick to the paddle attachment and a few flour streaks on the side of the bowl. If some parts of the dough are still dry and powdery and the flour is still sticking to the sides of the bowl, keep mixing and add another tbsp of water. Give it a few seconds to combine. If you need to, do it again with very little water.
5. Gather the dough with your hands and put it on a piece of plastic wrap. Form the dough into a ball with the plastic wrap, then flatten it into a disc with your hands so the plastic wrap is very tight. You can wrap it with another piece of plastic for extra safety.
6. Before you use it, put it in the refrigerator for at least an hour and up to two days. You can also put it in the refrigerator for up to 30 days.

ICE CREAM

201. PEACH ICE CREAM

Prep Time: 30 Minutes | Cook Time: 25 Minutes | Cool Time: 2 Hours 55 Minutes

Total Time: Minutes | Serving:

Ingredients

- 1 ½ cups of whole milk
- 4 medium peaches – peeled and sliced
- 2 cups of heavy cream
- 5 large egg yolks
- 1 ¼ cup of sugar – divided
- 2 Tbsp vanilla
- 1 tbsp lemon juice – freshly squeezed

Instructions

1. Using a Stand mixer attachment, put the bowl in the freezer for a full day (or at least 15 hours) before churning.

Temper the eggs:

2. Add the whole milk to a small saucepan and heat it on until the temperature reaches medium heat until it reaches 165 degrees. Stirring often. Do not boil.
3. Now, whisk the eggs and 1/4 cup of sugar well in a small bowl.
4. When the milk reaches 165 degrees, pour it into a small measuring cup of and pour it into the eggs while whisking hard. Don't stop whisking; keep adding a cup of hot milk while whisking.
5. Then, pour the contents of the bowl into the pan and turn the heat back on. Whisk the mixture and keep it warm until it reaches 165 degrees.
6. Take it off the heat and let it cool. Refrigerate.

Prep peaches:

1. Peel the peaches and cut them up. Mix with 1 cup of sugar and fresh lemon juice in a bowl. Mix it and let it sit. Let the peaches sit for about 30 minutes to form a rich, thick syrup.
2. Put peaches in a food processor and pulse them for a few seconds. You want to keep a few small pieces. Refrigerate.

Churn ice cream:

1. In a large mixing bowl, mix together all of the ingredients: the chilled, tempered eggs, the chilled, pureed peaches, the heavy cream, the vanilla, and a pinch of salt.
2. Start the mixer with the attachment before you pour in the liquid using a Stand mixer attachment. Then, pour in the whisked ingredients and let it churn until done. You'll know it's ready when the mixer starts to slow down, and the dough rises to the top of the bowl. It may take about 25 to 30 minutes.
3. Use a rubber scraper to get the ice cream out of the bowl and into a pan or other container.
4. Put the ice cream in the freezer until it's time to eat. The ice cream will be a little soft, so it needs a couple of hours to firm up.

202. VANILLA ICE CREAM

Prep Time: 5 Minutes | Chill Time: 15 Minutes

Total Time: 20 Minutes | Serving: 12

Ingredients

- (1) 12-ounces sweetened condensed milk
- 2 cups of heavy cream
- 2 cups of half and half
- 2 tbsp vanilla extract

Instructions

1. Once you've mixed all ingredients in a bowl, take the bowl out of the freezer and put the paddle (or dasher) inside.
2. Add the paddle to the frozen bowl, then lower the motor head and lock it.
3. Set the mixer to "stir" (the slowest speed).
4. Slowly pour the mixture into the stand mixer's bowl, which is frozen.
5. Turn the ice cream for up to 30 minutes or until it has the consistency of soft serve.
6. Add the soft-serve to a container that can go in the freezer and freeze it for 2 to 4 hours.

203. COFFEE ICE CREAM

Prep Time: 30 Minutes | Cook Time: 30 Minutes | Total Time: 60 Minutes | Serving: 16

Ingredients

- 1 cup of strong coffee
- 1 cup of granulated sugar
- 3 Tbsp vanilla
- 4 large egg yolks
- 2 cups of whole milk
- 2 cups of heavy cream
- 8 ounce toffee candy, chopped

Instructions

Temper the eggs:

1. Heat the whole milk to 160 degrees in a small saucepan, stirring occasionally. Do not boil.
2. Now, stir the eggs and 1/2 cup of sugar well in a small bowl.
3. When the milk reaches 160 degrees, pour it into a small measuring cup of and pour it into the eggs while whisking hard. Don't stop whisking; keep adding a cup of hot milk while whisking.
4. Then, pour the contents of the bowl into the pan and turn the heat back on. Whisk the mixture and keep it warm until it reaches 160 degrees.
5. Take it off the heat and let it cool. Refrigerate.

Make strong coffee:

1. Use any robust coffee for this recipe. Espresso is preferred, but cold brew works well, too, adding a refreshing touch to the coffee.

Make the ice cream:

2. Using a Stand Mixer attachment, put the bowl in the freezer for at least 15 hours or a full day before churning.
3. Mix the cooled tempered egg mixture (whole milk, eggs, and sugar), the heavy cream, the vanilla, the cooled coffee, and the sugar in a large measuring bowl. Mix well and put in the refrigerator until you're ready to use.
4. Using a Stand Mixer attachment, switch on the mixer with the attachment before pouring in the liquid. Next, pour in the whisked ingredients and let them churn until they reach the desired consistency. You'll know it's done when the mixer slows down and the dough rises to the top of the bowl. This process may take about 25 to 30 minutes.
5. Use a rubber scraper to move the ice cream from the bowl to a container in the freezer. Mix the broken-up toffee bars into the ice cream.
6. Freeze the ice cream until you're ready to serve it. The ice cream will be soft, so it will need a couple of hours to harden up.

204. COCONUT ICE CREAM

Prep Time: 45 Minutes | Cook Time: 15 Minutes

Total Time: 60 Minutes | Serving: 6

Ingredients
- 50 g sugar
- 1/2 tsp salt
- 450 g coconut milk
- 450 g coconut cream
- 80 ml agave syrup (or sweetener of choice)

Instructions
1. Whisk the coconut milk, coconut cream, agave syrup, sugar, and salt in a saucepan. Add kaffir lime leaves. Break the lemongrass into pieces and add it to the pot. Now, Bring to a simmer over medium heat while stirring occasionally. Once the mixture simmers, stir it for 2 minutes and then remove it from the heat.
2. Let the coconut mixture cool down. Take out the leaves of kaffir lime and lemongrass. Put it in a container with a lid and chill it overnight in the freezer or refrigerator.
3. Attach the Ice Cream Maker to the Stand mixer. Turn the mixer to "Stir" speed and pour the cold coconut ice cream batter into the Freeze Bowl while the mixer is running. Let the mixer stir the ice cream mixture for 20 minutes or until it looks soft-serve.
4. Put the ice cream in a container that won't let air in and put it in the freezer for three hours. Use it right away after freezing.
5. Add toasted coconut flakes.

205. BLUEBERRY ICE CREAM

Prep Time: 30 Minutes | Cook Time: 35 Minutes

Total Time: 1 hour, 5 Minutes | Serving: 8

Ingredients
- 4 large eggs
- 2 cups of heavy cream
- 2 cups of whole milk
- 2 Tbsp vanilla
- 1 large lemon – freshly squeezed
- 2 pints blueberries – or 24 ounces
- 1 ¼ cup of granulated sugar – divided

Instructions

Temper the eggs:

1. Put all the whole milk in a small pot on medium heat and let it warm until it reaches 160 degrees. Stir the milk often, but don't bring it to a boil.
2. Whisk the eggs and 3/4 cup of sugar well in a small bowl.
3. When the milk reaches 160 degrees, pour it into a small measuring cup of and pour it into the eggs while whisking hard. Don't stop whisking; keep adding a cup of hot milk while whisking.
4. Then, pour the contents of the bowl into the pan and turn the heat back on. Whisk the mixture and keep it warm until it reaches 160 degrees.
5. Take it off the heat and let it cool. Refrigerate.

Prep blueberries:

1. In a medium saucepan, mix the blueberries, the juice from freshly squeezed lemons, along with 1/2 cup of sugar. Use a potato masher to break the blueberries open while cooking on medium heat. It will take about 20 minutes to do this.
2. Pour the cooked berries through a strainer with a fine mesh into a bowl to catch all the juices. Push the berries with a spoon and let all the liquid drain.

Make the ice cream:

1. Using a Stand mixer attachment, put the bowl in the freezer for at least 15 hours or a full day before churning.
2. Mix the cooled egg mixture (whole milk, eggs, and sugar), blueberry juice (not the berry pulp), heavy cream, and vanilla in a large measuring bowl. Mix well and put in the fridge until it's ready to use.
3. Using a Stand mixer attachment, start the mixer with the attachment attached so that it's turning before you pour the liquid in. Then add the whisked ingredients and let it churn until done. It's done when the mixer starts to slow down, and the dough rises to the top of the bowl. It may take about 25 to 30 minutes.
4. Use a rubber scraper to move the ice cream from the bowl to a container in the freezer.
5. Mix the blueberry pulp well into the ice cream after adding it.
6. Freeze the ice cream until you're ready to serve it. The ice cream will be soft, so it will need a couple of hours to harden up.

206. RASPBERRY ICE CREAM

Prep Time: 30 Minutes | Cook Time: 25 Minutes | Chill Time: 2 hours

Total Time: 2 Hours, 55 Minutes | Serving: 8

Ingredients

- 5 large egg yolks
- 1 ¼ cups of whole milk
- A pinch of salt
- 1 pound fresh raspberries
- 2 cups of heavy cream
- 1-2 tbsp vanilla extract
- 1 ½ cups of granulated sugar, divided

Instructions

1. Run cold water over the raspberries. Pour into a medium bowl after straining. Then add a half cup of sugar and stir to combine. Let the raspberries sit on your countertop for about an hour until juice forms.
2. Pour the raspberries and juice into a blender. Pulse until the mixture is very smooth.
3. Remove the seeds and pour the raspberry puree through a fine-mesh sieve. It will lead to a smoother consistency.
4. In a bowl, blend the egg yolks and 1/4 cup of sugar. Put the whole milk in a saucepan and heat it over medium heat until the temperature reaches 165 degrees. Do not bring it to a boil.
5. Pour a quarter cup of at a time of the hot milk into the bowl containing the eggs and sugar while vigorously whisking. Reheat the pan to 165 degrees before adding the egg mixture back in.
6. Pour the hot mixture into a measuring cup of or bowl with a capacity of 8 cups. Let it cool down a bit, and then add the last 3/4 cup of sugar, the heavy cream, and the vanilla extract. Mix it well.
7. Place the raspberry puree into the ice cream mixture and whisk it together. Put it in the fridge until the food is cold.
8. Start the stand mixer, and while it's running, take the chilled ice cream mixture in the stand mixer's bowl. Till the ice cream solidifies, let the mixer run.
9. The ice cream will thicken and rise to the top of the bowl as you watch. The mixer might slacken. It may take about 25 to 30 minutes.
10. Any shallow, airtight container will work to receive the churned ice cream. Put the container in the refrigerator to allow it to set up more. The ice cream will initially be soft-serve in consistency; freezing it will firm it up.
11. If desired, top the ice cream with additional fresh raspberries before serving.

207. VANILLA BEAN ICE CREAM

Prep Time: 30 Minutes | Cook Time: 30 Minutes | Chill Time: 2 Hours

Total Time: 3 Hours | Serving: 8

Ingredients

- 2 ¼ cups of heavy cream
- 5 large egg yolks
- 2 whole vanilla beans
- 1 cup of granulated sugar – divided
- 1 ¾ cups of whole milk
- pinch of salt

Instructions

1. When using the Stand Mixer attachment, put the bowl in the freezer for at least 15 hours or a day before you churn.
2. When preparing vanilla beans, slice the beans lengthwise, keeping the underside whole, with a sharp knife. Remove the seeds with a scraper.

Temper the eggs:

1. Put the whole milk, freshly scraped vanilla bean, and vanilla pods in a small saucepan. While constantly stirring, heat over medium-low heat until it reaches 165 degrees. Avoid boiling.
2. To thoroughly combine the egg yolks and 1/4 cup of sugar, whisk them in a small mixing bowl.
3. Take a small measuring cup, and when the milk reaches 165 degrees, pour it into the egg mixture while vigorously whisking. As you whisk, gradually pour one cup of hot milk into the eggs. Continue whisking while pouring about a cup of hot milk into the eggs.
4. Then, add the bowl's contents back to the saucepan. The heating and whisking must continue until the mixture reaches 165 degrees.
5. Discard the vanilla pods, turn off the heat, and cool the mixture. When desired, strain the custard. Refrigerate.

Make the ice cream:

1. Combine the tempered egg mixture (whole milk, eggs, 1/4 cup of sugar, and vanilla bean seeds) with the remaining sugar, heavy cream, salt, and vanilla in a large measuring bowl. Mix thoroughly.

Churn:

1. Using a Stand mixer attachment, turn on the mixer first with the attachment before adding the liquid. Then, add the whisked ingredients and let it churn for the desired time. It will take about 25 to 30 minutes to complete; at this point, the mixer will begin to slow down, and the mixture will rise to the top of the bowl.
2. Pour the ice cream from the bowl into a pan or other container using a rubber scraper. Up until serving time, keep the ice cream frozen. Firming the ice cream will take a few hours because it will be soft.

208. COOKIES & CREAM ICE CREAM

Prep Time: 10 Minutes | Chill Time: 8 hours

Total Time: 10 Minutes | Serving: 6

Ingredients

- 14 ounces sweetened condensed milk
- 1 ¾ cup of heavy whipping cream
- 1 tsp vanilla extract
- 15 Oreo cookies
- 2 tbsp granulated sugar

Instructions

1. Put your mixing bowl and any attachments for your mixer in the freezer for at least 20 minutes before you start.
2. The cookies should be placed in a zip-top bag and smashed with a rolling pin into small to medium pieces while the mixing bowl is in the freezer. r. Don't crush them, or your ice cream will turn gray.
3. Take the heavy whipping cream and sugar to the cold mixing bowl and mix with the stand mixer until it has the consistency of whipped cream.
4. Add the vanilla and sweetened condensed milk to the mixture. Again, mix until smooth.
5. Mix the crushed Oreos by hand, then place the mixture into a 9x5 loaf pan.
6. Put the loaf pan in the freezer and let it stay there for at least three hours. Place the ice cream in the freezer for longer than 3 hours; this will make it "harder."
7. If the ice cream has been frozen for over 3 hours, set it out at room temperature for 5 minutes to soften it so it can be scooped and served easily.

209. OREO ICE CREAM

Prep Time: 20 Minutes | Cook Time: 30 Minutes | Chill Time: 2 hours, 30 Minutes

Total Time: 3 Hours, 20 Minutes | Serving: 10

Ingredients

- 2 cups of heavy cream
- 2 cups of 2% milk
- 3/4 cup of granulated sugar
- 4 large egg yolks
- 3/4 – 1 pound Oreo cookies – crushed
- 2 tbsp vanilla extract

Instructions

1. Stir the egg yolks and 1/4 cup of sugar in a mixing bowl. Put the milk in a saucepan and warm it to 165 degrees over medium heat. Never boil.
2. Whisk constantly when the milk is hot as you add 1/2 cup of to the eggs. Re-add the egg mixture to the pan. Once it reaches 165 degrees, pour the egg mixture back into the pan.
3. Add the remaining ingredients
4. In a big bowl or measuring cup of that holds 8 cups of pour the hot mixture. Next, add the remaining sugar, heavy cream, and vanilla extract. Whisk well.
5. Put the mixture for the ice cream in the fridge until it is cold.
6. Crush the Oreos using a food processor. I like to leave a few big chunks in place. If you don't have a food processor, you can quickly put Oreos in a plastic bag and crush them with the help of a rolling pin or other heavy object.
7. Using a Stand Mixer attachment, start the mixer with the attachment in place before you pour in the liquid. Then, pour in the whisked ingredients and let it churn until done. You'll know it's ready when the mixer slows down, and the dough rises to the top of the bowl.
8. Put the ice cream and crushed cookies in a container in the freezer. Mix things up.
9. Put the container in the freezer so it can harden even more. At first, the ice cream will be very soft, so putting it in the freezer for a few hours helps it get firmer.
10. If desired, garnish the ice cream with additional Oreo cookies.

210. MINT CHIP ICE CREAM

Prep Time: 25 Minutes | Cook Time: 25 Minutes

Total Time: 50 Minutes | Serving: 8

Ingredients

- 3 large eggs
- 2 ½ cups of whole milk
- 1 cup of granulated sugar
- 1 tbsp vanilla extract
- 4 ounce mini chocolate chips
- 1/4 cup of creme de menthe
- 2 ½ cups of heavy cream

Instructions

1. Using a Stand Mixer attachment to make this ice cream, make sure to put the bowl in the freezer for at least 15 hours before churning.

Temper the eggs:

1. Pour all the milk into a small pot on medium heat until the temperature reaches 160°F. Stirring often. Do not boil.
2. Whisk the eggs and sugar together well in a small bowl.
3. When the milk reaches 160 degrees, pour it into the egg mixture while whisking with a small measuring cup. Pour about an additional half cup of hot milk into the eggs.
4. Then, add the bowl's contents to the pan and re-adjust the heat. Whisk and heat the mixture until it reaches 160 degrees.
5. Take the pan off the heat and let it cool. Refrigerate.
6. Mix up the ice cream:
7. Mix the tempered eggs, heavy cream, vanilla, and creme de menthe in a large bowl. Mix everything well and put it in the fridge until you're ready to churn.

Churn:

1. Using a Stand Mixer attachment, start the mixer with the attachment in place before you pour in the liquid. Then, pour in the whisked ingredients and let it churn until done. You'll know it's ready when the mixer slows down, and the dough rises to the top of the bowl. It may take about 25 to 30 minutes.
2. Put the ice cream in a container in the freezer, add the chocolate chips, and stir well. Freeze it for a few hours to make it firm.

211. BUTTER PECAN ICE CREAM

Prep Time: 20 Minutes | Cook Time: 25 Minutes | Total Time: 45 Minutes | Serving: 16

Ingredients

- 4 large egg yolks
- 1 cup of chopped pecans
- 1 cup of brown sugar
- 3 cups of heavy cream
- 6 tbsp unsalted butter - browned
- 2 tbsp vanilla extract
- 2 cups of whole milk
- pinch of salt (optional)

Instructions

Brown the butter:

1. Put butter on the stove pan and turn the heat to medium. Let it melt, then stir with a spatula when it starts to sizzle. Let the butter keep cooking while stirring it often. On the bottom of the pan, you'll begin to see some brown bits. Let this continue for about a minute, and then take the pan off the heat.

Temper the eggs:

1. Put the pan back on the stove over medium-high heat and add the whole milk to the pan where the butter was. Stir the mixture and wait until a digital thermometer reads 165 degrees.
2. In a bowl, mix the eggs and brown sugar. When the milk and butter mixture reaches 165 degrees, pour some into the eggs while whisking hard with a small measuring cup. Keep mixing while adding about a cup of the mixture to the eggs.
3. Pour the contents of the bowl into the pot and turn on the heat again. Keep cooking until the temperature reaches 165 degrees. Take it off the heat and let it cool.

Continue with the process:

1. Mix the ingredients for the ice cream. In a large bowl, mix the tempered egg mixture (the browned butter, whole milk, eggs, and brown sugar), the heavy cream, vanilla, a pinch of salt, and the heated mixture to temper the eggs. Mix well, then put in the fridge until you're ready to use. Make sure it's nice and cold!
2. Warm up the pecans. Use a pan that won't stick, and heat it over medium heat. Add the chopped pecans to the pan. Toast until just golden brown. When they start to turn brown, you'll be able to smell it. Be careful not to burn! Take the pecans out and let them cool. Then, put it in a freezer bag and put it in the freezer until you are ready to use it.
3. Churn. Using a Stand Mixer attachment, start the mixer with the attachment already moving before you add the liquid. Then, carefully pour in the whisked mixture as it turns. Let it mix for about 25 to 30 minutes, or until the ice cream rises to the top of the bowl and the mixer slows down a bit.

4. Using a rubber scraper, move the ice cream from the bowl to a container in the freezer. Add the toasted pecans and stir them in well.
5. Put the ice cream in the freezer until it's time to eat. Put it in the freezer for a couple of hours to get firm.

212. PUMPKIN ICE CREAM

Prep Time: 30 Minutes | Cook Time: 30 Minutes | Chill Time: 2 Hours

Total Time: 3 Hours | Serving: 8

Ingredients

- 1/2 tsp pumpkin pie spice
- 1 tbsp vanilla extract
- 5 large eggs
- 2 ¼ cups of heavy cream
- 1 tsp cinnamon
- 1 cup of pumpkin
- 1 cup of brown sugar
- 1/4 cup of granulated sugar
- 1 ¾ cups of whole milk
- pinch of salt

Instructions

Make the pumpkin ice cream mixture:

1. Mix the whole milk, heavy cream, pumpkin, pumpkin pie spice, and cinnamon in a small saucepan and heat over medium heat. With a digital thermometer, heat it until it reaches 165 degrees and whisk it often. Don't boil.
2. Whisk the egg yolks, sugar, and salt in a small bowl.
3. When the milk mixture reaches 165 degrees, pour it into the egg mixture while whisking with a small measuring cup. Don't stop whisking; keep adding a cup of the hot mixture to the eggs as you whisk.
4. Then, pour the contents of the bowl into the pan and turn the heat back on. Whisk the mixture and keep it warm until it reaches 165 degrees.
5. Take it off the heat and let it cool. Add vanilla extract. You can also strain the custard at this point.
6. Put it in the fridge until it is cold.

Churn ice cream:

1. Using a Stand Mixer attachment, start the mixer with the attachment in place so that it turns before you pour the liquid in. Then, pour in the whisked ingredients and let it churn until done. You'll know it's ready when the mixer starts to slow down, and the dough rises to the top of the bowl. It may take about 25 to 30 minutes.
2. To get the ice cream out of the bowl and into a pan or other container, use a rubber scraper.
3. Put the ice cream in the freezer until it's time to eat. The ice cream will be a little soft, so it will take several hours to firm up.

213. BLACK FOREST ICE CREAM

Prep Time: 45 Minutes | Cook Time: 30 Minutes | Chill Time: 4 Hours

Total Time: 5 Hours 15 Minutes | Serving: 8

Ingredients

For the brownies:

- 1 large egg yolk
- 6 ounce Double Chocolate Ghirardelli brownie mix
- 3 tbsp unsalted butter – melted
- a splash of hot water

For the cherry sauce:

- 3/4 cup of granulated sugar
- 1 pound frozen dark cherries

For the ice cream base:

- 1 ¾ cups of whole milk
- 1/4 cup of granulated sugar
- 2 ounce dark chocolate
- pinch of salt
- 1 tbsp vanilla extract
- 4 large egg yolks
- 2 tsp cherry extract
- 1 ¾ cup of heavy cream

Instructions

1. Mix the brownie mix, melted butter, egg yolk, and a few tbsp of hot water in a small bowl. Stir to combine.
2. Grease a one-pound bread pan and pour the brownie batter into it, making sure it spreads evenly to all sides of the pan. Put the pan in an oven preheated to 350 degrees F and bake for 16 to 18 minutes or until the center is done.
3. After the brownies have cooled, cut them into small pieces.
4. In a bowl, blend the egg yolks and 1/4 cup of sugar together. Put the whole milk in a pot and heat it over medium heat until the temperature reaches 165 degrees. Do not boil.
5. When the milk is hot, pour in 1/2 cup at a time, whisking constantly, into the eggs and sugar. Then, pour the egg mixture back into the pan and heat it to 165 degrees.
6. Pour the hot mixture into a measuring cup of or bowl with 8 cups. After it has cooled down, add the rest of the sugar, heavy cream, and vanilla extract. Mix it well.
7. Mix the frozen cherries, 3/4 cup of sugar, and a splash of water in a small saucepan. For about 10 minutes, stir the food often while cooking over medium heat. Let it cool down a bit.
8. Pour the cherry mixture into a blender with a lot of power. Mix at high speed until everything is well mixed. Put the cherry compote and the other ingredients into the measuring cup.
9. Wrap the container in plastic wrap and put it in the fridge until the ice cream mixture is very cold.

10. Start the stand mixer and blend the chilled ice cream into the stand mixer's bowl while running. Turn the cherry ice cream with a mixer until it gets thick and creamy.
11. You'll see the ice cream thicken and rise to the top of the bowl. The mixer could slow down a bit. It may take about 25–35 minutes.
12. Put the ice cream in a container for storing ice cream with a rubber spatula. Add the brownie pieces and, if you want, some chopped chocolate pieces.
13. Put the airtight container in the freezer to harden even more. At first, the ice cream will be very soft, so putting it in the freezer for a few hours helps it get firmer.
14. A drizzle of chocolate sauce would go well with this ice cream.

214. PEANUT BUTTER ICE CREAM

Prep Time: 20 Minutes | Cook Time: 25 Minutes

Total Time: 45 Minutes | Serving: 8

Ingredients

- 2 cups of heavy cream
- 4 large egg yolks
- 3/4 cup of granulated sugar
- 1/2 cup of creamy peanut butter
- 2 tbsp vanilla extract
- 2 cups of 2% milk
- 36 extra mini Reeses peanut butter cups of – or about one cup chopped

Instructions

1. Mix the egg yolks and 1/2 cup of sugar in a bowl. Put the milk in a pot and heat it on medium heat until it reaches 165 degrees. Don't boil. When the milk is hot, pour 1/2 cup at a time into the eggs while whisking constantly. Then, pour the egg mixture back into the pan and heat it until the temperature reaches 165 degrees.
2. Stir the peanut butter into the egg mixture while it is still hot.
3. Pour the hot mixture into a measuring cup or bowl with a capacity of 8 cups. Then add the rest of the sugar, the heavy cream, and the vanilla. Mix it well.
4. Put the mixture for the ice cream in the fridge until it is cold.
5. Start the stand mixer, and while it's running, pour the chilled ice cream mixture into the stand mixer's bowl. Let the mixer mix the ice cream until it hardens. You'll see it get thicker and rise to the top of the bowl. The speed of the mixer may slow down.
6. Add the ice cream to a container that can go in the freezer and mix in the pieces of Reese's peanut butter cups. Stir together.
7. Put the container in the freezer so it can harden even more. At first, the ice cream will be very soft, so putting it in the freezer for a few hours helps it get firmer.
8. You may offer the ice cream with some extra Reese's peanut butter cups of on the side.

215. STRAWBERRY ICE CREAM

Prep Time: 25 Minutes | Cook Time: 30 Minutes

Total Time: 55 Minutes | Serving: 8

Ingredients

- 1 pound fresh strawberries – hulled
- ½ cup of granulated sugar
- 1 cup of granulated sugar – divided
- 1 ½ cups of heavy cream
- 4 large egg yolks
- 1 ½ cups of whole milk
- 2 tbsp Watkins vanilla – or good quality vanilla extract

Instructions

1. Add the sugar to the mix in three separate steps. Start by adding 1/2 cup of to the strawberry puree, another 1/2 cup of to temper the eggs, and finally, the last 1/2 cup for the final mixture.
2. Run cold water over the strawberries. Peel and cut them, then put them in a bowl. Then, add half a cup of sugar and mix well. Let the strawberries sit on your counter for about an hour until juice forms.
3. Put the juices and strawberries in a blender. Pulse until the mixture is very smooth. Put in the fridge to cool down. This puree is about the same as 2.5 cups.
4. Blend the egg yolks and 1/2 cup sugar in a mixing bowl. Put the milk in a saucepan and heat it over medium heat until the temperature reaches 165 degrees. Do not boil.
5. When the milk is hot, pour 1/2 cup of at a time into the eggs while constantly whisking. Then, pour the egg mixture back into the pan and heat it until it reaches 165 degrees.
6. Pour the hot mixture into a measuring cup or bowl with 8 cups . After it has cooled down a bit, stir in the sugar, the heavy cream, and the vanilla extract. Mix it well.
7. Place the ice cream mix in the fridge to chill until it is cold. When the ice cream mixture is cold, whisk in the strawberry puree.
8. Start the stand mixer and, while it's running, pour the chilled ice cream mixture into the stand mixer's bowl. Let the mixer mix the ice cream until it hardens.
9. You'll see it get thicker and rise to the top of the bowl. The speed of the mixer may slow down. It may take 30–35 minutes.
10. Put the container in the freezer so it can harden even more. At first, the ice cream will be very soft, so putting it in the freezer for a few hours helps it get firmer.
11. You may offer the ice cream with some extra fresh strawberries.

Printed in Great Britain
by Amazon